Patrick Pearse
and the Politics of
Redemption

Seán Farrell Moran

Patrick Pearse and the Politics of Redemption

The Mind of the Easter Rising, 1916

The Catholic University of America Press

Washington, D.C.

941.5082
P361Ym
1994

The paper used in this publication meets the minimum requirements of
American National Standards for Information Science—
Permanence of Paper for Printed Library Materials, ANSI z39.48-1984.

∞

Library of Congress Cataloging-in-Publication Data

Moran, Seán Farrell, 1951–
    Patrick Pearse and the politics of redemption : the mind of the Easter Rising,
    1916. by Seán Farrell Moran.
        p.   cm.
    Includes bibliographical references and index.
    1. Pearse, Padraic, 1879–1916.   2. Ireland—History—Sinn Fein Rebellion, 1916
    Biography.   3. Ireland—Politics and government—1910–1921.
    4. Revolutionaries—Ireland—Biography.   I. Title.
    DA965.P4M67   1993
    941.5082'1—dc20
    92-26449
    ISBN 0-8132-0775-4 (alk. paper)

In memoriam

Peter and Marilayne Moran

Contents

Acknowledgments

I am deeply grateful to a number of scholars and friends who have assisted me in the writing of this book. It would be impossible to credit adequately the help and wise counsel extended to me by Terence Murphy. Several other people have taken time to read or respond with useful criticism to parts of this work in the past, including Graham J. Barker-Benfield, Maurice O'Connell, Ruth Dudley Edwards, Alan O'Day, Roger Brown, Ted Rosche, and Pat Cooke. Likewise I am indebted to Cóilín Owens, Valerie French, Janet Oppenheim, Al Mott, David Rodier, Richard Brietman, Martha Murphy, Paul Michaud, Roy Kotynesk, James Graham, Anne Tripp, Paul Van der Slice, Rebecca Easby, James and Sheila Kelly, Jim Tierney, Tommy Lamb, and the late John Cameron for their encouragement as well as critical comments. Special acknowledgments must be extended to my family in Bailieborough, Patrick and Nancy Farrell, and to my editor, Susan Needham, whose expertise straightened many a tortured phrase.

I would like to express my gratitude to the Oakland University Faculty Research Committee, which provided funding for another project that tied up more than a few loose ends in this one. I would also like to thank the American University Office for Graduate Affairs for the support that led to the initial formulation of this work. I give many thanks to my colleagues in Oakland University's Department of History and to former colleagues at the History and Political Science Department of Montgomery College, as well as those with whom I used to work on the staffs of the Chestnut Lodge Hospital and Research Institute and the Mental Health Care Unit of Georgetown University Hospital.

Acknowledgments of permission to publish here work that has appeared previously must go to Mercier Press, for permission to publish pages 16–19 from *The Home-Life of Padraig Pearse* and to Thomas Kinsella for permission to publish "A Redeemer's Son" by Aogan O'Rathaille. An abbreviated version of chapter 1 was published as "Patrick Pearse, the Easter Rising, and Irish History," in *The Graduate Review* (Summer 1989), pages 2–19. An abbreviated form of chapter 4 was presented as " 'My Sons Were Faithful and They Fought': Patrick Pearse and the Easter Rising" (paper delivered before The Sesquicentennial Jonathan Swift and Irish Studies Conference, Notre Dame University, 18 October 1991). A shorter version of chapter 7 was published as "Patrick Pearse and the European Revolt Against Reason," in *The Journal of the History of Ideas*, 50, 4 (Oct.-Dec. 1989), pages 625–43, and presented in an earlier form "Patrick Pearse and the European Revolt Against Reason" (paper delivered at the Twenty-fifth Annual Meeting of the Atlantic Region of the American Conference of Irish Studies, Hofstra University, 6 November 1987).

Lastly, I must recognize the pre-eminent contributions of Julie Gilroy Moran, whose support was unstinting over the past ten years. I cannot help but remember several people who have passed on since I began the research for this book: Edward A. MacDowell, who gave me my love of ideas; JoAnne Munger, who convinced me that I should pursue the life of a scholar; and my parents, Peter and Marilayne Moran, who gave me my love of history.

*Patrick Pearse
and the Politics of
Redemption*

CHAPTER 1

The Individual and the Historical Event

Historians of Ireland widely regard Dublin's Easter Rising of 1916 as the most important event in modern Irish political history. The insurrection began on Easter Monday, April 24, 1916. It had been planned by a secret military council within the Irish Republican Brotherhood. The rebels did not attack military targets; instead they seized buildings and parks in the center of Dublin and waited for the British to come and attack them. Within a week, and after a bloody conflict, the rebels were defeated; British firing squads eventually executed most of the Rising's leadership.

Intended originally as the opening act of a national revolution, the Rising was a complete military failure. But it was intended to serve as a symbolic act, or in the words of Patrick Pearse, as "a blood sacrifice" shed on behalf of Ireland. While the Rising was not generally greeted with enthusiasm by the Irish people, the execution of Pearse and the others turned the rebels into national martyrs, and Patrick Pearse's idea of exemplary self-immolation on behalf of Ireland worked, as the executions helped reinvigorate the nationalist movement. Within three years, Irish republicans took to fighting a guerrilla war with Great Britain, which led ultimately to the establishment of the independent Irish Free State in 1922.

It is now clear that Patrick Pearse was the most important figure of the Easter Rising. As the thirty-seven-year-old Commandant-General of the insurrection, this writer, poet, and educator held firm nationalist convictions, and he loved the Irish language and culture. Quiet, shy, and socially awkward, he presented a most unlikely revolutionary, who nevertheless won his prominence within the republican movement largely on the basis of the speeches and writings he produced in the years just before the Great War. Pearse argued that death in service to Ireland could bring personal and national redemption that would ultimately liberate the Irish people. His use of this soteriological language established Pearse's historical eminence among Irish revolutionaries. It continues to convince many Irish nationalists that self-immolation is the way to win an ultimate victory for Ireland over England and English culture.

Pearse's ideas and the language he used to frame them produced a legacy vital to succeeding generations of Irish republicans. His ideas about blood sacrifice, redemptive violence, chiliastic expectation, and Irish national identity constitute the ideological heart of the physical-force republican tradition—to this day he remains a deeply controversial figure in Ireland. How and why Pearse developed these ideas necessarily constitute the core of any analysis of revolutionary politics in modern Ireland.

Despite his historical importance, Patrick Pearse remains an enigmatic figure.[1] Perhaps because he was such an unlikely hero, Pearse has generally been mishandled by historians, most of whom have wished to see him raised to sainthood or cast off as strange and a failure; Pearse the man has remained elusive and difficult to understand. How Patrick Pearse came to be a violent revolutionary and to play the critical role in Dublin's Easter Rising of 1916 has yet to be revealed adequately.

1. J. J. Lee, "In Search of Patrick Pearse," in Máirín Ní Dhonnchadha and Theo Dorgan, eds., *Revising the Rising* (Derry: Field Day, 1991), 122–38.

Patrick Pearse was exactly the right man at exactly the right moment in his country's history. Because of his background and the course of his personal life, he could address the major political issue of his time in a unique way. This does not mean that he was saintly, original, or profound; rather, his life and a great historical event were wholly intertwined. He has become a heroic figure because his private life and Irish political life met when each was undergoing a profound crisis; the solution Pearse sought and found for his own life was the same solution that changed Irish history—the Easter Rising of 1916. It was this coincidence that led to Pearse's enshrinement and has been the source of his unique standing in the history of his country.

The literature on Pearse has failed to draw the critical connections between Pearse and the historical event. Although considerable work has been done on Pearse and the Rising, much of it scholarship of great insight, none of it really helps us to understand how this improbable figure came to play a major role in such an extraordinary event. The improbability has been noted generally, and in most accounts the unusual event and the improbable figure are interrelated. Nonetheless, the questions remain: How are Pearse and the Rising connected and what is the significance of that relationship? How did this individual get caught up in such an event, when nothing in his life would seem to indicate that he would have? And in what ways was the Rising uniquely influenced by his participation?

The literature on Pearse and on the Rising has tended to be conventional in approach and conservative in tone. Despite the variety of recent writing in Irish history, as well as recent forays into Ireland's social history, Irish historiography has not been touched generally by the more innovative methodological approaches that have emerged elsewhere over the last thirty years. Perhaps this conservatism has been a result in part of the need for historians to erect the structure of Ireland's "story"; but it has manifested a distinctly positivistic bias in favor of political and administrative history.

Thus, historians of Ireland generally have not made extraordinary political events or unusual individuals very comprehensible. In the case of Patrick Pearse and the Easter Rising, the assumption that some kind of rationality will reveal itself has made both Pearse and the event seem fantastic and oddly unique: Pearse and his vital role in modern Irish and European history remain incompletely understood.

This is not to fault the source materials. Pearse published extensively in his brief life; he was a poet, a dramatist, an essayist, and a journalist. Nearly all of his writings and major public addresses are collected,[2] as is his personal correspondence, much of which has been published.[3] The various members of the Pearse family all have papers collected in Ireland,[4] and Pearse's never-completed autobiography was edited and published by his younger sister, Mary Brigid Pearse, in a single volume, with lengthy reminiscences from the rest of the Pearse family and friends.[5] Pearse has remained enigmatic not for lack of primary sources but as a result of the approaches employed by those who have written about him.

The writing on Pearse and his part in 1916 falls into several categories. The majority of works on this subject have focused on the political dimensions of Pearse's role in the Rising and include most of the general histories of modern Ireland. There also exist a large

2. Patrick Pearse, *The Collected Works of Padraic H. Pearse*, ed. Desmond Ryan, 6 vols. (Dublin: Phoenix Press, n.d., but published 1917-22); Seamas O'Buachalla, ed., *A Significant Irish Educationalist: The Educational Writings of P. H. Pearse* (Dublin: Mercier Press, 1980).

3. Patrick Pearse, *The Letters of P. H. Pearse*, ed. Seamas O'Buachalla (Atlantic Highlands, NJ: Humanities Press, 1980).

4. Pearse Family Papers, National Library, Dublin.

5. Mary Brigid Pearse, ed., *The Home Life of Padraig Pearse* (Dublin: Mercier Press, 1934; reprint ed., 1979). This work contains an extended fragment of Pearse's planned autobiography. It also contains several essays and remembrances by Pearse family members and close friends that were written in the early 1930s. The original documents at the St. Enda's school reveal that editing altered the autobiography only incidentally.

number of works that are hagiographical in tone and held sway over the subject until the 1970s, when a number of "revisionist" interpretations emerged to challenge both the political and hagiographical historical traditions. Lastly, there are those interpretive and more broadly "synthetic" works which have attempted to consider Pearse within some larger context.

General studies of the Irish history of this period include several that stand out.[6] Most of these histories have looked at Pearse from a political perspective. Their concern is with Pearse as an important political figure whose participation in the events of his time must be described and analyzed in political terms. Others have chosen to focus on policymakers and politicians and the failure of British political institutions to respond to nationalist hopes and aspirations.[7] Both types of analysis reveal a "liberal" faith in constitutionalism that failed to persuade either Pearse or his colleagues and has been rejected consistently by the republican tradition. Although these works recognize Pearse's uniqueness, that uniqueness is never

6. Without equal in this regard is F. S. L. Lyons, *Ireland Since the Famine* (London: Oxford University Press, 1971; paperback, 1973). For the period in question it is far better than J. C. Beckett, *The Making of Modern Ireland* (New York: Alfred A. Knopf, 1963; reprint ed., 1966). Lyons must be considered alongside of J. J. Lee, *Ireland 1912-1985: Politics and Society* (Cambridge, England: Cambridge University Press, 1989). A "revisionist" history is the stimulating R. F. Foster, *Modern Ireland, 1600-1972* (London: Oxford University Press, 1988). More specialized and useful is Robert Kee, *The Green Flag* (London: Wiedenfield and Nicholson, Ltd., 1972); later published in 3 vols.: *That Most Distressful Country, The Bold Fenian Men*; and *Ourselves Alone* (London: Quartet Books, 1976). See also Joseph Lee, *The Modernization of Irish Society, 1848-1918* (Dublin: Gill and Mcmillan, 1976); Pauric Travers, *Settlements and Divisions: Ireland, 1870-1922* (Dublin: Helicon, 1988); Dermot Keogh's *Twentieth Century Ireland: Unequal Achievement* (Dublin: Gill and Macmillan, 1988); P. S. Hegarty, *A History of Ireland Under the Act of Union* (London: Metheun and Co., 1952; reprint ed., New York: Kraus Reprint, Co., 1969).

7. George Dangerfield, *The Damnable Question: A Study in Anglo-Irish Relations* (Boston: Little, Brown and Co., 1976).

sufficiently analyzed and discussed in a way that explains his role. Perhaps it is this liberal predisposition in the literature that led the late F. S. L. Lyons to comment that the Rising continued to remain too big an event, with too great a change ensuing from it, to be entirely understood as yet.[8] Lyons made this assertion while admitting that in order to understand the Rising we must first understand Pearse.[9]

The temptation to explain Pearse from the political point of view has lured most of the serious historical scholars who have written specifically about Pearse, the Rising, and subsequent republicanism. Some have downgraded Pearse's contribution while they emphasized one of the other main characters instead, such as Eoin MacNeill or James Connolly.[10] Histories of the republican movement have been unrelentingly political in their viewpoints and have frequently obscured their analyses with polemical criticism or admiring advocacy. They have tended to see the Rising as a moment in an evolu-

8. F. S. L. Lyons, *Culture and Anarchy in Ireland, 1890-1939* (London: Oxford University Press, 1979; paperback, 1982), 33.

9. Lyons, *Ireland Since the Famine,* 334.

10. F. X. Martin, ed., *Leaders and Men of the Easter Rising, Dublin 1916* (London: Harper and Row, 1967); "1916—Myth, Fact, and Mystery," *Studia Hibernica* 7 (1967): 7-126; "The Easter Rising—Coup d'état or Bloody Protest?" *Studia Hibernica* 8 (1968): 106-37; D. George Boyce, *Nationalism in Ireland* (Baltimore: Johns Hopkins University Press, 1982). Boyce makes a fairly convincing argument that Connolly, whose early position was roughly syndicalist, moved toward nationalism in order to radicalize the republicans and the Irish Volunteers and thus had the crucial role in 1916. While persuasive, this argument scarcely needs repeating—Connolly moved to physical-force nationalism partly because it was tactically necessary and partly because, if he had not, the socialist revolution he wished for Ireland would never have occurred. More importantly, Boyce overlooks Connolly's despair over the war in Europe and the failure of British unions to support the Great Strike of 1913 in Dublin. His syndicalism had to be abandoned in favor of nationalism if Connolly was to have greater influence in Irish politics. In part, Connolly's change of philosophy was due to the increasing influence of the IRB.

tionary and inherently rational developmental process. The Rising can be seen as a problem of political logistics and timing more than as an event representative of any deeper phenomenon.[11]

The spiritual and mystical aspects of the Rising that Pearse consciously articulated are treated in several volumes of dubious value.[12] These hagiographic works are inevitably deeply flawed, yet even these books are useful, because of the proximity of some of the authors to Pearse and to the Rising. These works set out to establish Pearse's credentials as a national hero; their greatest usefulness lies in the influence that they had in making him a religious and patriotic martyr.[13]

In contrast to the work of the hagiographers and their success,

11. The standard work on the Fenians remains Leon O'Broin, *The Revolutionary Underground: The Story of the Irish Republican Brotherhood 1858-1924* (Totowa: Rowman and Littlefield, 1976) although it must be seen in light of R. V. Comerford, *The Fenians in Context: Irish Politics and Society 1848-1882* (Dublin: Gill and Macmillan, 1985). The standard works for the IRA are J. Bowyer Bell, *The Secret Army: The I.R.A. 1916-1979* (Dublin: The Academy Press, 1970; Cambridge, MA, 1983); Tim Pat Coogan, *The I.R.A.* (Glasgow: Pall Mall Press, 1970; paperback, 1980); Patrick Bishop and Eamonn Mallie, *The Provisional I.R.A.* (London: William Heinemann, 1987; paperback, 1988); for Pearse's republican political legacy see the seriously flawed Brian Murphy, *Patrick Pearse and the Lost Republican Ideal* (Dublin: James Duffy, 1991). For the ideological aspects of republicanism the choices are few and limited: see Maurice Goldring, *Faith of Our Fathers: The Formation of Irish Nationalist Ideology 1890-1930* (Dublin: Repsol, 1982); Ronnie Munck, "Rethinking Irish Nationalism: the Republician Dimension," *Canadian Review of Studies in Nationalism* 14, 1 (1986).

12. See Louis Le Roux, *Patrick H. Pearse*, trans. Desmond Ryan (Dublin: Talbot Press, 1932); Desmond Ryan, *The Man Called Pearse* (Dublin: Maunsel and Co., 1919); *Remembering Sion* (London: Arthur Baker, 1934); *The Rising: The Complete Story of Easter Week*, 4th ed. (Dublin; Golden Eagle Books, Ltd., 1969). A former student of Pearse's, Ryan is generally uncritical and sentimental, although his work does have value as a primary source and offers an evocative point of view.

13. Hedley McCay, *Padraic Pearse: A New Biography* (Cork: Mercier Press, 1966).

some revisionist historians have sought to temper the Pearse myth. J. J. Horgan's *From Parnell to Pearse*[14] is in this vein. But of much greater importance is an article by the Jesuit Francis Shaw, "The Canon of Irish History—A Challenge," which is an attack on the political ideology Pearse has come to exemplify.[15] Shaw argues that Pearse's political ideas were unoriginal and derivative, offering nothing new or profound.[16] For Shaw, Pearse's effect has been a glorified republican legacy of violence that has since monopolized the nationalist vision of a united Ireland—an effect that has proven deleterious to Irish nationalism. In addition, Pearse's supposed piety and courage have corrupted the nationalist movement, which has embraced the myth of Pearse uncritically and now has a vision fixed on the Easter Rising and its tactics.

Shaw's analysis, written against a background of escalating political violence in Northern Ireland, fails to do more than attack the work of Pearse's hagiographers. Shaw's position within the church is notable here because his heaviest attacks fall on Pearse's "heretical" and "unorthodox" views of the Catholic faith.[17] Though Shaw's is the most important revisionist view of Pearse and his legacy, it cannot dismiss the importance of Pearse in the nationalist tradition. With the exception of his analysis of Pearse's heterodoxy, Shaw does not clarify why the myth of Pearse has had such an important influence on Irish nationalism.

Another important revisionist, certainly the one with the highest visibility, is Conor Cruise O'Brien. If one can call the Irish "liberal" constitutional view "revisionist," then O'Brien's views on the Rising are revisionist.[18] He says that since Home Rule was going to be

14. J. J. Horgan, *From Parnell to Pearse* (Dublin: Gill and Macmillan, 1948).

15. Francis Shaw, "The Canon of Irish History—A Challenge," *Studies* 61, no. 242 (Summer 1972): 115–53.

16. Ibid., 121.   17. Ibid., 122ff.

18. Conor Cruise O'Brien, *States of Ireland* (London: Hutchinson and Co., 1972; paperback, 1973).

granted at the end of World War I, the Easter Rising was unnecessary. According to O'Brien, Pearse and the Anglo-Irish War of 1919–21 have left the mystique of the gunman as the predominant political theme in Irish nationalism. But the gunman mystique in Irish republicanism was well entrenched by 1916, and the Rising occurred within a tradition of political violence in Ireland, which had received its greatest boost from British subjects determined to resist Home Rule after 1912.

Most interpretive works have attempted to see Pearse within a larger context, generally, as a representative type, subject to forces beyond his immediate control or consciousness. These studies express dissatisfaction with the view of George Dangerfield and others that the Rising was an inevitable result of failure to reform the political system.

Patrick O'Farrell's *Ireland's English Question* and William Irwin Thompson's *The Imagination of an Insurrection: Dublin, 1916*[19] are brilliant and suggestive works. Both, while not about Pearse alone, consider him to be the critical figure in the Easter Rising. O'Farrell's thesis is that the problem between Ireland and England lies in the distorted picture each country has of the other, and this lack of understanding of the other's motivations and the reasons for the other's way of seeing things has led to an intense mutual antagonism; the relationship between the two countries is not quasi-colonial but is a protracted war in which the parties no longer understand the issues that separate them.

O'Farrell believes that an Irish cosmological view emerged that saw England as secular, materialistic, and unethical and saw Ireland as spiritual and moral. This Irish view was diametrically opposed to that of the English, who could not help seeing the "Irish problem"

---

19. Patrick O'Farrell, *Ireland's English Question* (New York: Schocken Books, 1971; paperback, 1975); William Irwin Thompson, *The Imagination of an Insurrection: Dublin, 1916* (London: Lindisfarne Press, 1967).

as primarily political with no larger connotations. While the Irish saw their struggle as a spiritual battle for the truth, the English saw it as a strategic and logistical question, which they had a moral responsibility to settle fairly. The Irish, accordingly, moved the conflict to a place far removed from the political realm. For the Irish, O'Farrell claims, the battle has been over the salvation of "holy" Ireland against "pagan" England; because of that view, Ireland's conception of national liberation has become eschatological and millenarian in nature, and Irish nationalism has come to be couched in chiliastic terms based on the "truth," which "sinful" Britain will never be able to know. Patrick Pearse's greatest achievement, according to O'Farrell, was to articulate this cosmic hope of Irish nationalism. By openly positing the problem as spiritual, Pearse could speak for the millenialist dream that had set itself into the political and public subconscious. By dying for Ireland, Pearse and his generation lived out a sacrificial role that would bring on the new age.

Ireland's English Question acted as a corrective to the conventional historical view of the Anglo-Irish problem as essentially political. But O'Farrell sees Irish identity as solely Catholic. This discounts the Protestant backgrounds of many Irish national martyrs; it also avoids the question of the hostility or indifference that the church, and the population as well, usually felt toward the revolutionaries— his schema asserts that massive public support developed in favor of each act of insurrection. O'Farrell has in effect fixed Ireland in stone, especially when he discusses contemporary Ireland. Although he shifted the balance in the writing of Irish history, he went too far and did not give political and economic factors their due. The pragmatic diplomatic discussions between the British and Irish governments in the late 1980s and the 1990s seem somewhat to belie his thesis that the religious dimension is an impossible hurdle to any dialogue between Ireland and England.

Thompson's *The Imagination of an Insurrection* is primarily a work of literary criticism; it depicts Pearse as one of a number of minor Irish artists who, faced with their failure to render a first-rate artistic creation, were forced to implement an artistic vision in politics. The transference of their feelings of failure, along with their maudlin Romanticism, led to their desperate need either to create or to destroy as acts of artistic expression. Thompson's view has great merit, but he overestimates the imaginative influences at work on Pearse. While Pearse's personal disappointment over his artistic shortcomings played a role in his movement toward political action, he never truly despaired over his lack of artistic success. He did, however, face deeper personal problems that both affected his life and writing and helped make political action compelling. Thompson makes little mention of this, and his failure to do so does not help us understand how Pearse could influence others who were not themselves contending with artistic inadequacy and failure.

Somewhere between Thompson and O'Farrell, Pearse as a human being and the world he lived in still need to be tied together. Probably the single most important work on Pearse, Ruth Dudley Edwards's *Patrick Pearse: The Triumph of Failure*,[20] comes as close as any book, yet it fails in much the same way as Thompson and O'Farrell. This is not to say that Edwards's biography is neither thorough nor critical; it is a very good biography, which was considered a revisionistic work when it was published. Given the primary sources currently available, it must still be considered insightful. Edwards, though, neglects to show why Pearse became personally committed to the use of force. She maintains that Pearse's sense of personal failure led him to the Rising. Obviously convinced by the financial and professional determinism of Thompson's thesis, Edwards still fails to present Pearse as subject to the kinds of forces or emotional stress that would make him go out on a suicidal mission. Suddenly Pearse is there at the General Post Office on Easter

20. Ruth Dudley Edwards, *Patrick Pearse: The Triumph of Failure* (London: Victor Gollancz, 1977; paperback, 1979).

Monday, 1916, and we are not really sure why he is there. We do know that he faced grave financial difficulties, but we are not given the connection between the political act and his life.

Edwards has looked at Pearse's life from a totally positivistic point of view. This kind of commitment to rational analysis would be fine if all the connections between events and motivations were rational and readily understandable. When Edwards has subjects to deal with which are "rational," her analysis is impeccable. The major problem that Pearse presents historically is not so rational, however, and any rationalistic attempt to explain his participation in the Rising, as well as his obsession with death and salvation, is destined to be inadequate.

In addition, Edwards betrays an iconoclasm wholly secularistic and perhaps ultimately hostile to her subject. Why did Pearse come to consider death and violence desirable and beneficial? Why did he become a major political figure when nothing in his past indicated that he had either proclivity or desire for political leadership? Edwards, as well as Thompson, believes that Pearse's political and military involvement was a result of his growing sense of artistic and personal failure. For each of them, success and failure are mutually exclusive ideas; Edwards in particular seems to impose a value system that automatically denies the hero his due. In any case, theories of failure still do not explain why Pearse resorted to these desperate answers instead of other, more reasonable ones, and they offer little insight into Pearse's enduring contribution to Irish nationalism.

In the cases of both Thompson and Edwards, Pearse's sense of failure is used to imply that the Rising was a suicidal way of achieving some kind of success, and there is certainly a commonly held political opinion that the Rising was a suicidal act. But a sense of failure is usually inadequate as a sole cause of suicide. According to most psychiatric works on the subject of suicide, a sense of failure is not one of the prime factors in suicide; in particular, W. C. Menninger found that financial failure is an inadequate explanation for suicide.[21] Failure would certainly not be adequate as a sole explanation for participating in the Rising. Furthermore, Pearse does not seem to have presented any of the classic features of depression. While the serious and earnest Pearse did experience sadness, disappointment, and frustration, he did not at any time in the period between 1911 and 1916 exhibit symptoms of either a major or an atypical affective disorder as defined in the current psychiatric literature. He most certainly did not present indications of bipolar disorder, a depressive disorder, or any kind of psychosis.[22] Pearse does not seem to have gone through writing farewell notes in anticipation of his death, giving away treasured objects, losing interest in his appearance, or any of the other classic signs of someone anticipating ending their life. On the basis of his behavior, Patrick Pearse was not a man who was considering suicide, and his conscious choice of going to his death in the Easter Rising was not due to a sudden or increasing sense of failure and inadequacy. Recent psychiatric work on suicide indicates that perhaps the most important element in suicide is the individual's loss of hope, yet one cannot say that Pearse ever lost hope; his language and demeanor remained optimistic until the very end.

Although Pearse's increasing sense of personal failure played an undeniable part in his emotional outlook during the period in question, it was arguably less than that shared by the other two "Easter Rising Poets," Thomas MacDonagh and Joseph Mary Plun-

21. A. T. Beck, H. L. P. Resnick, and D. Lettieri, eds., *The Prediction of Suicide* (Bowie, MD, 1974); N. L. Farberow and E. Shneidman, eds., *The Cry for Help* (New York, 1961); E. Shneidman et al., *The Psychology of Suicide* (New York, 1970); and W. C. Menninger and Leona Chidester, "The Role of Financial Loss in the Precipitation of Mental Illness," *Journal of the American Medical Association* (6 May 1938), 1398–1432.

22. See *Diagnostic and Statistical Manual of Mental Disorders*, 3d ed., rev. (Washington: American Psychiatric Association, 1987).

kett.[23] If artistic or financial failure was the major cause of Pearse's self-destructiveness, it is an inadequate explanation for the hard-bitten political and military pragmatists such as James Connolly and the young Michael Collins—their participation in a self-consciously suicidal mission seems incongruous.

Also unexplained is how Pearse, the least likely person to lead a military revolution—a shy and usually retiring individual, a person of few if any political abilities—became the public spokesman for the radical politics of his day. only did he become an important rhetorician for Irish republicanism, but he also helped lead hundreds of people into a hopeless struggle. The fact is that Pearse spoke to a time and a society that understood him. His irrational ideas became the clarion call for many Irishmen, even when practically everyone who responded on Easter Monday, 1916, was sure that it meant death and defeat. This response and the ideology that led men to do such an irrational thing are not explainable with a conventional, rationalistic historical approach.

By and large the literature on Patrick Pearse has failed. It has helped us to know him, and it has helped us to know the Ireland in which he lived; but the reasons why he, with all his hopes, aspirations, and fears, *wanted* to die as a sacrifice for Ireland has yet to be explained. Those who have written about Pearse's participation in events have mistakenly assumed that human motivation is always conscious, always freely made, and always rationally conceived. This simply is not the case, and especially not with Pearse. The facile recognition that Pearse had an obvious "obsession with death" fails to illuminate how or why it existed. Likewise the historical effect of a person so afflicted is unlikely to be discerned by merely recounting what occurred after his death. A different approach to the analysis of the individual and his relationship to events in history is required.

23. MacDonagh's sense of artistic frustration was profound, and Plunkett was critically ill with tuberculosis in 1916.

O'Farrell has perhaps given a clue when he says that Irish historical development has been determined by Great Britain: the course of Ireland's development has not been one of choice.

It is odd that the historical literature on Pearse has so readily accepted him at face value. This man, full of deep conflict and unresolved contradictions, played a decisive role in his nation's history, and yet his complex personality has not been openly and honestly discussed. Edwards has done considerable service in this regard, but she fails to explain the contradictions of the man and seems to have resigned herself to this fact. That resignation is true of most of the commentators on Pearse; the work of the revisionists has stood alone in confronting the reputation of a courageous national hero.

Both the failure of Pearse's admirers to make him other than a mythic figure and the revisionist attack on his political legacy are the result of an unwillingness to consider Pearse in light of the forces that molded him. As Ireland's course has been undeniably influenced by Great Britain, so also was Pearse's personal development shaped by larger forces. The man who came out on Easter Monday to lead a group of men in the opening battle of a revolution was not there by accident.

This is not to suggest that Pearse was solely the creature of his environment, that he could not have imagined and espoused such self-destructive behavior with such vigor if he had acted solely from conscious political motivations. Patrick Pearse was an unusual individual, recognized as such by his contemporaries; but he did not seem to be the kind of man to kill himself leading troops into a doomed cause. Precisely because his acts were irrational and drew an equally irrational response from men who were wholly unlike him, the historian is forced to consider a different approach—a methodological approach that recognizes human decisions as complex phenomena, neither wholly determined by forces from without nor freely chosen from within. The moral and ethical values involved in any choice cannot be adequately explained by a wholesale acceptance of the individual as either a free moral agent or a puppet. Only a methodology that taps the reservoir of modern social science has a chance of explaining what needs explanation—the psychological makeup of the individual who acts in an historic event.

The main problem in using psychology to interpret the data of a person's life historically is the question of placing an a priori psychological construction over that person's life story. The variety of psychological theories, and the arbitrary choice among them this multiplicity implies, compound the problem, but the situation is manageable if historians are willing to look at their subjects with an open mind. No one approach can possibly deal with the myriad forces in any person's life history, just as no one therapeutic approach has a universal applicability to living people in therapy. But the historian can look at the individual as an adult, at the kind of person he became; the historian can search for patterns in the subject's habits, dreams, and actions. Then the historian can look back over the course of that person's life to see if those patterns have the sort of precedents that modern psychiatry or psychology would expect for that kind of adult behavior. The credibility of this approach is based on the consistency with which one finds certain patterns of behavior, as well as the kind of critical events that psychiatry or psychology tells us will invariably have connections to certain classes of behavior.

The methodology used in this case is based on neo-Freudian modifications of classical Freudian psychoanalysis, with faith in the "scientific" insight that psychoanalysis has given about human beings, their conflicts, hopes, aspirations, and fears. Approaching Pearse as an analytical subject through two differing, but related, analytical schools of thought reveals a great deal.

The first school is the so-called "ego-psychology" school of psychiatry, practiced by Heinz Hartmann, Ernst Kris, Paul Lowenstein, and others. Ego-analysis modifies the Freudian emphasis on instinctual drives as the primary motivation in the human personality and emphasizes instead the ego and its attempts to deal with intrapsychic conflict. Analytically, the ego mediates between the demands of our instincts and the demands of society. It manufactures compromises among the competing forces in the personality, to help people adapt to reality while still meeting their instinctual needs. Ego-analysis gives more attention than does classical analysis to the defensive operations of the ego in the individual's maturation toward rational thought.

The second, and the school of thought most heavily relied on in this analysis of Pearse, is the so-called "developmental" analytical school of Erik Erikson. It emphasizes the psychosocial development of the individual in terms of the social relations and social reality faced by that individual at various points in his development. Stages in a person's development are punctuated by the resolution of "phase-specific" psychological conflicts, and those resolutions propel the individual forward in maturity and growth. Irresolution of any one conflict can be identified and treated analytically according to the psychosocial issues that are known to manifest themselves at the period when the specific conflict first emerges. An advantage of the Eriksonian model for historians is that it can be applied in a point-by-point way to every stage of life, thus freeing the historian from the absolute dependence on information about infancy that classical psychoanalysis demands.

This dual approach has been chosen for flexibility. On the one hand, the ego-analytical school leaves room for a certain measure of free will, rescuing the individual from the cold determinism of his instincts. On the other, the developmental approach allows an analysis of the individual throughout his development and not just in early childhood. The assumptions behind the developmental approach allow the adult some exercise of will and creativity. For the purpose of this study, the Eriksonian model will dominate, although the ego-analytical approach should be kept in mind, because it, too, has heavily influenced the formulation of this thesis.

It is important to note the inherent weaknesses in the psycho-his-torical approach and the problems it presents. The developmental school has yet to deal adequately with the problem of cultural diver-sity. Obviously people in different cultures are going to develop at different rates of growth. The danger in the developmental approach lies in its presumption of cultural uniformity. Development seems obviously influenced by one's culture to a great degree. Precisely this criticism was at the heart of R. D. Laing's criticism of modern psychi-atry. In works such as *The Divided Self*,[24] Laing argued that the con-cept of normality is obviously culturally determined, as is the con-cept of madness or abnormality. Both concepts are in a continual state of flux and evolution. The idea that human development is fixed in a schematic system fails to recognize that normality is at best the accommodation of the majority to the prevailing system of val-ues. This so-called "existential-analytical" school would criticize the developmental model of growth on the grounds that it fails to take into account that the society in which a certain individual lives might well be mad. In a society that is mad, the "mad" individual might well be healthy, because his madness represents a defensive shell erected by his ego in response to the widely shared pathology around him. Because of this possibility, systems like Erikson's are incapable of helping us determine what is or is not normal development.

It seems particularly important that the historian be careful not to judge the behavior of an individual without placing him within his cultural and social milieu. Works such as Erich Fromm's *The Anatomy of Human Destructiveness* and *Escape from Freedom* are attempts to take such historical factors into account.[25] In fact the school of psychoanalytic thought of which Fromm was a member,

24. R. D. Laing, *The Divided Self: An Existential Study of Sanity and Madness* (New York: Tavistock Publications, 1959; Pelican Books, 1965; reprint ed., 1977).

25. Erich Fromm, *The Anatomy of Human Destructiveness* (New York: Holt, Rhinehart and Winston, 1973; paperback, 1975); *Escape from Freedom* (New York: Holt, Rhinehart and Winston, 1941; paperback, 1969).

the "Washington Cultural School," emphasized the therapeutic need to consider individuals within the context of the world in which they live. The question of how normal Pearse's society was is not irrelevant; neither is the question of how much the people around him helped determine the choices he both faced and made.

Of equal importance to any consideration of Pearse is the problem of several coincidentally unresolved stages. Erikson believes that if an individual fails to resolve any one developmental crisis, he will remain fixed at the unresolved level of development. The individual would then be controlled by the issues before him at the crisis he failed to resolve, and would be unable to move onward to face a new set of psychological tasks. Erik Erikson's *Young Man Luther*[26] took Martin Luther as a subject for analysis in order to explain his role in the historical events at the beginning of the Reformation. Erikson looked at what he believed was the determining "identity crisis" in Luther's psychosocial development and how it was resolved. In the case of Pearse this scenario did not reveal itself so clearly. It would appear that Pearse only partially resolved several conflicts; thus he partially progressed on a variety of levels while failing to mature emotionally, intellectually, and sexually. Pearse was forced to be an adult, and he lived at times quite successfully, despite his obvious immaturity; but his inadequate psychosocial preparation led him to a desperate conflict between his need to act as a free, autonomous adult and his immaturity. His arrested personality, which demanded security and gratification, was increasingly unable to protect him from the conflicts he had avoided.

In his psychic search for resolution, Pearse manifested an ever-increasing preoccupation with death and violence. The search for a resolution of his personal crisis confronted the arrested development of Irish politics between 1912 and 1916. When Irish hopes of

26. Erik Erikson, *Young Man Luther: A Study in Psychoanalysis and History* (New York: W. W. Norton, 1958; paperback, 1962).

establishing Home Rule in Ireland were suspended because of potential violence in Ulster and a world war on the continent, Pearse's rhetoric offered a clear resolution. That resolution—one of self-destruction, violence, and conscious self-sacrifice—spoke to people who had expended themselves on a variety of approaches to the "Irish problem" only to come up short repeatedly; and his personal answer met their need and redirected the course of Irish nationalism. Pearse's resolution was not suicidal—an extermination of the self—but the embrace of martyrdom, which transcends the world of failure and fulfills the self by confirming the place of the individual within the culture. Pearse "enabled" those who followed him to realize their own place and worth within Irish history.[27] The positivistic inability to see martyrdom in this sense has clouded the ability of historians to see Pearse and his legacy for what they really are.

In a larger sense, Pearse's act was not that of a parochial man in the obscure place that Ireland usually occupies in European history. Throughout Europe in the period just before the Great War other men, such as Rupert Brooke and Charles Peguy, expressed the need for personal and national redemption which could only come through violence and death. Pearse was only another European expressing what seemed to be a sentiment of his age. Once the war loosed its vast bloodletting, with millions of human beings dying for ill-defined reasons, the lives of Pearse and his comrades were sacrificed for what were relatively clear ideals within a long history of similar events. His chiliastic vision, and the rhetoric he used to help realize it, were not without parallels in Western culture, nor was his narcissistic self-indulgence without precedence.

By looking at Pearse as a human being whose motivations were

27. For more on this kind of "enabling" see John E. Mack, *Prince of Our Disorder: The Life of T. E. Lawrence* (Boston: Little, Brown, 1976; paperback, 1976), xxvi.

both complex and unique, yet paradoxically were shared by many men of his age, we can arrive at a view of him which neither raises him on high nor seeks to deny his very real courage. If we look at him as a person, Patrick Pearse might retain some of his "greatness," or even increase in his historical stature, while gaining some of the humanity that has so long been denied him.

CHAPTER 2

The Making of a
National Hero

Much of the historical writing about Patrick Pearse's early life has
tended to look into his childhood uncritically and with an eye
toward sanctifying the child who was later to become a sainted martyr of the Easter Rising of 1916. But like all men, Pearse was once a
boy, and the story of that boy's life does have a considerable impact
on the ending of the adult's life. In that child the man who follows
will bear a striking resemblance to himself as a youth in many
ways—so much so that he was never to grow free of his childhood
dependency on his home.

Patrick Pearse's parents came from two different countries; more
importantly, they came together with different experiences, values,
and aspirations. His father, James Pierce, was born in London in
1839; in 1892 he changed the family name to the "more Irish" form—
Pearse.[1] His family were artisans, and James was to follow in their
footsteps. Initially, however, poverty bedeviled the family and James
and his two brothers moved to Birmingham in search of work while
he was still a young boy. At the age of eight, James took a job at a
chain-making factory, the first of many marginal jobs he was to take

1. McCay, *Padraic Pearse*, 16.

and dislike; but he was a stubborn and self-motivated individual, determined to make something of himself in the world. This determination fueled his fierce appetite for learning, and he became a fairly well educated man in spite of the economic hurdles he faced.[2]

One of his main interests was art, and his decision to become a stone carver probably followed a series of evening drawing classes.[3] Stone carving was a respectable and potentially lucrative trade, what with the substantial business created by the Gothic revival in architecture, with its emphasis on detail and ornamentation, and the steady market in Victorian funerary decoration. Pearse chose eventually to emigrate to Ireland to take advantage of a boom in Catholic church building.[4] He settled in Dublin as a journeyman[5] within a community of largely Anglo-Irish artisans, who, it appears, fully accepted him.[6]

By the mid-1870s, James Pearse not only was firmly established in the trade with a partnership of his own but also was the father of a daughter and son. While he was still young, he had married Emily Fox. His feelings about her after her death at the age of thirty in 1876 reveal that the marriage had been difficult; James bitterly blamed her for the death through "neglect" of one of their infant children.[7] A now-burgeoning business and children to be tended demanded a mother at home, and James soon married a nineteen-year-old young woman who worked at his local stationer's shop around the corner.[8]

Margaret Brady, later to become Patrick Pearse's mother, was by all accounts a simple, attractive young woman when she caught James Pearse's eye. Originally her Irish-speaking family was from

2. Ruth Dudley Edwards, *Patrick Pearse*, 1.

3. Ibid.   4. McCay, *Padraic Pearse*, 12.

5. Ruth Dudley Edwards, *Patrick Pearse*, 2.

6. David Thornley, "Patrick Pearse and the Pearse Family," *Studies* (Autumn-Winter 1971), 335.

7. Eamonn de Barra Papers, National Library of Ireland, Dublin.

8. Stephen Barrett MSS, Lennon to Sighle Barrett, 14 May 1958, National Library of Ireland, Dublin.

County Meath,[9] but during the potato famine of the 1840s they had been forced to move to Dublin, where they became members of the urban laboring class. Margaret's father, from whom the future patriot was to get his name, was later able to buy land, but at the time of her meeting with James she and her family were living in a North Dublin tenement house.[10]

When they married, James was thirty-seven and she a mere twenty. The difference in ages was almost as great as the differences between them in temperament and attitude. By 1877 he was a respected practitioner of his craft with a successful business. But there is evidence that James Pearse had objectives different from mere craftsmanship in mind. He was advertising himself as a "sculptor," and while there was some legitimacy to the claim, most of his work fell into the category of carving as opposed to that of a true sculptor.[11] He was well read, had broad interests, and expressed himself well if unimaginatively in writing. This was not the case with Margaret, whose writing was of a less than sophisticated hand, overly sentimental and almost without punctuation; indeed her writing betrays a maudlin romanticism and emotional immaturity that confirm that her gifts were considerably less intellectual than those of her husband. She was affectionate, loyal, and open-hearted, while he, especially in later years, was somewhat reserved and distant. Though their economic origins were similar, there is no doubt that James had inherited the English craftsman's fierce sense of pride and independence that could often come across as an air of superiority, especially to those of a working-class background such as the Bradys. Indeed James would have been very aware that Margaret Brady had married well.

9. Ruth Dudley Edwards, *Patrick Pearse*, 5.
10. Ibid.
11. Ruth Dudley Edwards maintains that the distinction between artisan and artist at this time was minor. She believes that James Pearse's claim to an artistic title was merely a device used to advertise his abilities. See Ruth Dudley Edwards, *Patrick Pearse*, 5.

A far greater difference than that of age, education, or social class stood between them—the question of religion. At the time of his marriage to Margaret Brady, James Pearse was formally a Catholic; in retrospect, his coming to the church seems more than a little suspect. His parents had been freethinkers and Unitarians,[12] and James seems to have converted out of fear of being denied work because of his religious opinions.[13] In spite of his desire to communicate the beauty and sensibility of religious sculpture,[14] nothing indicates that he had religious inclinations. In fact, his youth was marked by a firm denial of the validity of organized religion, legend having it that he rejected Christianity while a child because it could not respond adequately to his precocious questions.[15] While his library was full of comparative religious studies,[16] his anthropological interest in this subject appears to have been that of many Victorian agnostics and skeptics of the day. But when Catholic artisans wanted to know why he, a non-Catholic, was being given Church commissions, James realized the financial necessity of conversion, and in 1870 he brought his family into the Roman Catholic fold with him.[17] The sincerity of his motives was attested by the local parish priest.[18] But later actions and changes in his thinking laid open to question the depth of James's original spiritual commitment. In any case it would seem that his less than orthodox religious upbringing might have caused him no minor hurdles in coming "around" to the peculiarly Calvinistic Catholicism of Ireland.

Margaret on the other hand, had all the signs of the simple, pietistic, unquestioning, and conventionally devout believer. Letters between James and Margaret, especially those written during their courtship, show that James was not above mocking his future

12. Ibid., 1.   13. Ibid., 2.
14. Eamonn De Barra Papers, University College, Dublin.
15. Ruth Dudley Edwards, *Patrick Pearse*, 1.
16. Ibid.   17. Ibid.
18. Eamonn De Barra Papers, letter from Divine to James Pearse, 26 Dec. 1877.

bride's less rigorous thinking and emotional religiosity. In the years to follow, as James began to drift back toward reclaiming his heritage by affiliating himself with the English Radicals and espousing a kind of dogmatic skepticism, Margaret quietly yet resolutely resisted. The most obvious bone of contention in this regard would have been the raising of their children, where she undoubtedly was determined to keep them within the faith in which she had been raised and in which she believed absolutely.

Perhaps these differences between them, seen more objectively by her family than by Margaret, were part of the reason for their wish to delay the wedding. As some historians have pointed out, her family probably desired a delay because they disliked having a wedding so soon after the death of James's first wife—less than a year earlier. In an age of elaborate funeral observation with strict customs governing the proper social conventions regarding mourning and grief, the planning of a hasty marriage must have been unseemly to the rather conventional Bradys.[19] The more liberal James, while recognizing these feelings, probably saw this issue as less important; besides, the business and children could not wait for long.

Despite these family reservations, Margaret Brady married James Pearse, and within a short time bore three of their four children. A girl, named Margaret after her mother, was born in 1877; Patrick (given the middle name Henry after the American patriot) was born two years later; a second son, Willie, followed in 1881. Not long afterward the two children from James's previous marriage were married and out of the home, with the son, James Vincent, moving to England. Thus the new family had the house to itself and thrived, like the stone carving business to which it was attached.

Born in 1879, Patrick was reportedly bright, serious and, like his father, self-motivated. By his own account he was a healthy child; but his half-sister Mary Emily, fifteen years old at Patrick's birth,

19. Ruth Dudley Edwards, *Patrick Pearse*, 4.

later wrote that he had been shy and thoughtful from his earliest years and became more so as he grew older.[20] Mary Emily described his childhood nature as being one of "self-repression,"[21] at the same time that she described him as a "marvellously [sic] dominant personality."[22] Patrick later recorded that his parents, and in particular his father, seem to have had few personal friends.[23] At home he rarely dealt with adult visitors, but since home and business were in the same building, he probably had to deal with visitors at least formally on occasion. His withdrawn demeanor seems to have worn off by late adolescence, though Patrick was shy and socially awkward all of his life. He grew up, then, a homebody, much more open around his siblings and mother than with others, counting few friends apart from his relatives. To the bright and self-conscious Patrick, his home remained a safe and secure refuge in which he was continually able, perhaps forced, to amuse himself.

The rhythm of the house was determined by the activities of the business, occasional vacations at Margaret's uncle's farm, the children's schooling, and the normal religious obligations of an Irish-Catholic family. As is so often the case, Patrick's description of his elder sister, Margaret, makes her out to be a bit of a boss, and at times she must have been trying to her younger brothers. Another girl, Mary Brigid, came along in 1883, two years after Willie; these younger children lived forever in the shadows of their more assertive and imaginative siblings. Willie especially emerged as a sensitive and extremely gentle personality who developed an intensely close relationship with his brother. Later in life, after her brothers had been put to death, Mary Brigid developed into a somewhat neurotic sycophant, dwelling and living on her deceased brothers' fame.

20. Emily Pearse McGloughlin, "An Elder Sister's Recollections of Padraig Pearse," in Mary Brigid Pearse, ed., *The Home Life of Padraig Pearse*, 44.
21. Ibid.   22. Ibid.
23. P. H. Pearse, "My Childhood and Youth," 22.

As a youth Patrick exhibited an extraordinary capacity for fantasy.[24] He reveled in it constantly, usually seeing himself as a great Gaelic hero of the past, alive again and saving others from distress. This seems to have gone on into early adolescence—not so unusual perhaps—but Patrick's unusually vivid memory of this habit seems psychologically significant. Also as a youth, he often dressed up in the clothes of women or beggars, usually with Willie, complete with makeup; and with the help of a sister or female cousin, they would go out and roam the streets.[25]

Young Patrick had a serious devotion to the serving of his religious obligations, especially in matters of indulgences. He dressed up as an acolyte[26] and took special delight in May devotions before the altar of the Virgin.[27] One of the few traumas we know of from his childhood is recorded by his sister Mary Brigid, who remembers him running into the house one day with blood streaming down his face. It seems that Patrick, overanxious to get to church, jumped from a tram while it was still moving, fell, and severely cut his face, and was distressed that he had missed a holy day of obligation.[28]

This childhood religious devotion joined hands with his delight in fantasy on more than one occasion: he wrote and "produced" plays with himself cast as a priest complete with the giving of sacraments and blessings to his cooperative and approving brother and sisters.[29] In fact, this writing and producing of family dramas was one of the

24. Ibid., 20.

25. This practice of dressing up in female clothes and wandering in the street is attested to by both of Pearse's sisters and was confirmed by his female cousin. See Mary Brigid Pearse, "Our Home Recollections of Padraig," in Mary Brigid Pearse, ed., *The Home Life of Padraig Pearse*, 40–42; Margaret Pearse, "Patrick and Willie Pearse," *Capuchin Annual* (1943), 87. While Ruth Dudley Edwards notes that Pearse dressed in disguise, her discussion of him is not analytical. See Edwards, *Patrick Pearse*, 8–9.

26. Mary Brigid Pearse, "Our Home Recollections of Padraig," 50.

27. Ibid., 52–53.   28. Ibid., 53.

29. Ibid., 50–52.

major diversions of his youth. *Macbeth* was a favorite, and the children produced it often, with Patrick in the title role and Mary Brigid cast as Lady Macbeth;[30] once when Willie had the lead role, Patrick cheerfully ruined the scene.[31] He also loved reciting songs and other readings of a patriotic nature, more than once giving interpretations of pieces his father performed at the few parties given by the Pearses.[32]

Patrick's emotional and aesthetic sensitivity was coupled with a lack of self-assurance. At school he was reserved and shy, although it is obvious he was respected by his peers for his intellectual abilities.[33] There are grounds to believe that he seemed somewhat effeminate to the boys around him.[34] Instead of the usual games of boys his age, he chose less physical and more cerebral games such as draughts.[35] Both of the Pearse boys were nonathletes and Patrick was to be totally uninterested in athletics as an adult.[36] Nonetheless he did play occasional games of football and hurling as a boy, and a former classmate told of Patrick punching someone who laughed at his poor skills.[37] It is likely that his physical abilities were poor, and his humiliation at having those shortcomings pointed out publicly must have been keen indeed. On more than one occasion he even challenged adults toe-to-toe when he thought that they were being unfair to him, but especially to others. His sister records that Patrick had his share of fights, and she thought that he found them to be intoxicating as tests of his ability to meet danger.[38] With the history

30. Ibid., 47.   31. Ibid., 48.

32. Thornley, "Patrick Pearse and the Pearse Family," 340.

33. Eamonn O'Neill, "Some Notes on the School and Post-School Life of Padraig Pearse," in Mary Brigid Pearse, ed., *The Home Life of Padraig Pearse*, 103.

34. McCay, *Padraic Pearse*, 11.   35. Ibid.

36. Mary Hayden, "My Recollections of Padraig Pearse," in Mary Brigid Pearse, ed., *The Home Life of Padraig Pearse*, 114.

37. Eamonn O'Neill, "Patrick Pearse, Some Other Memories," *Capuchin Annual* (1935), 38.

38. Mary Brigid Pearse, "Our Home Recollections of Padraig," 59.

we have so far, it is not difficult to see why he enjoyed these confrontations—his sister was probably right, he did look at these incidents as opportunities to test himself. One can imagine that he was taunted frequently about the shyness that his family found so appealing. In his need to be sure of himself, he could not give any ground to anyone who challenged him.

Several things in his manner probably did not help his sense of security. In later life he had to overcome a pronounced stammer in order to speak in public;[39] perhaps this accounts for the peculiar "pistol-like" and "jerky" delivery he had when talking.[40] He had a distinct cast in his left eye, which led him to pose for pictures always showing his profile.[41] And to add insult to injury, he had to wear spectacles as a child[42]—no doubt a source of occasional discomfort, as with all children. Roger Casement observed that Pearse, as an adult, seemed physically awkward and had a "curious heavy gait,"[43] and even his admirers later commented on "that peculiar voice of his."[44]

Patrick was extremely afraid of the dark and suffered from frequent nightmares that required adult comforting to assuage his fears.[45] It is unlikely that his father gave that comfort. Patrick's relationships with his parents were marked by widely differing levels of affection and interaction. While his mother was loving and doting to

39. Joseph Holloway Diaries, 5 Jan. 1899, National Library of Ireland, Dublin.

40. Ibid. This seems to have been not only a part of his speeches but also characteristic of his conversational speech. One of his faculty recorded that "he spoke in abrupt, nervous phrases." F. O'Nolan, "Prophet and Martyr," in Mary Brigid Pearse, ed., *The Home-Life of Padraig Pearse*, 123.

41. Ruth Dudley Edwards, *Patrick Pearse*, 24.

42. Ibid.

43. Roger Casement, *The Black Diaries of Roger Casement*, ed. Peter Singleton-Gates and Maurice Girodins (New York, 1958), 395.

44. Martin Daly (pseud. Stephen MacKenna), *Memories of the Dead* (Dublin, 1917), 176.

45. P. H. Pearse, "My Childhood and Youth," 19.

the point of excess, his father was distant and very reserved. Patrick's adult memories of his father are remarkably vague, as if he could not remember much about him because he hardly knew him. His sisters also relate little about their father, and his absence in the family's collective memory is striking—in death Patrick dominated the Pearse women's memory of the family with hardly a mention ever made of his father. Patrick described his father as wholly absorbed in his business:

> My father came up to our room [the family room over the shop] only once or twice in the day, and at evening. He was big, with broad shoulders that were a little round. He was very silent, and spoke only once or twice during the course of the meal; breaking some reverie to say something kind to my mother or something funny to one of us. At times, indeed—but these were very, very seldom—he would, in order to please my mother, rouse himself to exercise the wonderful social gift that he had and then my mother's face would flush with pleasure, and we would laugh in pure happiness, or join shyly in the conversation.[46]

In Patrick's autobiographical writing, and in later writings by his two sisters, the father's distance from the family becomes very obvious. For example, the only story we have of Patrick and his father together comes from Mary Brigid. It is about one of the occasional family lantern shows put on by James Pearse for friends of the family and the children, featuring Patrick as narrator. Even years later his sister recognized the pressure to please his father that Patrick felt on these occasions.[47]

James Pearse's relationship to his family might well have been normal for a Victorian father; nonetheless it is obvious that his father seemed indefinite and unreal to Patrick, a problem later compounded by his father's death when Patrick was twenty and about to embark on his adulthood. What did impress itself upon Patrick as a

46. Ibid., 26–27.
47. Mary Brigid Pearse, "Our Home Recollections of Padraig," 83.

boy—it was in fact his earliest childhood memory—was the sound and sight of his father's workshop downstairs,[48] where imagination and will overcame and transformed lifeless stone and shaped it into living things. The kind of carving done in the shop doubtless impressed itself as well into his subconscious; statues of the bleeding Savior, the Virgin, tombstones, angels, and the like, which out of necessity dealt with the spiritual and seemed perhaps more than a little macabre to a young boy. For Patrick, his father was not only a God-like figure—the creator and potential destroyer of his existence—but also evidently able to create entire universes, the kind that existed only in Patrick's fantasy.[49]

In 1879 James Pearse was forty, and the age difference between his two sets of children makes it understandable that he left the child-rearing to his younger and more energetic wife. But the birth intervals of James and Margaret Pearse's children raise significant questions about the relationship between James and Margaret and the possible cause of their growing estrangement. Within six years, Margaret gave birth to four children, all of them approximately two years apart. After the birth of Mary Brigid, the couple had no more children despite Margaret's being only twenty-seven years old. Even though James was in his mid-forties by this time, the failure to have more children must be regarded as abnormal in the absence of some proof of impotence or infertility. In the context of Catholic Ireland in the 1890s, it is highly doubtful that Margaret, a woman of relatively little education and of serious Catholic principles, would have pursued or allowed voluntary contraception. James, however, was an admirer of Charles Bradlaugh and would have been keenly aware that Bradlaugh and Annie Besant had been put on trial for their distribution of sex education and birth control information in 1877.[50]

48. P. H. Pearse, "My Childhood," 12–13.

49. See Appendix.

50. Walter Arnstein, *The Bradlaugh Case: Atheism, Sex, and Politics among the Late Victorians* (Columbia, MO: University of Missouri Press, 1983).

The Besant and Bradlaugh affair caught the attention of those Dubliners who wished that their rather provincial capital was not nearly so isolated from the mainstream of life in London: everything points to James responding in a similar fashion. That he would have chosen to control his family's size makes even more sense in the general intellectual and economic climate of Liberal Britain, where both intellectual and economic justification for birth control seem to have overtaken the middle classes at this time. Furthermore, a desire to see at least one son all the way through school furnished substantial reason for James Pearse to limit his family's size.[51]

Margaret and James probably came to some kind of peaceful coexistence on this issue, but it is unlikely that Margaret ever would have given in to James. Her difficult delivery of Willie might have been a factor leading to abstinence.[52] Thus one could infer that as time went by the Pearses' physical relationship, whether because of inability, fear of pregnancy, or ideological differences, grew colder, and that their sexual relationship was probably unsatisfactory to them both. The possible personal repercussions would have been frustration, anger, disappointment, and a sense of self-vindication on both sides.

Shortly after Patrick was born, Margaret wrote a letter to her husband that indicates a major falling out between them had already taken place. "[N]othing will ease me now but death alone and only for me poor little ones I would be freely satisfied to go if my peace

---

51. See J. A. Banks, *Prosperity and Parenthood: A Study of Family Planning among the Victorian Middle Classes* (London: Routledge and Kegan Paul, 1954), for the most important analysis of contraception and birth control in the late Victorian period; for an update of the argument, and a statistical look at the issues of income and aspiration in conjunction with birth control, see J. A. Banks, *Victorian Values: Secularism and the Size of Families* (London: Routledge and Kegan Paul, 1981).

52. See Appendix.

was made with God Almighty. . . . I hope you are not angry with me about this afair [sic] . . . to live knowing you are not fond enough to be jealous I wish to God I had that to say to you if so I would think less of this afair [sic]. . . ."[53] Whatever caused this "afair," the problems in the relationship had deep origins; as Ruth Dudley Edwards has pointed out, after this incident James increasingly retreated into his self-education and Margaret into the raising of the family.[54]

James Pearse's claims to the title "sculptor" were occasionally realized. At his death, his achievements were noted in the Irish press, especially the sculpture on the front of the Bank of Ireland. But the stock in trade of his business was ornamental and decorative carving. Although James's artistic achievements had merit, most of his time had to be spent on the details of carving, often repetitively, and his continued claim to the title of "sculptor" represents wishful thinking. Whether he was frustrated about this we cannot be sure; but we can say that his insistence on the loftier title is curious.[55] Why did he call himself a sculptor? The answer lies in his own notions of class, where he had come from, and where and what he wanted to be.

A conflict seems to have presented itself here: James considered himself to be an artist despite the fact that his work usually filled some more pragmatic function designed mostly by others. In other words, he usually did not create wholly original works of art to be admired on their own merit but carved instead those things that served a primarily decorative function. He was a typical artisan, well within the Liberal-Radical tradition, and probably very familiar with the "socio-aesthetic" criticism of John Ruskin and William Morris,

53. James Pearse Papers, letter from Margaret Pearse to James Pearse, 16 Sept. n.d., National Library of Ireland, Dublin.

54. Ruth Dudley Edwards, *Pearse*, 8.

55. Especially if, as Edwards maintains, the difference between a carver and a sculptor was largely semantic and did not alter his position among those in the trade (ibid., 5).

and thus saw his craft as art serving a social and moral function. Nonetheless, he lived at a time when the debate on this issue was especially lively, and he could not have been ignorant of the significance of his adoption of the artistic title, in an era when strict aestheticism had emerged to challenge Ruskin and Morris. James's claim to the artist label was just, and it reflected his belief that his craft was a noble and creative one. Nonetheless his subject and personality seemed to be at odds. His work centered on religious themes, yet he seems to have exhibited few religious sensibilities.

To some extent this wishful thinking about his artistic position stemmed from his fear of a return to the poverty he had known in his youth. From poverty he had come, and he always remembered it; as he frequently told his children, he had been born in two rooms and a garret, and "'You must not forget the garret!'"[56] The fact that the memory of that admonition stuck in the minds of his children meant that James's background had great importance both for him and for them. His attitudes about his past and the desire he had to improve himself indicate that he did not think of himself as a working man but as somewhat better and different. This sensibility was symptomatic of that part of the working class described by several historians as the "labor aristocracy" of the Late Victorian period.[57] Having grown out of and away from the poverty and drudgery he had known as a youth, James was prepared to take credit for his accomplishments and stand apart from his past. His skilled trade and his relatively sophisticated education had come together to establish within him the "self-reverence" that characterized the emerging middle-class labor aristocrat during the last decades of the century.[58]

56. Eamonn de Barra Papers.

57. For the most coherent discussion of the "labor aristocracy" see Eric Hobsbawm, *Labouring Men*, (London: Wiedenfield and Nicholson, 1971; paperback, 1973), esp. the chapter "The Labour Aristocracy in Nineteenth Century Britain."

58. Standish Meacham, *A Life Apart: The English Working Class, 1890-1914* (Cambridge, MA: Harvard University Press, 1977), 195.

Because of his sense of achievement, James had come to see himself in contrast to the kind of worker he had once been. With his sense of accomplishment grew a desire to improve not only his own station in life but also that of his children.[59] Their improvement was to be a confirmation and validation of his own life and values.

This attitude would have been another source of conflict between him and his wife. While his whole experience seemed to confirm the validity of individual initiative and free will, Margaret clung to the deterministic moralism of Irish Catholicism and her romantic views of Irish nationalism. Against the odds James had, through skill and tenacity, secured and improved his standing within his trade and the community. His artistic claims were attempts to better himself still further. When Patrick later turned toward choosing a legal career, it is difficult to believe that this choice was his own as much as it represented a fulfillment of James's desires for his son and his family's improvement.

James clearly moved intellectually more and more toward the English radicals of the day. Whatever had existed of his Catholic enthusiasm eroded.[60] Also, developing a political appetite, he became a staunch supporter of the Irish Parliamentary Party leader, Charles Stewart Parnell, and in 1886 reacted with fury to a published attack upon Parnellism by a Fellow of Trinity College Dublin. Out of his own pocket, he published a reply entitled "England's Duty to Ireland as Plain to a Loyal Irish Roman Catholic." This twenty-thousand-word pamphlet argued for giving Irishmen their constitutional rights with fair representation in Parliament. Despite his radical leanings, a defense of Parnell along these lines was rather unimaginative and predictable. James stressed that, while Ireland was not entitled to any kind of separate national existence, nevertheless it was, and should be, fully an equal member of the United Kingdom.

59. Ibid., 22.
60. Ruth Dudley Edwards, *Pearse*, 10–11.

The tone of this pamphlet was sincere but stentorian; the James Pearse who emerges from these pages was "a formidable if somewhat pompous individual."[61] What also emerges is a father whose conclusions about Irish nationalism are considerably different from those found in the romantic tales that Patrick dreamed for himself, where political compromise and debate had no place.

James Pearse published a second pamphlet in 1888, this one in the form of a fictitious dialogue between James's new idol, the Radical M.P. Charles Bradlaugh, and Henry Hyndman of the Social Democratic Federation. In this tract, "Bradlaugh" argues against the use of force and the idea of class warfare in favor of democracy and private ownership of property with state control and regulation of the economy.

Such intellectual and political changes on the part of a husband would, if she understood them, be likely to disturb the orthodox Irish Catholic mother and force her to shelter her young children from any potentially harmful effects on their faith. It appears that this was indeed to be the case, and Margaret did so with the assistance of her Aunt Margaret. This aunt was a small, dark woman, described as usually dressed in black (a color later to be much favored by Patrick), and she played a major part in the raising of the Pearse children at this time.[62] Pearse was later to refer to her as "Auntie Margaret," describing her as "my dear fosterer and teacher."[63]

At Auntie Margaret's knee the children heard gilded nationalistic tales of Wolfe Tone, Robert Emmet, John Mitchel, and the Fenians, especially O'Donovan Rossa[64]—later to be the subject of a famous Pearse eulogy. Her advanced age must have given her an air of great wisdom in the eyes of the children, and Patrick Pearse believed

61. Thornley, "Patrick Pearse and the Pearse Family," 338.
62. P. H. Pearse, "My Childhood," 23.
63. Ibid., 12.   64. Ibid., 29.

unquestioningly her tales of the famine, the rebellions of 1848 and 1867, even her accounts of eyewitnesses she had met who supposedly knew the beloved Tone and Emmet.[65] In addition she also told tales of ancestors who fought and died in the rising of 1798.[66]

Pearse's mother and great aunt obviously both had special feeling for him, and they argued on at least one occasion over the right to care for him when he was ill, his aunt arguing that Patrick and she were closer.[67] As an indication of just how close he felt toward his aunt, he later recalled suffering a prolonged and severe bout of scarlatina, his only memory of which was his aunt at his bedside, singing rebel songs.[68] Pearse later credited her as the source of his appreciation of the Fenians.[69] His mother and aunt adored him, and they came to represent in his mind the incarnation of love and acceptance. His emotional experience with them was wholly different in spirit and tone from that with his too-distant father.

An equally important inheritance from them was Patrick's romantic Irish Catholic nationalism, reinforced in popular literature and history, that tended to be unexamined and intensely emotional, feeding his life of fantasy. Where his father's nationalism was pragmatic and constitutional, the national view that Patrick developed was intensely idealistic and romantic. In the stories he heard, Ireland's patriotic heroes came to life and passed on to him eternal truths that he would have to address as an adult.

If a fairy tale is a story told repeatedly and rooted in reality with characters from everyday life, then the patriotic stories Patrick heard from his mother and his aunt were fairy tales.[70] They differed from more conventional fairy tales in their overwhelmingly negative and

---

65. Ibid., 28-29.   66. Ibid., 28.
67. Ibid., 12.   68. Ibid., 28.
69. *An Claidheamh Soluis*, 19 May 1906.

70. For an analysis of the role of fantasy and fairy tales in childhood along these lines, see Bruno Bettelheim, *The Uses of Enchantment: The Meaning and Importance of Fairy Tales* (New York: Vintage Books, 1977), 3-45.

despairing endings; Bruno Bettleheim holds that fairy tales traditionally end in triumph and optimism as the stories serve to order for the child a disordered and threatening universe by elaborating fantasy. The content of the fairy tale fits the unconscious fantasy, thus enabling the child to cope with the content of this real struggle. Through the fairy tale the child performs a kind of self-analysis. These tales present not only good but also bad things that exist in life and must be accommodated and overcome. The child's reaction to the story is identification with a heroic figure, not because that figure is good but because the figure arouses within him feelings of sympathy and pathos.[71]

Both Patrick's mother and his aunt supplied him with stories in which the characters were noble but doomed to defeat in spite of the righteousness of their cause. Because of the overwhelming odds against them, the characters went down to a death that was preordained but embraced nonetheless. The stories exalted the death of the hero as long as the hero died well.

In the period in his life critical for his first efforts to grasp the nature of the human condition and to find meaning in the face of that condition, Patrick was receiving a uniquely pessimistic image of the "good" presented to him on an almost daily basis. Central in the content of conventional fairy tales and fantasy is the adult world, which waits to be appropriated by the child's diligence, courage, and cunning. Once the child controls it, he is secure in his abilities and power. The question is to what extent was Patrick, living a life of constant fantasy which had a pessimistic vision of human existence and the world, able to be secure in his own abilities and freedom? His fantasy world held no security or reassurance. It offered only defeat, suffering, fame, and no condolence. If he had been secure in his real world, the world of fantasy would have receded.[72]

71. Ibid., 9.
72. Bettleheim warns, "The more insecure a man is in himself and his place

In a house where he would never be a boss, where he was isolated and later protected from his father's ways, where his whole life was dominated by women whom he was never going to have the opportunity to dominate, Patrick's feelings of inadequacy were virtually assured.[73] In the most important stage of the development of the child's new sense of individual initiative, between the ages of about four and six, Patrick had to find his own way of initiating in order to succeed. The only success open to him was in his own fertile imagination, where he could overcome the obstacles and ambivalence within himself.[74]

One must also wonder about the inevitable confusion that must have taken place early in Patrick's life as he attempted to deal with three older females—a mother, sister, and aunt—all having the same name. He was to feel obligated and attached to many a Margaret—all of whom loved him, doted on him, and in the end came to worship him. While his father increasingly withdrew from his son, Patrick received female attention in abundance. While James sought to convince others of the validity of his atheistic and materialistic faith in the noble ideals of democratic representation and business, the women in Patrick's life cultivated a vastly different view of the world.

Patrick went to the nearby Westland Row Christian Brothers School for his intermediate schooling, primarily because it had a

---

in the immediate world, the more he withdraws into himself because of fear, or moves outward to conquer for conquest's sake" (ibid., 51).

73. See Erik Erikson, *Identity and the the Life Cycle* (New York: W. W. Norton, 1979), 78–87; cf. Erikson, *Childhood and Society*, 2d ed. (New York: W. W. Norton, 1963), and R. D. Laing, *The Divided Self*, esp. chap. 3 on "Ontological Insecurity."

74. See Jean Piaget, *The Child's Concept of the World* (New York: Harcourt, Brace, 1929), for discussion of the child's animistic relationship to the inanimate world; and for an analysis of the nightmare and its relationship to fantasy see Ernest Jones, *On the Nightmare* (London: Hogarth Press, 1931; reprinted 1949).

reputation for getting good examination results.[75] Despite his respectable early academic achievements, the educational style of this school forced Pearse within himself, and he became ever more introspective and less socially competent. This inwardness reached its peak in his early adolescent years—when a young person's search for identity confronts the harsh realities of the academic need to prepare for the future. It was undoubtedly the kind of education that his father would have died for, and James would have seen it as most practical and useful, rigorous enough to help further the family name by preparing his son for university and a professional career.

It is interesting to note that Pearse later became the greatest and most effective Irish critic of the teaching he had experienced as a child. Its goal-oriented curriculum, with an emphasis on rote memorization, the recitation of long passages, and the strict, even cruel, discipline, was in Pearse's mind horribly dispiriting for students. In his essay on Irish education, *The Murder Machine*, published as a pamphlet in 1916, he argued persuasively that the contemporary Irish educational system, based on an English model, was purposely designed to destroy the will of Irish children; in effect it created "willing or at least manageable slaves."[76] In its place he advocated a more humane system, with an attempt made to talk to the boys rather than to punish them for transgressions. He argued with equal conviction that there was a critical need to stimulate boys with a more interesting and diverse curriculum, based as often as possible on native Irish texts and achievements, as opposed to the English ones.[77] Although Pearse was not alone in criticizing this type of education, his vision of an "indigenous" Irish form of schooling was innovative and unique; through a rejection of the old system the

75. Ruth Dudley Edwards, *Patrick Pearse*, 12.

76. P. H. Pearse, *A Significant Irish Educationalist: The Educational Writings of P. H. Pearse*, ed. Seamus O'Buachalla (Dublin, 1980), 372.

77. Ibid., 381–82.

national dream would be realized: by tapping the natural creativity and spontaneity of the child, Irish culture would be saved from the English.[78]

It is important to consider the kind of child Patrick was and how difficult the regimentation was for him. Patrick deeply felt the tension (about which he was later to write so knowingly) between his child-like desire to "know" absolutely, incorporating the world around him into his life, and the school system in charge of preparing him for adulthood and getting him through his examinations; hence it is not surprising that, although he did fairly well in school, the pressures of it influenced him to an unusually high degree.[79] His only victory over that system was due to his indefatigable imagination, and it consisted of an absolute immersion in Irish language and literature; indeed, the legends of heroic deeds and romantic love, along with his ability to imagine himself into that past, had a vividness and satisfaction not experienced in memorizing Horace or Milton.

When he graduated from Westland Row in 1896, Pearse identified his main intellectual interest as Gaelic studies (in the fall of that year, he joined the young Gaelic League under Douglas Hyde's leadership) and he was proficient enough in the language to get a quasi-teaching position in Irish at his old alma mater. He planned to sit two years later for the matriculation examination for the Royal University, though his results on the preparatory examination were unremark-able.[80] Because of the abundance of time on his hands and his intense interest in the subject, he and a few friends founded a literary society to consider weekly subjects in Gaelic literature. He was elected president, and, as Edwards has shown, most of the programs of this grandiosely titled "New Irish Literary Society" centered on his, or his sister Margaret's, work.[81] This kind of concentration was

78. Ibid., 381ff.
79. Ruth Dudley Edwards, *Patrick Pearse*, 12.
80. Ibid., 16.   81. Ibid., 17.

quickly to yield rewards—Patrick gave papers at meetings in 1893 that he was to eventually publish.[82] In addition, he made great strides in the Gaelic League, even though he was yet in his teens, and both he and the fledgling Literary Society received regular attention in official Gaelic League publications.

In 1898 he passed his matriculation examination with first honors in Irish but little else of extraordinary note.[83] He also became a member of the Gaelic League Executive Council that year at the age of nineteen. He entered the Royal University and King's Inns to study law. But he concentrated more on the things he loved. As the University was little more than an examining body, he had few responsibilities regarding classes.

One wonders how deep was his desire to enter the university and prepare for a legal career, for nothing in his life suggests that this particular student at this time would ever have chosen to study law. Here was a person of considerable creative talent who, although withdrawn and self-conscious, had overcome handicaps when presented with a subject that interested him. The study of Gaelic, augmenting his lifelong love of Irish history and culture, had released him from many of those fears that had held him back as a child; because of this he approached the subject with the passion of a zealot. But less engaging subjects could barely sustain his interest. Can one believe that Patrick was interested in studying law and had come to that decision freely? The answer would seem to lie with his father.

Patrick was the eldest son of the Pearse family. His brother Willie, two years younger, was not up to a university degree. Willie showed some of his father's ability with stone, but in fact, was only very good at being a follower of his brother, a following Patrick took on gladly. At one point, Willie became a vegetarian just because his older brother had done so.[84] It was obvious to everyone that Willie's

82. Raymond J. Porter, *P. H. Pearse* (New York: Twayne Publishers, 1973), 34.
83. Ruth Dudley Edwards, *Patrick Pearse*, 23–24.
84. Mary Brigid Pearse, "Our Home Recollections of Padraig," 93–94.

future lay in other places than a regular university education. Patrick represented the family's hope for the future.

To an artisan like James Pearse, the bar represented a great step in education, prestige, and money. A son practicing at the bar would display his father's diligence and ability. But James Pearse knew Patrick only secondhand; anyone else could have seen the unlikelihood of Patrick's success at the bar. In fact, although he fared relatively well lecturing before his own Literary Society, Pearse was stiff and boring before his fellow students at the university and King's Inn debating societies.[85]

More is at issue here than merely a father and son who might not have seen eye-to-eye on the proper vocation for the son, even if it was one for which the father had worked and saved and was prepared to pay. After a lifetime of relative neglect, Patrick's father's wishes came back into Patrick's life. James attempted to mold his son's life according to James's own desires. He seems to have given little consideration to Patrick's strengths and weaknesses or desires. Nothing indicates that Patrick would willingly have taken this path, although there is no evidence that any disagreement ever transpired between the two of them about his future career. In any case it is unlikely that Patrick would have rebelled openly against the reserved and somewhat mysterious figure who came up to the family room only once or twice a day. Since Patrick was the eldest son, the family and Patrick had probably assumed such a career, and the goal had become reified into a prevailing and unquestionable principle.

Here, James Pearse sought to manipulate the boy at a very critical phase of his development without having won the right to be heard. The father was ready to interject himself into his son's future, partially out of that normal parental phenomenon of fulfilling oneself through the success of a child—a kind of success he had been

85. Pearse tried only one case and he lost it. See Ruth Dudley Edwards, *Patrick Pearse*, 48.

denied. At a crossing of important phases in both their lives—Patrick was nineteen and his father fifty-nine, the future opening for one and starting to close for the other—Patrick was forced to choose, and his choice seems to have been made subconsciously. When Patrick later failed to pursue his legal career, it was ostensibly to serve in his deceased father's place as head of the family firm; however, it seems that his real motive was the desire to write, teach, and proselytize for Gaelic Irish culture. That pursuit had freed his tongue and heart and could save him from a vocation that would have inhibited him.

Patrick muddled through law with no obvious enthusiasm, and James Pearse died suddenly in 1900 while visiting in Birmingham. According to the historical literature, James's death had an oddly incidental and anticlimactic impact on his family. Edwards points out that within a week, Patrick was back in full swing at school and involved again with the Gaelic League.[86] The silence of the family, and of the biographers, is testimony to the uncertain emotions that the death of the father stirred, probably because of his distance from their emotional lives.

Some time later Patrick was to write of his father with more than a bit of sadness: "If ever in an Irish church you find, amid a wilderness of bad sculpture, something good and true and lovingly finished, you may be sure that it was carved by my father or by one of his pupils."[87] Patrick recognized that what his father wanted to be thought of himself and what he had aspired to would be hidden and forgotten rather than remembered.

There is more than a little ambivalence expressed in Pearse's remembrance of his father, whose detachment from, and yet domination of, the family had taken its toll on the eldest son's affections. In August 1915, when Pearse gave his famous eulogy over the repub-

86. Ibid., 46–47.
87. Eamonn de Barra Papers.

lican O'Donovan Rossa's grave at Glasnevin cemetery, he was deeply aware that he had visited the place often as a child and much of his father's work had been placed there. Glasnevin had already been established as the burial place for Irish patriots and republicans. In giving his oration over one of his childhood heroes, Pearse lived out the ceremonies he had fantasized as a child.[88]

Like any young man, Patrick looked to his father for approval and guidance, but he never received a steady diet of approval from his increasingly inaccessible father. The genesis of this lack of approval was probably James's and Margaret's disaffection. Perhaps Patrick's mother was determined to make her favorite child what her husband had proved not to be, and James resented the fact. The boy was to bear the burden of a situation entirely out of his hands. It is obvious that because of Patrick's lack of ability or desire, Willie became the heir presumptive to the artistic side of the business.

Moreover, Patrick's overwhelming interest in things Irish seems to have been a reaction against his father. Throughout his life, he rebelled against English manners, English schooling, English art, and English rule. Even though James had supported Parnell, his political point of view remained distinctly British, and he spoke of himself as an Englishman. His ties to England were more than superficial: in the late 1880s he thought of returning to Birmingham because of a business interest he had inherited there.[89] To the rest of the family, whose whole heart was in Ireland, the thought of leaving must have been unsettling.

The emotional chasm that had developed between James and Patrick meant that the only way the son could ever establish any kind of identity was in reaction to what his father stood for. With his father's death came regret and loss, but also an abatement of his need to establish autonomy and self-confidence. Late adolescence is

88. P. H. Pearse, "My Childhood," 18. See Appendix.
89. Ruth Dudley Edwards, *Patrick Pearse*, 11.

the critical phase in the development of an autonomous identity able to assert itself confidently. With this sense of freedom from dependency and restriction, the individual also needs to establish a sense of values and morals in order to decide freely and consistently.[90] The achievement of adulthood requires a certain amount of functional resolution of an individual's psychosocial arrangement. This resolution integrates the identifications and fantasies that had once ordered life, and thereby resolves the sources of conflict that spurred or hindered the individual's growth. At this point, the individual moves from childhood to adulthood without those conflicts that inhibit the adult sense of identity, security, and self-worth.[91]

For Patrick Pearse these developmental issues were difficult, not only at twenty, but also later, when he articulated a political and spiritual position that demanded moral choices with great cost to himself and others. From a developmental point of view, Pearse was never to leave the lap of his mother, where the fantasies and morals of his youth were not forced to encompass an ever-widening world view. In Eriksonian terms, he never resolved the issue of autonomy versus guilt and shame that characterizes the second stage of development.[92] He never was forced to do so because he had been driven to her by his father's unilateral withdrawal of attention; hence, he never went through the necessary breakup of the child's relationship with his mother. Although he was sandwiched between an elder sister and two younger siblings, Patrick remained the family favorite; and when his mother or sisters were inattentive, the magical Auntie Margaret was often there to fulfill his needs. Because the women of the family were obsessively devoted to Patrick, and because he rejected his father and his father's ways, Patrick over-identified with

90. Erik Erikson, *Young Man Luther: A Study in Psychoanalysis and History* (New York: W. W. Norton, 1958; paperback, 1962), 14-15.

91. Ibid.

92. Erik Erikson, *Identity and the Life Cycle* (New York: W. W. Norton, 1959; paperback, 1979), 129.

the women of his childhood and prevented the emergence of his own identity. Almost as if in parody, he became the absolute paragon of all Irish Catholic sons.

This lack of firm male identity is the source of his expeditions in female dress through the streets of Dublin. The Pearse family lived for most of Patrick's early life at 27 Great Brunswick Street,[93] in an area sandwiched between perhaps the two most notorious red-light districts in late-nineteenth-century Dublin. To the north, just across the Liffey River and past the Customs House, along what was then Mecklenburgh Street, lay the "Monto" district, infamous for its vice trade catering to the whims of sailors from the quayside and soldiers from the army barracks just up the street. To the immediate southwest of Westland Row lay Grafton Street, in the 1870s world-famous for prostitution; some fifteen hundred prostitutes lined the street in front of some of Dublin's fanciest shops.[94] Despite official attempts to crack down on illicit activity, there appears to have been little or no decline in the numbers of prostitutes during the last decades of the nineteenth century.[95]

Patrick, frequently wandering in such an environment with his brother, both in women's dress, often in the company of their sisters or a female cousin, had to be have been aware of this world. This is not to suggest that Patrick engaged in conscious transvestitism; however, he could easily have been propositioned. The age of consent was a mere thirteen, and child-prostitution in British cities of the day was extensive.[96] His cousin related that Patrick dressed in his

93. The family did move to Sandymount when Patrick was five but moved back to the shop on Great Brunswick Street when he was ten or eleven. See Ruth Dudley Edwards, *Patrick Pearse*, 9.

94. See Joseph O'Brien, *Dear, Dirty Dublin: 1899-1916* (Berkeley: University of California Press, 1982), 189-93; Peter Somerville-Large, *Dublin* (London: H. Hamilton, 1979), 270-72.

95. O'Brien, *Dear, Dirty Dublin*, 192-93.

96. For more on this subject, see George Behlmer, *Child Abuse and Moral*

elder sister's clothes as a poor woman and went with his cousin to Amiens Street,[97] a trip that took them into the very heart of Monto. It is hard to believe, especially since Patrick continued this practice until he was in his teens,[98] that these expeditions were entirely innocent. For a boy as withdrawn and obviously immature as Patrick, no doubt the disguises furnished him the opportunity to participate surreptitiously in a world he was not allowed to experience. The fact that the sights to greet him were often fascinating makes his behavior all the more understandable.[99]

Patrick's social immaturity mirrored his overwhelming sexual immaturity. His adult relationships with women, none of which we can say were sexually consummated, were as distant as those he had known in his voyeuristic trips into the red-light districts. He idealized women without knowing them,[100] and his libidinal feelings, detectable in his writing, seem increasingly to have been focused on boys as he grew older.

Patrick's immaturity is surely responsible for his excessive love for the boys at his "Irish" school in the years before 1916. By being sensitive and open to the needs of boys, he not only rejected his father, but also sought to be a bit of a mother. In his plays, poetry, and letters, he sought to establish his equality with his boys. This served to validate his identity when he did not have the emotional ability to secure it by adult means alone.

Young Patrick Pearse suffered from an overwhelming depen-

Reform in England, 1870-1908 (Stanford: Stanford University Press, 1982); Judith Walkowitz, *Prostitution and Victorian Society* (Cambridge, England: Cambridge University Press, 1982).

97. Mary Brigid Pearse, "Our Home Recollections of Padraig," 41.

98. Ibid., 40.

99. For an analysis of Victorian obsession with sexual aberrancy, see Stephen Marcus, *The Other Victorians: A Study of Sexuality and Pornography in Mid-Nineteenth Century England* (New York: W. W. Norton, 1964).

100. Mary Hayden, "My Recollections of Padraig Pearse," 115.

dency on those he loved most, and in his adulthood we shall see in him an ever-increasing expression of nostalgia and fantasy as his needs for that kind of certainty increased. Forced to act without a wholly developed sense of his ability to do so, he retreated and sought the past everywhere—in his religion, in his writing, even in his politics. In a real sense, Patrick Pearse was held back from being a free man. Held back by both his fear of the outside and the responsibility incumbent in that world, he was in effect denied the means to break free psychologically. He looked obsessively toward the past in the attempt to make something of his life in the all-too-complex present.

Because Patrick adored his mother, he was wholly dependent upon her and the rest of the family for emotional support and for the sense that he was doing all right. But existing in tension with this need for safety was the normal adult need to establish himself in an independent way. Thus, in the end, he faced the future needing to forget what he came to see as an idyllic childhood. His conflict was not only that of a mama's boy. It was and is the fundamental struggle of every individual to establish their own sense of who they are in a world that requires autonomous action. For Patrick Pearse the death of his father meant the loss of the one person who could cultivate that sense. Without that influence, he was forced into a difficult search for identity and freedom that finally resulted in his denial of the present for the future and the past.

The marriage of James Pearse and Margaret Brady suffered problems that might have been somewhat common in a marriage of their day, but the immature young man of 1900, who emerged as a national hero in 1916, faced some extraordinary difficulties in finding himself within the conflicts of that union. Pearse recognized that the source of conflict within himself lay in his own relationship to the different characters who had created him. He wrote in his *Autobiography:*

For the present, I have said enough to indicate that when my father and mother married there came together two very widely remote traditions—English and Gaelic. Freedom-loving both, and neither without its strain of poetry and its experience of spiritual and other adventures. And these two traditions worked in me, and, prised together by a certain fire proper to myself—but nursed by that fostering of which I have spoken—made me that strange thing I am.[101]

That strange creature desired both to be safe and to escape, to retire to that same place where his dreams were sufficient and to fulfill his normal human desire to break free. Freedom for Pearse meant a sense of breaking loose from the conflicting emotions that held him captive—in the same way he had once done as a child, through heroic activity and adventure. Pearse was never given a firm foundation in which he could freely make life a choice of adventurous acts. Instead he emerged from childhood deeply ambivalent about making his own way in life. He later described this conflict in the terms he knew best: "The woman in us loves to sit by our own fireside; the man in us urges us forth on divine adventures."[102]

The immediate issue for Patrick Pearse at the age of twenty was whether or not he would practice law. His interest in Gaelic would not provide a substantial living for his mother and siblings, but his inheritance provided him the opportunity to pursue that interest while abandoning his legal career. It also allowed him to await with disastrous results the days when he would be forced to choose adventure or the fireside.

101. P. H. Pearse, "My Childhood," 11.
102. Ibid.

CHAPTER 3

The State of Ireland

The Literary Movement and the Search for a National Culture

In a speech in 1899, Standish O'Grady made a powerful prophecy about the future course of Irish history. Speaking before a group of literary colleagues he said, "We have now a literary movement, it is not very important; it will be followed by a political movement, that will not be very important; then must come a military movement, that will be important indeed."[1] O'Grady correctly forecast the outline of the next quarter of a century of public history in Ireland. What was not knowable then, and would only become apparent in 1916, was the extent to which some men would come to feel a need to act decisively in a violent fashion in order to rectify the failures of the movements O'Grady had foreseen.

At the turn of the century, Ireland was in the midst of one of the more surprising cultural renaissances of modern times. The Celtic Revival was the artistic manifestation of an Irish search for a national and cultural identity, which it promised to establish by reviving interest in pre-English Ireland in particular its myths and

1. William Butler Yeats, *The Autobiography of William Butler Yeats* (New York: Macmillan, 1926; paperback, New York: Collier Books, 1974), 284.

folklore. Many believed that through an emphasis on the mythic past, models for present-day Ireland could be found that would one day serve as the basis of a newly resurrected Irish nation. While part of this search for national identity was bound by nationalist considerations, even racialist ones, typical of European Romanticism earlier in the century, there was a distinctly anti-colonial and anti-modernist cast to much of Ireland's cultural revival. The artists and intellectuals who gathered around the leaders of this movement had in mind the "salvation" of Ireland from the "hands" of England and English culture.[2]

There were two main facets of the Celtic Revival: one, most forcefully and clearly articulated by the Gaelic League, stressed the Irish language and Irish customs as the root of national identity; the second, an aesthetic movement, attempted to reinterpret the Irish past in the art of the present. In 1892 Douglas Hyde gave a paper entitled "On the Necessity for De-Anglicizing Ireland" before a meeting of the National Literary Society, which he and William Butler Yeats had founded earlier that year.[3] The views and goals outlined in Hyde's paper were soon to become those of Hyde's Gaelic League, co-founded with the Irish medievalist Eoin MacNeill in 1893. Hyde's argument, not wholly original, urged the rejection of English cul-

2. Robert Kee, *The Bold Fenian Men* (London, 1972; paperback, 1976), 133. In this sense they were "cultural nationalists" of the type described in John Hutchinson, *The Dynamics of Cultural Nationalism: The Gaelic Revival and the Creation of the Nation State* (London, 1987). Hutchinson contrasts cultural and political nationalism, even though both share an antipathy to the bureaucratic state. Political nationalists see nationalism in terms of a *polis*, whereas cultural nationalists see it in terms of the end product of a unique historical process (12–13). A key to this conception of the nation is an attendant sense of modernization's erosion of the distinctive national culture. Thus the cultural nationalists strive for a "moral regeneration" (16) of their culture through the revival of its distinctive characteristics of language, art, literature, etc. The implication is obvious: political nationalists move in spheres of moral and cultural compromise.

3. Kee, *Bold Fenian Men*, 133.

ture and the embracing of a modern Irish culture based on the Irish language; the language was to be taught to everyone, in order to make accessible the non-English forms of ancient Ireland's culture and values and thus to establish a distinctly Irish cultural identity. With the emphasis on language came a great variety of native "Irish" expressions—literature, poetry, and to a lesser degree the plastic arts, even the preference for Irish tweed rather than "English second-hand trousers."[4] Hyde equated Anglicization with modernization and in the process obscured the similarities and the clear distinctions between the two things. In D. P. Moran's *The Leader*, founded in 1900, anti-English sentiment was invariably tied to anti-modernist themes. In his weekly pieces in *The Leader* and in a series of polemics published as *The Philosophy of Irish Ireland*, Moran took to task those who did not recognize that the answer to the search for national identity lay in Irish traditions and native values and not in England's "modern ways." Ultimately "Irish-Ireland" and the bulk of support for the new cultural nationalism was committed to conservative, atavistic, and even racialist principles.[5]

The revivalists followed a path laid out for them by the Young Irelanders of the 1840s but even more clearly the precedent set by the establishment of the Gaelic Athletic Association (GAA) in 1884. In the same era that games such as English football and American baseball saw the establishment of administrative organizations with codified sets of rules, the largely Anglo-Irish Athletic Association, which advocated the development and supervision of English games in Ireland, was challenged by a new self-consciously anti-English GAA. The GAA was founded on the anti-English ideas of Archbishop Croke of Cashel,[6] but it was in practice largely the creation of the Irish-speaking Michael Cusack of Clare. Cusack was dictatorial in

4. *An Claidheamh Soluis*, cited by Kee, 136.
5. R. F. Foster, *Modern Ireland* (London: Oxford University Press, 1988), 450ff.
6. Lyons, *Ireland Since the Famine*, 226–27.

his running of the fledgling organization, and from 1886 to 1971 GAA members were forbidden from belonging to organizations that played "English" games.[7] From the beginning the organization was interpenetrated by members of the Irish Republican Brotherhood, and many of the GAA's leadership were active members of the secret society.[8] The GAA's impact was felt mostly in the countryside as it helped to focus national feelings and national pride into distinctly non-English, nonmaterialistic, and anti-modern physical activities.[9] In the Gaelic League the Revivalists put onto paper and into ideological form the sentiments of anti-Anglicization already abroad in Irish society.

The revivalists were not totally united in their opinions, however. Sharp differences in emphasis and philosophy created difficulties within the literary movement from the beginning. Early on, leading proponents of the language movement—Hyde, for instance, and especially Charles Gavan Duffy—preferred fostering the study of the Anglo-Irish literature of the nineteenth century, such as the works of Davis and Moore. But Yeats, whose eponymous book, *The Celtic Twilight*, gave the aesthetic part of the revival its name, advocated resurrecting the old Celtic mythic cycles and tales in new artistic forms, especially through drama and poetry.[10] To realize these goals, Yeats helped found an Irish Literary Society in London

7. Marcus de Búrca, *The G.A.A.: A History of the Gaelic Athletic Association* (Dublin: Cumann Luthchleas Gael, 1980), 65–66.

8. Ibid., 34ff.

9. Foster, *Modern Ireland*, 448–49.

10. An excellent analysis of the various factions and developments in the cultural movement can be found in Malcolm Brown, *The Politics of Irish Literature*, 5th ed. (Seattle: University of Washington Press, 1972), 348–70. There appear to be close affinities between these developments in Irish culture and the "Welsh revival" of the mid-nineteenth century. See Prys Morgan, "From a Death to a View: The Hunt for the Welsh Past in the Romantic Period," in Eric Hobsbawm and Terence Ranger, eds., *The Invention of Tradition* (Cambridge, England: Cambridge University Press, 1983), 43–100.

in late 1891 and the National Literary Society in Dublin two years later. He helped to establish the Irish National Theatre in 1897 (soon to be known as the Abbey Theatre), to foster the staging of this new artistic expression of Irish nationalism. Hyde, on the other hand, wanted to resurrect the language because he believed that its daily use was the key to any cultural renewal of the nation; further, this renewal would happen only when the language was learned within a modern context. Yeats believed that the nation's political revival would develop only after the essence of the nation's culture had been resurrected and re-understood, and he viewed the language as a way to open up the mythic culture both intellectually and emotionally in order that it might serve that revival. Yeats saw the language as a tool for understanding the past rather than a goal in and of itself. Moreover, Yeats believed that the past had distinct advantages in presenting constructive nationalist models instead of the "noble failures" Tone and Emmet, who had been the modern models for the Young Ireland movement in the 1840s.[11]

In 1901 a debate raged between the revivalists and those arguing for the need of more imaginative political leadership. Yeats argued against the idea that Ireland's deliverance lay in a political solution complete with messiah. He and his associates in the avant-garde in the Celtic Revival were convinced that salvation for Ireland would be artistic: only through an artistic revival would a national idea strong enough to "save" Ireland emerge and make possible a political solution.

The political significance of the Celtic Revival was that it gave dynamic artistic expression to Irish nationalism. The foundations for their achievement had been laid by the Young Ireland movement in the 1840s,[12] whose Romantic and rather derivative nationalism was expressed in the newspaper *The Nation*. But the Revival stressed truly new work, much of it influenced by the European avant-

11. Kee, *Bold Fenian Men*, 138.
12. Thompson, *Imagination of an Insurrection*, 50–51.

garde,[13] and its success played a special role in raising public awareness of the value of Ireland's indigenous cultural heritage. The immediate political results of the artistic movement were mixed; no one should overestimate the numbers of people who were directly influenced by, or could even understand, what Yeats or Hyde meant at the time.[14] Those who were literate in Irish were even fewer than those who could speak it.[15] Much of the debate in the Gaelic League over fine points of grammar and style overlooked an essential fact: there was not a very large group for its members to address. Although the League grew from fifty-eight branches in 1897 to nine hundred branches by 1905 with a membership of around 100,000, its distinctly middle-class membership forced the League to fight against frequent accusations of snobbery.[16]

As William Irwin Thompson has pointed out, the man in the street was far more likely to respond to the simplistic and grossly romantic style of nationalism presented in publications like *The Nation* than to articles written by Yeats for *Dublin University Review*.[17] All of the revivalists basically preached to the converted, failing to recognize that the biggest hurdle in the hoped-for national revival was the ignorance and hostility of the very people they wished to save. The Ireland they believed in was an idealized one, and it served their interests. "The revivalists sought in Ireland the kind of dignity and kind of wealth that the industrialized world, the modern world had lost; the Ireland they loved had an enormous West Coast and no northeast corner."[18]

13. Foster, *Modern Ireland*, 451ff. See also G. J. Watson, *Irish Identity and the Literary Revival: Synge, Yeats, Joyce and O'Casey* (London, 1979); Richard Fallis, *The Irish Renaissance*, (Syracuse: Syracuse University Press, 1977).

14. Kee, *Bold Fenian Men*, 136.   15. Ibid., 139–40.

16. Ibid., 135–36.

17. Thompson, *Imagination of an Insurrection*, 14.

18. Conor Cruise O'Brien, "1891–1916," in *The Shaping of Modern Ireland*, ed. Conor Cruise O'Brien (Toronto: University of Toronto Press, 1960), 21.

In order to achieve their goals, the Revivalists had to do more than write poetry and produce plays or teach people how to read Irish or play hurling. All of the many parts of this movement were, in the early stages, very optimistic about their chances of success; their enthusiasm suffered substantially when their ideas received a less than jubilant public response. From the beginning, the revivalists made the mistake of believing that others would be moved intellectually and, thus enlightened, come to the same convictions as had they.

Behind the naïveté of the revivalists lurked a set of assumptions that became matters of faith and led to endless arguments over points of dogma in order to determine the canons of the new orthodoxy of the believers. One such idea, almost universally accepted by the revivalists, was that of the "Irish race." At the time, of course, and not only in Ireland, many people believed that race was the determining principle in the definition of any national identity. The revivalists' conception of race was somewhat unusual in that they defined the Irish race in contradistinction to other races, especially the English. In 1900 Moran would argue that the idea of an Irish nation was inconceivable without the revival of its unique racial language. Without a revived language, the idea of a distinct Irish nation was a farce, as was any concept of an Irish race.[19] Thus Moran helped to determine the schema in the search for an Irish national identity. It began by identifying those characteristics that were undesirable in other races, and then it defined one's own race in contrast to the previously identified characteristics; the Irish race was most often defined on the basis of what the Anglo-Saxon race was not.

The goal of most of the Revivalists was to restore the Irish race to its proper place by discovering and resurrecting those qualities, institutions, and customs that were most Irish or "most racial, most smacking of the soil."[20] Implied was the belief that the Irish race was,

19. Kee, *Bold Fenian Men*, 136.
20. Cited in Lyons, *Ireland Since the Famine*, 228.

despite persecution and oppression, a great race, able to bear witness to a nobler and more humane set of values. For many nationalists an imperative developed to determine nationalist orthodoxy—in other words, to identify "Irish" Ireland versus all "false" Irelands. Synge, whose criticism of the revival often mirrored Moran's,[21] was to be excoriated by the Irish-Irelanders in the riotous reception given to his plays *In the Shadow of the Glen* (1906) and *Playboy of the Western World* (1907) because he suggested the Irish were less than a pure and noble race. The reception given to Synge's work opened a breach within the cultural movement that was perhaps inevitable. It made it quite clear that the avant-garde were in fact artists whose cultural nationalism was based upon a modernist aesthetic that went way beyond the confines of Irish Ireland.[22] Yeats, from his usual Olympian perspective, saw the conflict as being between the boorish mob and the aesthetic elite.[23] But for most Irish people with an interest in the problem, the push was on to find a pure vision of Ireland untainted by the Anglo-Irish culture that supposedly infected Yeats and Synge.

This kind of doggedly nonrational thought might have indicated the dogmatism and mysticism that would emerge in future manifestations of Irish nationalism. The faith placed in ideas such as the nobility of the Irish peasant, an Irish race, and a "Golden Age" of Gaelic greatness could not have withstood probing examination, and these ideas soon became articles of faith that brooked little disagreement or dissension.

In the end, neither the linguistic nor the artistic revival had audiences large enough to make a great social or political difference. In

21. J. M. Synge to Stephen MacKenna, 13 July 1905, cited in R. F. Foster, *Modern Ireland*, 455.

22. John Hutchinson, *The Dynamics of Cultural Nationalism: The Gaelic Revival and the Creation of the Irish National State* (Boston: Allen and Unwin, 1987), 182–83.

23. Ibid., 183.

general their constituencies were small and privileged. The revivalists failed to make the necessary connections between what they hoped for and the political world they actually faced. But the Celtic Revival had a serious impact on many younger Irish intellectuals of the next generation, and some of them, such as Pearse, eventually made a considerably different kind of nationalist statement. In part because of what they had learned from the cultural movement, but especially because the cultural movement was to come up short in the end, they were determined to bring about a concrete affirmation of the nationalist ideal through some kind of action that was not just the hopeful creation of intellectuals and academics. "Since the fall of Parnell, the nationalists had spent a decade in the new enthusiasms; but small meetings, literary banquets, and a lonely reading of books were not enough. The intellectuals longed to address themselves to the multitude; they were in flight from 'The Decadence' and the solipsism of the Aesthetic Movement, and they longed to give their individual excitement a collective intensity."[24]

Eventually the cultural movement came up bankrupt in the face of reality; as Pearse was to say in late 1913, "The Gaelic League as the Gaelic League is a spent Force. . . . The vital work to be done in the new Ireland . . . will not be done so much by the Gaelic League as by men and movements that have sprung from [it] or have received from the Gaelic League a new baptism and a new life of grace."[25] By mid-1915 Pearse was calling for the Gaelic League to adopt an active political position.[26]

The possibility for the literary movement's politicization had always been there: Hyde in particular had been careful to keep the Gaelic League out of the political arena. He lost this fight in 1915 when he was eased out of the organization he had helped to found,

24. Thompson, *Imagination of an Insurrection*, 57.

25. Pearse, *Political Writings and Speeches*, 91–92.

26. Janet Egleson Dunleavy and Gareth W. Dunleavy, *Douglas Hyde: A Maker of Modern Ireland* (Berkeley: University of California Press, 1991), 326.

because he would not support its joining in direct political action.[27] By 1915, many people had come to believe that force was probably inevitable and necessary; any man who believed the things that Hyde espoused was now in a poor position to deny others their own notions about the national idea. At the root of the cultural revival existed a desperate desire to believe absolutely and without question. It was a legacy on which others were quickly to build.

The Political Movement and the Search for Independence

Standish O'Grady's prediction that there would be a political movement to follow the literary one reveals a great deal about the generally depressed state of Irish politics at the turn of the century. In 1899, the major political issue in Irish politics had been the same for nearly forty years—Home Rule. After Home Rule became the principal factor in British politics during the 1880s, there was every reason to expect it to remain in the political forefront during the next decade, but with the political demise of Charles Stewart Parnell and the subsequent splitting of his once-powerful Parliamentary Party, this was not to be.[28] The inability to find able political leader-

27. Ibid., 326–28.
28. The tortured history of the Irish Question is well represented in the literature. Some of the works already mentioned include Mansergh, McCaffrey and P. S. Hegarty. O'Farrell's *Ireland's English Question* is the most important revisionist view of the "Question," most useful if looked at in conjunction with Eric Strauss, *Irish Nationalism and British Democracy* (New York: Columbia University Press, 1951), and some of the standard English histories of the period: R. C. K. Ensor, *England 1870–1914* (Oxford: Oxford University Press, 1936); Llewellyn Woodward, *The Age of Reform 1815–1870* (Oxford: Oxford University Press, 1962); and A. J. P. Taylor, *English History 1914–1945* (Oxford: Oxford University Press, 1965; paperback, 1970). See also F. S. L. Lyons, *The Irish Parliamentary Party, 1890-1910*, (London: Oxford University Press, 1951); Oliver MacDonagh's *Ireland: The Union and Its Aftermath* (Englewood Cliffs, NJ: Prentice Hall, 1968;

ship acceptable to all parts of the party led to a decline in the party's influence for most of the decade after Parnell's death in 1891, and in the 1890s hope of attaining Home Rule waned.[29]

This decline was not solely the result of party disorganization and internecine strife. Part of the credit for calming the troubled waters of Irish politics must go to Britain's Conservative Party which had begun, even before Parnell's death, to see reform as a way to "rob Home Rule of its strength by disemboweling the social and economic causes which fed it."[30] Unionism became an essential element among the Conservatives after the Liberal Party came out in favor of Home Rule in 1886. Unionism rallied Conservatives and eventually

---

rev. ed., London: George Allen and Unwin, 1979; paperback, 1979) and *States of Mind: A Study of Anglo-Irish Conflict 1780–1980* (London: Allen and Unwin, 1983); R. D. Black, *Economic Thought and the Irish Question* (Cambridge, England: Cambridge University Press, 1960); Kevin B. Nowlan, *The Politics of Repeal: A Study in the Relations between Great Britain and Ireland, 1841–50* (London: Routledge and Kegan Paul, 1975); and Conor Cruise O'Brien, *Parnell and His Party, 1880-1890* (London: Oxford University Press, 1957).

29. The continual political failure of the political process to arrive at a pragmatic solution to the problem arose in part because of the inability to reconcile the nonrational forces arrayed on each side of the issue. People such as Pearse believed that a political solution would never be found that recognized the national vision he and others held—a fact that was directly to influence the thinking of the rebels of 1916.

The political malaise described above was felt by both British and Irish contemporaries to be true. Yet recent historiography has attempted to resurrect a revision of the traditional view. In particular John Redmond's and William O'Brien's accomplishments are being touted as being far more substantial than has been thought previously as examples of pragmatic attempts to accommodate the opposition. This development seems heavily influenced by the climate of the late 1980s negotiations between the various parties over Northern Ireland. For the essence of this argument see R. F. Foster, *Modern Ireland*, 431ff. and Patricia Jalland, *The Liberals and Ireland* (New York: St. Martin's Press, 1980). An important analysis is Catherine Shannon, *Arthur J. Balfour and Ireland: 1874–1922* (Washington: The Catholic University of America Press, 1988).

30. D. George Boyce, *Nationalism in Ireland*, 261.

gained control of the government with the support of some Liberals who had joined them under a "Unionist" banner. Through a strategy of gradual acquiescence on issues of land reform, and occasional political initiation at Westminster, the Unionists brought forth agrarian and social reforms in order to blunt the Irish sense of grievance.[31] On the whole the strategy proved a success; Home Rule, furthermore, had lost much of its momentum and had become merely "a cause of routine orthodoxy,"[32] without which the Irish political world could not exist, at the same time that agrarian unrest and terrorism declined. The issue of Home Rule had become a given in Irish politics even when it was not addressed directly.

In 1900, the Irish Parliamentary Party at Westminster reunited under the leadership of John Redmond and his deputy-chief, John Dillon. The party's hopes were tied, as they had been in Parnell's time, to the fortunes of the Liberal Party, which had come to grief over the defeat of two Home Rule bills. A unified Irish party stood to wield once again considerable clout because the Liberals needed them to gain power and to keep control of the government. This meant that they would return to the "militant constitutionalism" that had once served Parnell.

The first opportunity for Redmond and Dillon to exploit their strategic position arose in 1907. Attempting to mollify both the Nationalists and the opposition, the Liberals offered a devolution scheme instead of a true Home Rule measure. It sought to give Ireland its own council of administrative control, with final approval over the council's actions residing in London. In a striking display of party unity, the Parliamentary Party rallied behind Redmond in rejecting the Irish Council Bill of 1907, and the result was to increase the base of Home Rule support within the Liberal Party.

It was not until 1910 that such an opportunity presented itself

31. Kee, *Bold Fenian Men*, 111.
32. Ibid., 109.

again, when the Liberals' thin margin in the House of Commons meant that they were dependent upon Irish support in order to stay in power. Redmond received from the Liberals a guarantee of a Home Rule Bill, even though its passage would aggravate the constitutional crisis the government already faced over the issue of veto power in the House of Lords.

The importance of the final failure of this Home Rule Bill in 1912 was in its political side effects. For one thing, the failure to win Home Rule played a major part in the formulation of the Parliament Act of 1911, which established a procedure for overriding any future vetoes by the House of Lords; second, the public debate over Home Rule flushed out belligerent anti-Home Rule resistance. After stalling Home Rule for decades, the Unionists were not surprising anyone by resisting Home Rule, but the ominous way in which they resisted was to alter Ireland's political climate considerably. At a large rally at Craigavon House outside Belfast on 23 September 1911, Unionists under the leadership of Edward Carson and James Craig threatened "extra-constitutional resistance" in Ulster to any Home Rule Bill that forced all of Ireland to come under its sway.[33] Obviously, Unionist rhetoric had developed its own anti-Catholic, anti-Gaelic ideology to counter nationalist conceptions of the true Irishman.[34]

The Parliamentary Party was not the only party representing Irish nationalists in the political arena. There arose concurrently a clear political alternative to those bent on constitutionalism and Home Rule: although it was not to be the only new political movement, Sinn Fein was to be the most important; it eventually surpassed the Parliamentary Party and became the dominant political expression of Irish nationalism in 1918.

Why alternatives arose at this time is not altogether clear. Disillu-

---

33. A. T. Q. Stewart, *The Ulster Crisis: Resistance to Home Rule, 1912–1914* (London: Faber and Faber, 1967; paperback, 1979), 47–48.

34. Ibid., 26ff. See also Lee, *Ireland 1912–1985*, 1–13.

sionment or dissatisfaction set in among some long-time supporters of the Irish Parliamentary Party.[35] Additionally, the cultural awareness arising out of the Celtic Revival had led many to place their hopes in a separatist political movement that would secure the separate Irish spiritual and intellectual revival. Home Rule would not provide the degree of independence that could satisfy these separatists, as increasingly it smacked too much of compromise. The continued defeat of Home Rule, together with a new political party and an ideological position stressing Irish self-reliance, led many politicians to consider more assertive forms of political action.[36]

Sinn Fein was largely the invention of Arthur Griffith. Griffith had been born a Dubliner and had spent two years in South Africa during the 1890s before returning to edit the *United Irishmen* newspaper. While he was at the paper, Griffith's ideas began to develop an unmistakably unique, nationalist perspective. Griffith had been heavily influenced by the cultural separatism of the cultural revivalists and the political separatism of the Fenians. Although he did not espouse either the revolutionary doctrine or the violent tactics of the republicans, he was a strict separatist and claimed that Sinn Fein accepted "the nationalism of '98, '48 & '67 as the true nationalism of Ireland."[37]

His ideas were at first disseminated largely through the *United Irishmen*. Mouthpeice of his first political organization, Cumann na nGaedheal (established in 1900), Griffith's paper advocated massive civil disobedience and economic non-cooperation. He proposed, through passive resistance, to disrupt British rule in Ireland and then, through continual disruption, to render it unworkable. Griffith argued that such a policy would require economic self-reliance

35. Lyons, *Ireland Since the Famine*, 247.

36. Donal McCartney, "The Sinn Fein Movement," in *The Making of 1916: Studies in the History of the Rising*, ed. Kevin B. Nowlan (Dublin: The Stationary Office, 1969), 31.

37. Cited in Lyons, *Ireland Since the Famine*, 248.

for Ireland and political abstention from the Parliament at Westminster. Cumann na nGaedheal was not very successful in its stated purpose to confederate the nationalists,[38] although it had some following, but it provided Griffith with a forum for his ideas.

Whatever else could be said about Griffith, one could never accuse him of being unimaginative in his approach to the national problem. In *The Resurrection of Hungary*, published in 1904, Griffith expanded upon an idea he had brought before Cumann na nGaedheal two years earlier: Ireland should declare itself politically and economically free from Great Britain, withdraw from Parliament, and then act as if it were, indeed, a free and separate state. He based this idea on his rather quixotic reading of the Dual Monarchy established in Austria-Hungary in the 1860s. His model of two individual kingdoms united under a single monarchy was entirely original in the Irish context and affected enough people's thinking to be instrumental in the founding of a political party out of a reconstituted Cumann na nGaedheal in 1907. Sinn Fein ("Ourselves") represented a clear middle ground between the parliamentarians committed to Home Rule and the advocates of physical-force separatism, even while it could clearly claim members of both.[39]

It is true that Griffith's analysis of the *Augsleich* was superficial (although one could see his discussion of it as a tactical decision to reduce it to its essence), but his "Hungarian Policy" was as uniquely systematic in its approach as it was unorthodox.[40] For one thing, Griffith included considerable detail about the possible economic problems that could face an Ireland committed to the path he had laid out. For another, he envisioned a constitutional monarchy as Ireland's model government, complete with a parliament, all to be brought about by unilateral withdrawal from the union with Britain.

38. *United Irishman*, 15 March 1900.
39. Foster, *Modern Ireland*, 457–58.
40. Lyons, *Ireland Since the Famine*, 252–53.

Griffith's Hungarian model, however, was too exotic to command many Irishmen's attention while Home Rule still had a hope of passage, and Sinn Fein remained politically obscure, seeing little success until 1918, when it represented the sole political alternative to the Redmondites. At its pre-1916 height, Sinn Fein never numbered more than 150 chapters, most of which were in the Dublin area;[41] the rural areas remained relatively unresponsive to Sinn Fein's calls for support. The party lost its only serious election attempt in 1908.[42]

The Irish Parliamentary Party was the only broad-based political movement to capture the majority of the people's support between 1890 and 1910. For much of that time, the party was divided, disorganized, and, in effect, adrift, but Sinn Fein also remained weak, had a narrow base of support, and failed to gain ground over its enfeebled opposition. Thus the most powerful alternative to Redmond's party had relatively little impact on the political events of those years. When it finally succeeded in 1918, it did so not only because of the collapse of its opposition, but also because of its successful retention of its integrity, its connections to the Celtic Revival, and its apparent inheritance of the separatist tradition resurrected by the physical-force men of 1916.

By 1912 two failures had transpired: that of the Celtic Revival, which had done nothing more than to heighten some people's awareness of their cultural heritage, and that of Home Rule, which would never gain true national independence from Great Britain. A critical division had appeared, a division between those who were separatists and those who were committed to the constitutional process. This was no mere difference of class or style, but a matter

41. Donal McCartney, "Hyde, D. P. Moran and Irish Ireland," in *Leaders and Men of the Easter Rising*, ed. F. X. Martin (Dublin: Harper and Row, 1967), 38.

42. Although Sinn Fein ran what seems to have been a strong candidate, the Parliament Party candidate beat Sinn Fein by nearly a three-to-one margin in North Leitrim. See Kee, *Bold Fenian Men*, 158–60.

of profoundly differing moral commitments—and one side was determined to bring about a change no matter what the cost, because the cause was right.

> In truth the difference between the rival parties was temperamental. It was in this respect the difference between the Feuillants and the Jacobins in the French Revolution, the difference between those who believed in the expediency of Burke and those who gave uncompromising allegiance to the ideology of a theocratic conception. In Ireland this division, which finally resulted in civil war, was obscured during the first decade of the century.[43]

The criticism leveled against Irish parliamentarians was aimed at their commitment to the constitutional process as well as to Home Rule. In 1901, the mayor of Limerick, had anticipated what would develop:

> Any man in Ireland worth his salt today will spit upon the words constitutional agitation. The war clouds hang over China. France is uneasy, no man knows what Germany may do, and in it all the opportunity for Ireland to strike will surely come. See that you are prepared for the emergency and well prepared, for it is going to be a death struggle.[44]

What did in fact develop was widespread dissatisfaction with the nature of the discourse on Ireland's future.

Sinn Fein was failing to gather support for a variety of reasons. Its programs were perhaps too novel in the Irish context. Both Sinn Fein and the revivalists were limited to bourgeois support in a largely agrarian society; in terms of class, neither represented a clear-cut alternative or addition to constitutional nationalism. Sinn Fein's

43. Nicholas Mansergh, *The Irish Question, 1840–1921*, 3d ed. (Toronto: University of Toronto Press, 1966; paperback, 1975), 249.

44. *Chicago Sunday Times Herald*, 3 March, 1901, cited by Alan J. Ward, *Ireland and Anglo-American Relations 1899–1921* (Toronto: University of Toronto Press, 1969), 11.

lack of popular support, and the narrowness of that support, were problems that needed to be overcome.

Both Sinn Fein and the Revival bore a critical inability to amalgamate republican nationalist sentiment with the Catholic heritage of Ireland.[45] Neither the Cultural Revival nor Sinn Fein had any particular problems with the church, although in both cases they benefited from some Anglo-Irish support, but both failed to make the Catholic sense of grievance against England an integral part of their approaches.[46] Home Rulers got agrarian Catholic support by virtue of the long-standing relationship constitutionalism had to the church, dating to Daniel O'Connell. Sinn Fein and the Revival both failed to garner clerical support and suffered because of it.

In order to succeed, political movements in Ireland needed to combine the cultural and religious sentiments at work within the political process, in a manner similar to that of O'Connell's Emancipation campaigns in the late 1820s. By taking up the banner of the rebels of the 1798 Uprising, and that of Catholic Ireland, together with an apparent commitment (however rhetorical) to go to the limit in resistance to Britain, O'Connell became the embodiment of a movement and succeeded in gaining his initial objectives. But when O'Connell advocated repeal of the Act of Union in the late 1830s and 1840s, he lost control of the nationalist movement, because he was widely perceived to have backed away from confronting the English in the way he had promised. The Repeal campaign died when O'Connell revealed himself to be no revolutionary when he chose not to confront the authorities at a "monster" rally scheduled at Clontarf in October 1843. The famine merely sealed the fate of a movement that had already lost a battle over its integrity.

45. For the definitive discussion of Irish Republicanism and Catholicism, see O'Farrell, *Ireland's English Question*, 223–46.

46. Ibid., 107–14.

Redmond's Parliamentary Party, despite its problems, represented the sole nationalist political force in the years before the Great War to have widespread credibility. Behind the scenes, however, a much more important alternative to either the cultural or political movements was developing: many individuals—mostly younger than the generation of Hyde, Griffith, Redmond, and Yeats—were moving toward more concrete forms of action. Influenced by the revival, struck perhaps by the uniqueness of Sinn Fein, and alienated by the politics of Redmond, they were to emerge in late 1913 committed to the idea of resolute action to affirm an independent Irish identity. By and large, they had become dissatisfied with the political status quo, and from their position outside of it they became the prime political movers of their time.

Although Home Rule and the Irish Parliamentary Party seemed heirs to O'Connell's mantle and support, they too were unwilling to use violence to gain their objective. There was, furthermore, considerable sentiment for much more than Home Rule. People were emerging who were prepared to attain, by any means, a separate and equal Irish nation and identity. They were committed to leading the way in demonstrating their oneness with the revolutionary tradition and Ireland's unique Catholic national identity.[47] Their emergence, in sufficient numbers, helped at a crucial moment to force Irish politics into new channels of thought and action. Their presence in Irish politics meant the resurrection of the violent Republican tradition of Wolfe Tone and the Fenians, along with an emphasis on the cultural and spiritual heritage of Ireland. It was time for O'Grady's predicted military movement.

47. See Seán Farrell Moran, "Patrick Pearse and Patriotic Soteriology: The Irish Republican Tradition and the Sanctification of Political Self-Immolation," in Yonah Alexander and Alan O'Day, eds., *The Irish Terrorism Experience* (Aldershot: Dartmouth Press, 1991), 9–29; David Berman, Stephen Lalor, and Brian Torrode, "The Theology of the I.R.A.," *Studies* (Summer 1983): 137–44.

The Resurrection of the Military Movement

Tom Clarke and the Irish Republican Brotherhood

Few would have realized in 1908 that the return of Thomas Clarke to Dublin would turn out to be a critical moment in modern Irish history. Fifty-one years old, a small and unprepossessing man, Clarke looked more to be a soon-to-be-retired Fenian come home after decades of imprisonment and exile than the inspiration of a soon-to-be-revived Irish Republican Brotherhood. But, indeed, Clarke helped to resurrect and to lead the moribund IRB back into a position of power. In fact, he returned to Ireland from America to lead the IRB into a new era.[48]

Clarke had been born in England to a career British army officer and an Irish Catholic mother. He nearly entered the army at his father's behest,[49] but he chose instead to spend a lifetime in service to a sworn enemy of the British Army. Because of his IRB activities, Clarke spent fifteen years in British prison, and the long harsh imprisonment hardened his anti-British resolve into fanatical hatred.

Clarke's absolute commitment and his single-minded integrity led an Ulster Quaker named Bulmer Hobson to meet with John Devoy—head of Clan na Gael, the American group that financially supported the IRB—in 1907 with the intention of bringing Clarke back to Ireland.[50] Clarke's prison experience had changed his life profoundly and that, along with his personal involvement with Clan na Gael, had made him the perfect man for what they had in mind. Tom Clarke himself wrote that the horrors of his convict cell had

48. Louis N. Le Roux, *Tom Clarke and the Irish Freedom Movement* (Cork: Talbot Press, 1936).

49. Ibid., 14.

50. Leon O'Broin, *The Revolutionary Underground: The Story of the Irish Republican Brotherhood, 1858–1924*, Totowa, NJ: Rowman and Littlefield, 141.

changed his life forever. As one of his biographers wrote: "What had burned into his soul was something akin to Miltonic hate, unconquerable will, and a study of revenge, and most certainly a courage never to submit or yield until the flame of insurrection and flash of rifles rounded off the tragic integrity of his life."[51]

The IRB also needed to find a trustworthy go-between to link them and their American supporters in Clan na Gael.[52] Thus, when the little man with the quiet demeanor, piercing eyes,[53] and large mustache set up a tobacco shop in 1907 in what is now 25A Parnell Street in central Dublin, a most unusual man with a most important role to play in Ireland's future had indeed arrived.

In the early 1900s, the health of the once-powerful IRB was poor at best. It had seen its numbers diminish substantially since its glory days thirty-five years earlier. Part of this decline in strength, sharpest in the 1890s, resulted from lackluster and complacent leadership, and differences within the organization were played out within the GAA. The IRB had already suffered in the aftermath of Clan na Gael's being torn apart by factionalism in the late 1880s. Perhaps the most critical factor in the decline of the IRB was the generally favorable state of the Irish economy in the 1890s.[54] Despite some increase in republican support during the Boer War, where there was considerable public support for the Boers, the IRB seemed headed for a slow death, and the organization bore few signs of life by 1907.[55] These factors, compounded by the IRB's need to maintain secrecy and selectivity, had had the net effect of killing the organization.

51. Le Roux, *Tom Clarke*, 14.

52. Desmond Ryan, "Stephens, Devoy, Tom Clarke," in *The Shaping Modern Ireland*, ed. Conor Cruise O'Brien (Toronto: University of Toronto Press, 1960), 36–37.

53. Ward, *Ireland and Anglo-American Relations*, 24.

54. Le Roux, *Tom Clarke*, 213.

55. Kevin B. Nowlan, "Tom Clarke, MacDermott, and the I.R.B." in *Leaders and Men of the Easter Rising*, ed. F. X. Martin, 110–11.

It is not surprising that the IRB had entered the twentieth-century in a condition resembling the trance of death itself. Its membership was said to be so small that it would scarcely have filled a large-sized concert hall.[56] As with any movement that depended on the emotional conviction of its membership, the IRB's original vision, which had inspired its founders to extraordinary sacrifice, had failed to sustain itself in the leadership of the succeeding generations. This appears to have been especially true in the face of an improving economic situation and the Government's commitment to some measure of social reform. At the same time that the organization had to face the obstacle of "good times," it also had to deal with an old opponent—the church. Not only had the church long since banned membership in the IRB because it was a secret society, but it had also consistently supported the constitutional efforts of the Nationalist Party at Westminster.[57] On top of these obstacles, a militant and highly organized labor movement in both Dublin and Belfast took away a large part of the IRB's traditional urban constituency.[58]

The IRB was small and getting smaller, with little reason to suspect it would expand anytime in the immediately foreseeable future. It had become so insignificant and ineffectual that Diarmuid Lynch related he did not even know of its existence until he was told about it by Seán T. O'Ceallaigh in 1908.[59] Even the British, who had ample reason to suspect Clarke's sudden reappearance in Dublin, were largely ignoring the IRB.

56. Ibid.

57. Dangerfield, *Damnable Question*, 94.

58. John H. Whyte, "1916—Revolution and Religion," in *Leaders and Men of the Easter Rising*, ed. F. X. Martin, 216.

59. Lynch maintained that the IRB's early support came from evicted tenant farmers forced to move to the cities for work. He claims that this newly urbanized group, with a strong sense of grievance and deprivation, joined the IRB out of the lack of alternatives. With the organization of Irish workers in the late nineteenth and early twentieth centuries, the IRB lost members of this group to

All of this was to change, and Tom Clarke was the major reason for the changes that were to come. Although his organizational ability was minimal, he had an unusual gift for picking talented young men and inspiring them to do the organizational work that was needed if the IRB was ever to regain its vitality. His greatest gift to the "physical-force" movement was nurturing men eager to work, and he impressed them with his charisma and his unswerving faith in the rightness of the cause.[60] Clarke drew into the IRB men of outstanding ability such as Denis McCullogh, Sean MacDiarmida, and P. S. O'Hegarty along with already-committed activists like Bulmer Hobson and John MacBride, who quickly rebuilt the organization and almost as quickly replaced the old republican leadership. With his connections in America, a significant infusion of Clan na Gael money, the "Young Turks" of his tobacco shop, and a news agency, Clarke was in a position to make his presence known; not surprisingly, he and his cadre had taken over the IRB's Supreme Council by 1911.[61]

Perhaps of even greater importance for the future was the successful infiltration of other nationalist groups by members of the newly resurrected IRB. Typically, IRB men entered and quickly rose to positions of leadership and responsibility where they could influence the making of policy. This infiltration took place in all kinds of groups, regardless of their popularity or ideology; for example, Sinn

---

the labor movement. Thus in 1913 the Irish Citizen Army benefited from former IRB members swelling its ranks.

This analysis seems superficial. The IRB's leadership was overwhelmingly drawn from the ranks of the educated middle class, and its members would have gone only to a movement with a strong nationalist point of view. The early Irish labor movement was not within the mainstream of Irish nationalism and was brought into it only when Connolly "converted" to nationalism after the Great Strike of 1913. See Diarmuid Lynch, *The I.R.B. and the 1916 Rising*, ed. Florence O'Donoghue (Cork: Mercier Press, 1957), 42.

60. Ibid., 20.   61. Dangerfield, *Damnable Question*, 99.

Fein was heavily penetrated by the IRB, despite Griffith's anti-republican bias.[62]

This strategy of infiltration and subversion, critically important in 1916, worked largely because of Clarke's ability to get the right men, mostly of an impressionable age and willing to sacrifice a great deal in both his and the IRB's behalf. He inspired a new generation to embrace the old republican tradition of physical force for the Irish nation; "for the younger members of the IRB he was the incarnation of Ireland, militant, suffering, unbroken and unbreakable."[63] Clarke was so loved and respected by these men that he was honored, under Pearse's orders, by being the first to enter the General Post Office in 1916[64] and the first to sign the Proclamation of the Republic (written by Pearse).[65]

One must not overestimate the contribution of the IRB to politics in the pre-Rising period. Its operations and successes were largely surreptitious, and few people noticed any of the comings and goings at Clarke's shop. In order for the IRB to do more than stage violent protest actions, a very different political climate than that which existed before 1912 would have been necessary. Ironically, the IRB's opportunity came from the hands of British politicians at Westminster with the introduction of another Home Rule bill in the spring of 1912.

The Home Rule Crisis of 1912-14

The passage of the Parliament Act of 1911 assured Home Rule's eventual passage over the objection of the House of Lords. But the fervor of Unionist resistance took an ominous turn in September of that year when two leading Unionists, Edward Carson and James Craig, called for the organization of popular Unionist support. By

62. Ward, *Ireland and Anglo-American Relations*, 24.
63. Nowlan, "Tom Clarke," 113. 64. Ibid., 111-13.
65. David Thornley, "Patrick Pearse," *Studies* 55 (Spring, 1966), 12-13.

mobilizing the Orange Lodges and Unionist Clubs of Ulster in anticipation of the need for massive civil and military resistance to pre-
vent Home Rule, they successfully recalled to life the possibility of
conflict between the Protestants of the North and the Catholics of
the South. They were playing the "Orange Card" for more than mere
effect and appealing not solely to Ulstermen; Carson had been born
in Dublin to a mother from Galway and a father from Scotland.[66]
Unionism had considerable support in Britain and Ireland as a
whole. Nevertheless, the imbalance of Ireland's religious populations
and the concentration of a large minority of Protestants in Ulster—
unwilling to be immersed in a sea of Roman Catholic sentiment—
posed a difficult political problem. The Liberal government's Home
Rule Bill of 1912 contained no provision that recognized the Unionist's desire to remain British.

The Liberal government, under the leadership of H. H. Asquith,
appeared unresponsive to the Unionist plight. At a pro-Union rally
at Blenheim Palace in July 1912, the recently elected Conservative
Party head, the Canadian-born Andrew Bonar Law, sitting on the
dais with both Carson and F. E. Smith (the future Lord Birkenhead),
claimed in a remarkably inflammatory speech that Protestants had a
constitutional right to resist Home Rule. He implied that Home Rule
could come about only through a "corrupt parliamentary bargain"
and would deprive Ulster Protestants of their birthright as British
subjects. Because of this, "they would be justified in resisting such an
attempt by all means in their power, including force."[67]

On 28 September 1912, Carson led a vast crowd in Belfast to sign a
"Solemn League and Covenant," which bound over 400,000 signers
to resist Home Rule at all costs.[68] The Ulster Unionist Council went
so far as to establish its own anti-Home Rule militia, the Ulster Volunteer Force or UVF, in January 1913. Within six months, the gov-

---

66. Stewart, *Ulster Crisis*, 40.   67. Lyons, *Ireland Since the Famine*, 303.
68. Stewart, *Ulster Crisis*, 65–66.

ernment believed, the UVF numbered in excess of ninety thousand men.[69]

It was clear that resistance to Irish Home Rule was hardening, and Asquith implied to both sides that his government could support a scheme that partitioned Ireland along religious lines. This gerrymander satisfied neither side. By January of 1913, however, Carson and the Unionists seemed to accept partition in principle if it allowed for a nine-county Ulster remaining as part of the United Kingdom. Although Asquith rejected the proposal, he appears to have settled on some kind of partition as the only realistic compromise. Both Liberal and Nationalist leaders had become convinced of the possibility of a "worst case" scenario, and the government committed itself to a six-county partition compromise in November 1913, telling Redmond he had to take it or leave it.[70] Redmond reluctantly accepted Asquith's terms two months later.

The Ulster Crisis played a vital role in the development of popular acceptance of the possibility of violence over the Irish question. Only a short time earlier, any kind of large-scale public outburst of this kind would have been inconceivable. Constitutional politicians held sway over the political arena in the conventional way, with some interest in the cultural expressions of nationalism, but there was no hint of the rapid change in public attitudes that was to come.

Until the Ulster Crisis, Redmond's tactics appeared to have both time and inevitability on their side. By actively suppressing such alternatives to its political hegemony as Sinn Fein,[71] the Parliamentary Party grew in power at the expense of its opposition.[72] But Redmond's very commitment to the constitutional process, combined

69. Ibid., 70–71.   70. Kee, *Bold Fenian Men*, 183–85.

71. McCartney, "Sinn Fein Movement," 42.

72. Desmond Fitzgerald, "The Geography of Irish Nationalism, 1920–1921," *Past and Present* 78 (1978), 113–44 passim.

with his acceptance of the partition compromise, damaged both his and his party's integrity.[73] Although he had the difficult task of finding some acceptable road between all the competing factions, his party rendered disreputable the process by which they had operated because of the compromises they had to accept. Thus the party in part helped to create the climate which made other kinds of action possible or even necessary. In accepting partition and not resisting the Unionist threat, the party was widely perceived by many nationalists to have abandoned its banner of "pure nationalism" in favor of peace, Liberal support, and the maintenance of its own political supremacy among Irish voters.[74] The resulting lack of confidence in the party, promoted by the Irish Republican Brotherhood, led to a hitherto unimaginable mobilization of pro-Nationalist support.[75]

In July 1913, Michael O'Rahilly, the editor of the Gaelic League periodical *An Claidheamh Soluis*, contacted Eoin MacNeill, a Professor of Early Irish History at University College, Dublin.[76] O'Rahilly suggested that MacNeill write an analysis of the current political situation. MacNeill's paper was published on 1 November 1913 and was entitled "The North Began."[77] Even though MacNeill had been a well-known Redmond supporter and a political moderate, his analysis argued that the mobilization of Unionists in Ulster provided a model for the nationalists to emulate. Within the month a committee— meeting under MacNeill's leadership—approved a plan to set up a pro-nationalist militia along the same lines as the Ulster Volunteer

73. Mansergh, *Irish Question*, 44–45.

74. Bulmer Hobson, *A Short History of the Irish Volunteers* (Dublin: The Candle Press, 1918), 13.

75. Kee, *Bold Fenian Men*, 201.

76. Lyons, *Ireland Since the Famine*, 320. Dangerfield maintains in *The Damnable Question*, p. 97, that Hobson was the one who approached MacNeill. This is unlikely, as Hobson denied any personal acquaintance with MacNeill at the time and O'Rahilly was a major figure in Gaelic circles.

77. Lyons, *Ireland Since the Famine*, 32.

Force.[78] This Provisional Committee, with Hobson, The O'Rahilly (as he was known), and MacNeill as executive officers, formally established the Irish Volunteer Force on 25 November. By July its membership numbered somewhere around seventy-five thousand.[79]

Several factors account for this change in the temperament of Irish nationalism. The long and arduous fight for Home Rule had not borne fruit, and for more than a few people, any kind of action was preferable to inaction continued on behalf of Irish nationalism. Another factor was the fear that Orange resistance to Home Rule would result in an incomplete realization of the nationalist dream. Not to be underestimated was the seemingly contradictory sense of satisfaction and inspiration some nationalists felt at seeing Unionists take up arms against England.[80]

Despite the obvious changes in nationalist willingness to agitate aggressively on behalf of their cause, the Irish Volunteers was not a radical group by any means. On the contrary, those who joined the Volunteers were overwhelmingly supporters of Redmond, and if anything, they were out to show their support for Home Rule.[81] But, unknown to the public and most of the Volunteers, the membership of the Provisional Committee had a disproportionately high representation of radicals with ties to the IRB.[82] Of thirty members on the

78. Although reports in the *Westmeath Independent* claimed that a new Volunteer movement had been established in Athlone and had organized nearly five thousand men in a march on 22 October 1913, there is room for suspicion about this so-called "Midland Volunteer Force." F. X. Martin and F. J. Byrne argue persuasively that these numbers were inflated if not wholly fabricated. They cite British intelligence reports made from eyewitnesses estimating the number of marchers at only fifty-four men with twenty-two rifles. See F. X. Martin and F. J. Byrne, *The Scholar Revolutionary* (Dublin: Harper and Row, Inc., 1975), 123ff.

79. Lyons, *Ireland Since the Famine*, 323.

80. Ibid., 321.

81. O'Hegarty, *A History of Ireland Under the Act of Union*, 675.

82. Kee, *Bold Fenian Men*, 204.

Volunteer executive body, twelve were IRB men.[83] In fact, The O'Rahilly and Hobson were both members of Clarke's inner circle, and the course of events suggests that, from the very outset, the Volunteers were engineered into existence by the Republicans. MacNeill furnished the IRB with a well-respected and widely known name behind which the IRB could bring together various unsuspecting nationalist factions under Republican influence and control.[84] Mac-Neill was duped into being the leader of an organization a substantial part of whose membership had far more radical ideology than his own;[85] his tragedy lay in his belief that he was in charge, not realizing until it was too late the size and aims of the forces arrayed against him. His suspicions about the radical leadership was justifiable, however; he and Roger Casement found the more radical members of the Provisional Committee "untrustworthy" types—especially Patrick Pearse.[86]

At this stage, the IRB was not the only group committed to the use of force. In August 1913, transport workers went on a massive strike in Dublin. The strike led to a long, bitter, and violent confrontation between the owners and the workers. In light of later developments the most important aspect of this strike was the founding of an Irish Citizen's Army under the leadership of James Connolly, a Scots-born socialist. With protection of the workers its prime objective, the ICA emerged as an effective and cohesive force by the end of the strike in January 1914.

One cause of the owner's victory over the strikers was a sudden desertion from the ranks of the ICA. Sean O'Casey, the secretary of the ICA at the time, credits this to the Volunteers, who stripped away members of the labor organization.[87] O'Casey found the Volunteers's nationalism suspect because of their ties to the Irish Parliamentary

83. Ibid.

84. Martin and Byrne, *Scholar Revolutionary*, 158.

85. Ibid., 133–35.   86. Kee, *Bold Fenian Men*, 212.

87. Seán O'Casey, *The Story of the Irish Citizen Army* (London, 1919; reprint ed., 1980), 8–9.

Party, and he bitterly criticized its leadership as being both too bourgeois and too heavily supported by the same owners against whom the transport workers had struck only months before.[88] By mid-1914 the Irish Citizen Army settled down to a small, highly committed number, most of whom embraced Irish nationalism over socialist internationalism. So many left for the ranks of the Volunteers that James Stephens later called the ICA "the most deserted from force in the world."[89]

James Connolly argued that, in Ireland, the national cause was wholly indistinguishable from the class struggle. But the Irish proletariat was small and still as much concerned with the struggle for Irish national identity as with the modes of production. Connolly wrote in July 1913: "The movements of Ireland for freedom could not and can not be divorced from the world-wide movements of the world's democracy. The Irish question is a part of the social question, the desire of the Irish people to control their own destinies is a part of the desire of the workers to forge political weapons for their own enfranchisement as a class."[90] Thus Connolly held a position

88. O'Casey's history of the ICA is very biased. His personal dislike of Connolly and Connolly's rise to power within the movement, in effect replacing not only James Larkin but also O'Casey, is the dominant theme of the book. He also distrusted nationalism, which Connolly fostered in the Irish labor movement. This ideological dispute prompted O'Casey eventually to quit the ICA. He attacked those who were drifting to nationalism. "Many, no doubt, preferred Caithlin Ní Hoolihan in a respectable dress than a Caithlin in a garb of a working woman. Many also realized that the governing body of the Volunteers was eminently influential, and that the ban which was over the Citizen Army, like a dark cloud, because of its arterial connection with the Transport Union, was not chosen as a shelter, when they could radiantly enjoy the National halo that glittered around the whole structure of the National Volunteers" (O'Casey, *Story of the Irish Citizen Army*, 9).

89. James Stephens, *The Insurrection in Dublin* (Dublin, 1916; reprint ed., Gerard's Cross: Colin Smythe, 1978), 47.

90. Owen Dudley Edwards and Bernard Ransom, eds., *James Connolly: Selected Political Writings* (New York: Grove Press, 1974), 150.

not terribly dissimilar from that held by most of the leadership of the IRB.[91]

With these developments, there was definite resistance to the Volunteers from many within the Irish Parliamentary Party. The formation of the Volunteers was a seemingly spontaneous event, for which the party could take no credit, and it had brought a new group of leaders to the forefront of popular political recognition.[92] The old party leadership never appreciated fully the extent to which the movement toward direct action was out of its hands. That movement had received inspiration from the Unionists and had been engineered by the IRB. The failures that had dogged nationalists on the cultural and political fronts led many to endorse more assertive and confrontational politics. An example had been set on the streets of Dublin during the Great Strike, enough so that Padraic Colum was to credit the ICA as the real inspiration for the Volunteers.[93] This assessment may give the Citizens Army too much credit, but, as O'Casey claimed, a number of ICA members, fresh from the street battles in Dublin during the fall of 1913, took their experience and conviction to the Volunteers. An undeniable connection would accordingly seem to have existed between the two groups.

These were exciting times for the leadership of the IRB. But they needed to make a critical connection with the majority of those in the Volunteers who were surely less committed to the use of force. To move those Volunteers closer to the IRB's point of view, a man was needed to articulate the necessity of action—a man whose political integrity and nationalist credentials were beyond reproach and who had, in some way, participated in and could speak to all of the major nationalist movements. His rectitude would enable him to speak for them in a way that made action, no matter how violent or desperate,

91. Ibid., 169.

92. Hobson, *A Short History of the Irish Volunteers*, 15.

93. Maurice Joy, ed., *The Irish Rebellion of 1916 and Its Martyrs: Erin's Tragic Easter* (New York: Devin-Adair, 1916), 53.

acceptable and even attractive. And, finally, he had to be a man who felt an intense need to act, in order that those who followed the IRB would be assured of the rightness of their feelings and their decision. The IRB found the man they were looking for in Patrick Pearse.

CHAPTER 4

Ireland and the Politics of
Redemption

The existence of a tradition of revolutionary violence in Irish politics is hardly remarkable. The antagonistic relationship between Britain and Ireland fostered the development of a physical-force movement committed to overthrowing the perceived oppressor. However, as with many questions in Irish history, the tradition of violence has psychodynamics that more conventional historical approaches fail to reveal.

The development of a republican tradition committed to violent revolution is usually explained in evolutionary terms, with each stage in the tradition's development seen as an increasing commitment on the part of revolutionaries to the use of violence. Historically, it is true that in the Irish case the politics of violence have evolved in organization and perhaps even in ideology and have always produced factions committed to the use of physical force. What has made Irish politics unique is the extent to which violence has been raised to the level of myth. This myth has been reaffirmed in the periodic rededication of individuals to violence and death—self-immolation to bring redemption to the individual and the country.

But the personal motivation for self-immolation had to be more compelling than purely abstract or theological reasons. Individuals would sacrifice themselves consciously only on behalf of a cause worthy of the ultimate price. A concept of the nation was required that struck a chord deep enough in the psyche of the individual to motivate him to consider violence and his own death as desirable.

Ernest Jones identified problems in the Irish national identity that might be the source of this concept of the nation. In a 1922 essay, "The Island of Ireland: A Psycho-Analytical Contribution to Political Psychology," Jones suggested that Irish rancor toward Great Britain is a result of the Irish people's thinking of Ireland as an "island home."[1] Jones observed that, almost without fail, island peoples manifested psychological complexes attached to the idea of the "island home," which were "those of woman, virgin mother and womb, all of which fuse in the central complex of the womb of the virgin mother."[2] Isolated and untrammeled, the island has a psychological significance of the mother as virgin. This virgin image is a fundamental constituent in the Oedipal complex of the son who cherishes the fiction of his mother's virginity in order to repudiate his father—the main obstacle in the son's way toward sexual union with the mother.[3]

Jones offered considerable evidence to support this association of the virgin mother and the island in Western thought, finding this theme common in both literature and dreams. Jones believed it is no accident that island peoples tend to see the homeland overwhelmingly in feminine terms;[4] one of Britain's allegorical representations is the feminine figure of Britannia.[5] This is no less true for Ireland, which has a host of feminine representations: The Old

1. Ernest Jones, "The Island of Ireland: A Psycho-Analytical Contribution to Political Psychology," in *Psycho-Myth, Psycho-History: Essays in Applied Psychoanalysis*, 2 vols. (New York: Stonehill Publishing, 1974), 97–99.
2. Ibid., 98.   3. Ibid.
4. Ibid., 98–99.   5. Ibid., 99.

Woman of Beare, Caithlin Ní Houlihan, Roisin Dubh (the little black Rose), Shan Van Vocht (Old woman), Dark Rosaleen, and Deirdre of the Sorrows.[6] While it is true that island nations often have masculine representations as well as feminine, Jones's analysis of the Irish tendency to represent Ireland as a woman is consistent with both Irish literature and nationalist thought. Throughout Irish history the representation of Ireland in mythology, art, politics, and popular culture has always been feminine. For Jones, the significance of this form of national identity is that the feminine form of representation demands protection, or as in the case of its conquest and subjugation, acts of redemptive violence and self-sacrifice on its behalf.

The tradition of feminine representation in Irish mythology dates from the *Táin* and pre-Norman Ireland, but it can most clearly be seen in the post-conquest Gaelic poetry of the seventeenth and eighteenth centuries. The peculiar combination of erotic attraction to the suppressed nation in female form can be seen in the first three verses of the poem "The Redeemer's Son" by the poet Aogan O'Rathaille (1675–1729).

> A Bitter vision I beheld
> in bed as I lay weary:
> a maiden whose name was Eire
> coming toward me riding
> with eyes of green hair curled and thick,
> fair her waist and brows,
> declaring he was on his way
> —her loved one *Mac an Cheannai.*
>
> Her mouth so sweet, her voice so mild,
> I love her maiden dearly,
> Wife to Brian, acclaimed of heroes
> —her troubles are my ruin!
> Crushed cruelly under alien flails
> my fair-haired slim kinswoman:

6. Ibid., 102.

She's a dried branch that pleasant queen,
    till he come, her *Mac an Cheannai.*

Hundreds hurt for love of her.
    —her smooth skin—in soft passion:
kingly children, sons of Mile,
    champions, wrathful dragons.
Her face, her countenance, is dead,
    in weariness declining
and nowhere is there relief,
    till he come, her *Mac an Cheannai.*[7]

The famous Irish nationalist song, "The Little Black Rose," was taken from an anonymous folk poem of the late eighteenth century entitled "Roisin Dubh." The last verses capture the idea that, at least for the individual, redemption can come out of service to Ireland.

If I had six horses I would plough against the hill—
I'd make Roisin Dubh my Gospel in the middle of Mass—
I'd kiss the young girl who would grant me her maidenhead
and do deed behind the *lios* with my Roisin Dubh!

The Erne will be strong in flood, the hills be torn,
the ocean be all red waves, the sky all blood
every mountain valley and bog in Ireland will shake
one day, before she shall perish, my Roisin Dubh.[8]

The Gaelic tradition of feminine representation of Ireland was reinforced in Irish Catholicism, which has historically depended greatly upon a strong and enduring dedication on the part of Irish Catholics not only to the Blessed Virgin Mary but also to a host of women saints identified with Ireland itself, most notably St. Brigid, the supposed "Mary of the Gaels."[9] Born a slave in Kildare in the

---

7. Seán O'Tuama, ed., *An Duanaire 1600–1900: Poems of the Dispossessed*, trans. Thomas Kinsella (Philadelphia: University of Pennsylvania Press, 1981), 157.

8. Ibid., 308.

9. Eoin Neeson, *The Book of Irish Saints* (Cork: Mercier Press, 1967), 34–35.

fifth century, Brigid has long been thought of as the patroness of Ireland, and around her grew a near-cultic following peculiar to Ireland. Many early scholars speculated that Brigid was a Druidic high priestess who commanded a community of women who converted en masse to Christianity.[10] In virtually every representation of Brigid, she is portrayed as a matronly figure replete with symbols such as the shamrock to identify her as a titular national figure.

The tendency toward feminine allegory was continued by the artists of the Young Ireland movement of the 1840s. The Young Irelanders were precursors to the Revivalists in using old Gaelic themes as the basis of a nationalist literary revival. The writings of Thomas Davis (1814–45) and James Clarence Mangan (1803–49) later proved to be very influential for the Irish-Irelanders and Gaelic League writers of Pearse's era.[11] Mangan's best-known poem, "Dark Rosaleen," has all of the themes that Jones emphasized in his analysis of Ireland's "island-home" mentality. Here Ireland is cast not only in the figure of Dark Rosaleen but also as a virgin whose cause demands violent action as confirmation of one's devotion.

> I could scale the blue air,
>   I could plough the high hills,
> Oh, I could kneel all night in prayer,
>   To heal your many ills
> And one . . . beamy smile from you
>   Would float like light between
> My toils and me, my own, my true,
>   My Dark Rosaleen!
>   My fond Rosaleen!
> Would give me life and soul anew,
> A second life, a soul anew,
>   My Dark Rosaleen!

10. H. Patrick Montague, *The Saints and Martyrs of Ireland* (Gerrard's Cross: Colin Smythe, Ltd., 1981), 21.

11. Thompson, *Imagination of an Insurrection*, 38.

O! the Erne shall run red,
  With redundance of blood,
The earth shall rock beneath our tread,
  And flames wrap hill and wood,
  And gun-peal, and slogan cry,
  Wake many a glen serene,
Ere you shall fade, ere you shall die,
  My Dark Rosaleen!
  My own Rosaleen!
The Judgment Hour must first be nigh,
Ere you fade, ere you die,
  My Dark Rosaleen![12]

Even the more conservative poets of Mangan's generation used the feminine allegory for the nation. Sir Aubrey De Vere (1814–1902) was an intimate friend of Tennyson, Carlyle, and Wordsworth, and his work betrays the influence of the British Romantic poets, as well as the neo-Gothic eroticism later used to great effect in the poetry of Patrick Pearse and Joseph Plunkett.

SONG

The little Black Rose shall be red at last!
  What made it black but the East wind dry,
And the tear of the widow that fell on it fast?
  It shall redden the hills when June is nigh!

The Silk of the Kine shall rest at last!
  What drave her forth but the dragon-fly?
In the golden vale she shall feed full fast
  With her mild gold horn, and her slow dark eye.

The wounded wood-dove lies dead at last:
  The pine long-bleeding, it shall not die!
—This song is secret. Mine ear it pass'd
  In a wind o'er the stone plain of Athenry.[13]

12. Brendan Kennelly, ed., *The Penguin Book of Irish Verse* (Baltimore: Penguin Books, 1970), 149–50.
  13. Ibid., 218.

By the late nineteenth century the allegorical use of the feminine figure had become established as a literary convention in nationalist thought. In the last verse of her poem "After Death," Fanny Parnell (1854–82), a sister of Charles Stewart Parnell, sees her country glorified after a war of liberation.

> Let me join with you the jubilant procession,
>   Let me chant with you her story;
> Then, contented, I shall go back to the shamrocks,
>   Now mine eyes have seen her glory.[14]

In her poem "The Clogher Massacre" this liberation is to take place through the blood of men whose sacrifice sows the seeds of a crop of freedom.

> The blood of martyrs is the choicest seed God sows.
> A thousandfold, at last, the wondrous harvest springs,
> From every fertile crop a Truth triumphant grows,
> And to the living from the slain Hope's mission brings.[15]

Yeats's play *Cathleen Ni Houlihan* (1902) has as its protagonist an old woman cast as the spirit of Ireland. This woman draws young men to her—men who abandon all for her, including their brides on their wedding nights. This personification of Ireland was recognized instantly by audiences. Yeats had already written about Ireland in this way in his *Stories of Red Hanrahan*, where the hero realizes his love of Ireland and a woman simultaneously and in the process is redeemed.[16]

These themes of femininity, violation, violence, and redemption became central in Irish nationalist art and were not limited to literary works. Popular Irish songs from the sixteenth century onward

14. Ibid., 277.

15. *Celtic Monthly* 5, 3 (September 1880), 241.

16. For more on the relationship between men's love of women and of Ireland, see John Wilson Foster, *Fictions of the Irish Literary Revival: A Changeling Art* (Syracuse: Syracuse University Press, 1987), 86ff.

have resorted to the same imagery. A popular nationalist song of the late eighteenth century had as a chorus:

> Midst danger, wounds and slaughter,
> Erin's green fields its soil shall be,
> Her tyrants' blood its water.[17]

The extent to which the imagery had been accepted in popular Irish culture by the twentieth century can be seen in the work of Sean O'Casey. A sometimes bitter critic of the revolutionary tradition, O'Casey employed the colloquial language of his time; invariably his characters described Ireland as an oppressed female.

More recently, Irish literature has repeatedly described Ireland's relationship with Britain in the metaphor of rape, with Ireland as a woman whose violation will inevitably lead to retribution. Perhaps the most notable example of this is Seamus Heaney's poem "Act of Union" in which the narrative voice is that of a masculine England who realizes that the consequences of the union with an unwilling feminine Ireland will mean the rising up of a male resistance intent upon violent retribution.[18]

This image of Ireland's national spirit as an oppressed and violated woman calling her sons to fight and die in her behalf has played a direct role in making violence endemic to Irish national politics and its theme of sacrificial death has roots deep in Irish consciousness. The eighth-century epic tale the *Táin Bo Cuailnge* (*The Cattle-Raid of Cooley*) has as its hero the great and precocious warrior Cúchulainn, a semi-divine being conceived through the union of supernatural and human beings. His prowess at warfare is matched by his moral integrity. Like Homer's Achilles, Cúchulainn's fatal flaw is exploited by his enemies, and he dies so that Ulster might survive, suffering death at the hands of those more devious

---

17. Quoted in Kee, *That Most Distressful Country*, 145.

18. Seamus Heaney, *Selected Poems, 1965–1975* (London: Faber and Faber, 1980; paperback, 1981), 125–26.

than he.[19] Cúchulainn died on behalf of his "homeland" pure, guileless, and morally superior to his conquerors. He was defeated only because, like Jesus, he allowed himself to be defeated. In so doing, Cúchulainn, like Jesus, took on the role of the "child-hero redeemer" whose death gains him immortality and redeems those who are to learn from his example.

The Cúchulainn myth resonates in Irish historical consciousness in part because of Ireland's recurrent historical pattern of conquest and rebellion. Since the Anglo-Norman invasion in the twelfth century, Irish history has been defined by the constant tension between conquests that never completely succeed in winning control of Ireland and rebellion against the oppressor. For those who rebel, the exercise of violent resistance amounts to a moral stand against injustice and an assertion of the essential righteousness of the national cause. More importantly, in Irish politics violence became its own standard of that which was right—a myth reaffirmed in the commitment to use it and to die from it.

Random violence appears to have been common in post-Reformation Ireland and even before that time, when many early European visitors considered it to be a distinctive Irish trait. By the eighteenth century, Dublin had become a very violent city, and religious pilgrimages near the city often degenerated into violent confrontations with the authorities.[20] Throughout the eighteenth and nineteenth centuries, agrarian violence was commonplace.[21] Terroristic organizations such as "The Defenders," "Whiteboys," "Ribbonmen,"

19. The *Táin* passed into the Celtic Revival largely through two works by Standish O'Grady. According to Yeats, O'Grady's *History of Ireland I: The Heroic Period* (1878) and *History of Ireland II: Cúchullain and his Contemporaries* (1880), were a major influence upon his own generation of Irish cultural nationalists. See William Butler Yeats, *Autobiographies*, 220ff.

20. Patrick J. Corish, *The Catholic Community in the Seventeenth and Eighteenth Centuries* (Dublin: Helicon, 1981), 113.

21. W. E. H. Lecky, *A History of Ireland in the Eighteenth Century* (Chicago: University of Chicago Press, 1972), 113–24.

and "Peep O'Day Boys" pervaded the Irish countryside by the late 1700s,[22] especially in areas of extensive agricultural enclosure. By an Irish Parliament Act of 1765, people who went by night in parties of five or more, committing crimes of agrarian violence, were made liable to death. This law was to have lapsed in 1767 but was prolonged instead and saw the addendum ten years later of a whole list of new and similar misdemeanors as capital offenses. Whiteboy disturbances were especially common in the 1760s,[23] with much of the attention being directed at the issue of the tithe rates.[24] Especially in the more remote rural areas, clergymen became the subject of threatened hangings.[25]

Official efforts to stop agrarian terrorism were largely ineffective. After mass executions of Defenders failed to curb their violence, one English official admitted that the policy had led to the exact opposite of that intended: "Defenderism puzzles me now more and more; but it certainly grows more and more alarming daily, as the effect of the executions seems to be at an end and there is an enthusiasm in defying punishment."[26] Despite attempts to downplay and discredit the rebels, their appeal proved to be impossible to eradicate. Some of the popular support for agrarian rebellion was most certainly a direct result of British misrule, but the hold that violence

22. See Lecky, 126–27. A wonderfully vivid story that captures these kinds of groups is William Carleton's "Wildgoose Lodge," written in the 1850s but showing the author's familiarity with such events. See William Carleton, *Traits and Stories of the Irish Peasantry*, 4 vols. (New York: Books for Libraries Press, 1971). The volumes were originally published in 1853.

23. The Whiteboys are notable for their use of the figure of "Queen Sive" for Ireland in letters and slogans. Sive is associated with the Fionn sagas in Celtic literature, especially in the countryside of Kilkenny and Tipperary, where Whiteboy outrages were most common. See Patrick Corish, *The Catholic Community in the Seventeenth and Eighteenth Centuries*, 124ff.

24. Lecky, *History of Ireland*, 129, 214–15.

25. Beckett, *The Making of Modern Ireland*, 177.

26. Quoted in Kee, *That Most Distressful Country*, 59.

had in the popular imagination was profound. The British attempt to suppress violence led to the Irish exaltation of those who suffered punishment, and the elevation of violence proved consistently bewildering to the British.[27]

Agrarian terrorism even developed its own martyrs, such as the parish priest Nicholas Sheehy, who was executed at Clonmel in 1766 for the supposed murder of a Whiteboy informer. His grave soon became a site of religious and nationalist pilgrimage.[28] Violence, and the willingness to use violence, moved the popular imagination in important ways even in the face of the usual ineptitude of its advocates.[29] Men like Wolfe Tone, Robert Emmet, and the "Manchester Martyrs" were failures by any practical standard; yet their commitment to violence in the face of overwhelming odds and inevitable defeat led to their enshrinement as heroic figures. If anything, their failure made them national martyrs: because they took action in an impossible situation, they were seen to be sacrificing themselves for the sake of Ireland.

The British generally were not able to appreciate the psychological appeal that self-immolation had for Irish Catholics. A changing, urbanizing and industrializing society such as Victorian Britain found the whole idea of blood sacrifice and martyrdom increasingly difficult to grasp. The inherent meaning of violence and sacrifice, which was obvious to Catholic Ireland, remained alien and obscure to the British.[30]

27. In fact, the Ribbon Lodges were the prime sources for Fenian recruiting in the 1860s and 1870s. See D. George Boyce, *Nationalism*, 178–79.

28. John Brady, *Catholics and Catholicism in the Eighteenth-Century Press* (Maynooth, 1965), 140–41,

29. In this sense Irish agrarian violence during the eighteenth century bears all the characteristics of early modern "primitive rebels" seen elsewhere in Europe. See Eric Hobsbawm, *Primitive Rebels*, (New York: Frederick A. Praeger, 1959).

30. See O'Farrell *Ireland's English Question*, especially chap. 1, for the differences between "Catholic Ireland" and "Protestant England."

Because of their religious heritage, the Irish could spiritualize freedom and victory as an eternal and ultimate state attainable after death. Only in the realm of the transcendent could they hope for some ultimate beatific experience and vision of freedom. This particularly Catholic understanding of the role of death had non-Christian precedents back to the *Táin* and formed a central motif in the Irish mythos that was to become a critical part of republican thinking and in the Easter Rising of 1916. Many men became national heroes, even though their political accomplishments were negligible, because of their commitment to violence. Failure to be aligned with the politics of violence in some way, no matter how reasonable the objections to its use, cost some of Ireland's greatest politicians wholehearted admiration from Irish posterity. The degree to which violence has become the standard of political validation can be clearly illustrated through a comparison of the reputations of the two most important Irish politicians of the nineteenth century.

By 1830 Daniel O'Connell was the most powerful man in Ireland. He had won the most important constitutional political victory of his day, Catholic Emancipation, and it had led to his leadership of a bloc of M.P.s with which he could pursue the Repeal of the Act of Union. Nonetheless, the Repeal crusade failed disastrously, despite O'Connell's mobilization of even greater agitation than that developed in support of Emancipation.

Emancipation succeeded where Repeal failed because, in the first case, the Government did not challenge O'Connell's seeming willingness to unleash the forces of violence.[31] The popular belief that O'Connell would be willing to resort to violence brought out even greater numbers to clamor for Repeal. In a series of huge political rallies O'Connell emphasized that violence would result if Repeal

31. Patrick O'Farrell, *England and Ireland Since 1800* (Oxford: Oxford University Press, 1975; reprint ed., 1979), 138.

was not won; but in October 1843, when the largest of the Repeal rallies was planned for Clontarf, the Government called his bluff. O'Connell called off the meeting when he believed that he faced determined and armed Government opposition to the meeting. The result was massive disaffection from the cause, as well as the diminution of O'Connell's power. The critical difference between the two campaigns was the belief that, if O'Connell was not given Emancipation, the forces of revolution would be let loose; in the Repeal campaign, the Government never considered giving in, as Repeal threatened Ireland's constitutional relationship with Britain. Instead, it chose to force O'Connell's hand, and he backed down. O'Connell's choice not to confront the Government directly led to the fragmentation of his support and the ultimate disaffection of the Young Ireland nationalists, who had argued for a more aggressive course in the fight for Repeal.[32] Although he remained the most important Irish politician of his day, he never again enjoyed the following that he had had before Clontarf.

After his takeover of the Irish Parliamentary Party in 1878, Charles Stewart Parnell also fought for the elusive prize of Home Rule. His rapid ascent to leadership took place in a period of extensive agrarian violence. The poor state of Irish agriculture in the 1870s had led to increasingly widespread outbreaks of agrarian outrages and retributive attacks on landlords. Parnell manipulated the rural situation brilliantly, often seeming to indicate he would support violence if all else failed. Despite many setbacks, his threat that violence would result as a consequence of the failure to win Home Rule played a major part in his rallying united nationalist support behind him.[33] Eventual dissatisfaction with Parnell's leadership in his own party forced him in 1890 into a by-election in Kilkenny in order to maintain his leadership. He lost the North Kilkenny by-election, and this defeat was followed by two more electoral defeats that marked Parnell's last hurrah. During these campaigns Parnell made an

32. Kee, *That Most Distressful Country*, 240–55.
33. Lyons, *Ireland Since the Famine*, 261–80 passim.

appeal to the "hillside men" (assumed by most people to mean the IRB), indicating that if Home Rule was not granted he would be forced to endorse their tactics.[34] This move appears to have failed him, and the defeats, in addition to the revelation of his involvement in an adulterous relationship, led to his fall from power. Within a year of his departure from the political scene, Parnell died a disgrace in the eyes of many of his countrymen.

Because his career ended abruptly and because his appeal to the "hillside men" never was to be tested, the debate on how committed Parnell was about using force is moot. Parnell's leading biographer believed that Parnell's appeal to the "hillside men" was just another brilliant tactical move that unfortunately failed.[35] But Parnell's ambiguous and unchallenged relationship to violence allowed him to be enshrined in the nationalist pantheon in ways that were denied ultimately to O'Connell. In Ireland, opinions held for or against him soon became a litmus test of one's political allegiances; many believed that Parnell had succumbed to his enemies only as a result of their treachery. Because many people believed that he was betrayed by his party and the church, his motivations and tactics remained relatively unquestioned by die-hard nationalists, and for the generation of 1916, Parnell was to remain the pivotal figure in the determination of political allegiances.

Acceptance of the myth of the betrayal of Parnell also meant an acceptance of his tactics, and the myth continued despite the fact that he had failed to deliver Home Rule. By any standard, O'Connell was a more successful politician—Parnell won nothing nearly so significant as Catholic Emancipation. What established Parnell as a mythic figure was the nature and means of his failure and his betrayal at the hands of the Irish Church. His enduring fame has had little to do with his success or lack of it. What he had that

34. *Freeman's Journal*, 22 December 1890.

35. F. S. L. Lyons, *Charles Stewart Parnell* (New York: Oxford University Press, 1977), 614–16.

O'Connell had not were the credentials of an Irish nationalist martyr who could sustain his cause long after his death. Herbert Howarth has commented on Parnell's martyrdom: "The Irish committed the crucial act of killing their prophet, and the guilt, the desire to purify the guilt, the belief that his gift sanctified, the belief that sacrifice assures rebirth, gave them irresistible vigour in the next generation."[36] Parnell's popular appeal has actually less importance than the way he legitimized revolutionary violence for the public. His relationship to violent politics marked him as the only "unfallen" parliamentarian in Irish history—without sin because he had never repudiated outright the use of violence. Because he did not shrink from the politics of violence, he gave its usage more authority and moral legitimacy than it had ever had before.

Howarth's statement about Parnell is highly significant as it links his advocacy of violence and the problem of guilt. Brigid Brophy has identified guilt as a critical factor in the appeal to violence on behalf of one's country.[37] She believes that guilt motivates men toward violence out of a sense of obligation to their country or to a leader.[38] The appeal of any kind of real gain from the exercise of violence—freedom, for example—is impotent in comparison to the overwhelming power of guilt.[39] Brophy maintains that guilt, like any motivation, is not one-sided; while failure to meet an obligation might appear to be the source of guilt, in reality the soldier's personal Oedipal conflict, and the guilt that it invariably brings upon the child who wishes his father out of the way, is the source of all guilt. Brophy thinks all men share this deep sense of guilt; thus, the appeal of patriotism is universal to all men because it taps a giant reservoir of human emotions and psychological needs.

Brophy maintains that equally powerful is the sense of inadequacy

36. Herbert Howarth, *The Irish Writers 1880-1890* (London, 1955), 4-5.
37. Brigid Brophy, *Black Ship to Hell* (New York: Harcourt, Brace and World, 1962).
38. Ibid., 39.   39. Ibid.

that a child feels before a seemingly omnipotent father. Because the male child knows he is guilty of wishing his father's death, he fears the retribution he believes might have befallen the women around him—castration. To compensate for his fear of this fate, he begins to see that perhaps a woman's lot in life is not bad and that it could even be desirable. Along with his emotional compensation goes a certain fascination with the female sense of sexual pleasure, and he begins to speculate what it would be like to experience it in a similar way. Brophy maintains that combat would be intolerable without making its results, the possible penetration of one's own body, attractive; thus, the attraction of violence lies in one's potential homoerotic experience of penetration.[40]

To many Irishmen, whose identity has effectively been castrated by another country, the allure of retributive violence on Ireland's behalf could be strong. But though Ireland's cause was just, the odds against any real victory over Ireland's oppressor were overwhelming. This could not rationally be denied, as Ireland was only a fraction as strong as England, but the inevitability of failure did nothing to halt the psychological imperative to go forth. The only answer was to win the conflict on a cosmic level above the plane of certain defeat. In that way, the actual outcome of the conflict was inevitable, whatever the setbacks in the political struggle. If the conflict between Britain and Ireland was transcendent, failure could become success, ineptitude and folly could become virtues, and the shedding of one's blood could be both an act of atonement and a testimony of one's faithfulness. This transformation of failure was critical to the Irish in the face of their inability to do their duty and right the wrong done to their country.[41]

40. Ibid., 49.

41. Since service in behalf of the cause of Irish freedom has almost always led to defeat and death, one must ask to what extent choosing the politics of violence within the Irish context represents a suicidal choice. For more on this subject see Seán Farrell Moran, "Patrick Pearse and Patriotic Soteriology: The Irish

On a less cosmic level, violence can attest the moral legitimacy of one's cause. Not only is violence an attempt to deny one's helplessness, it also serves to ease the individual's guilt. Instead of accepting the reality of inadequacy before the father, one seeks to overcome him by drawing from him the violence that justifies violence as a response.[42] Because the weapons of death happen to be those able to pierce the body, violence can fulfill the human desire for sexual penetration and union. Death can thus be eroticized into a desirable experience that has the potential to beatify the individual: it allows in death what has been denied and repressed in life—union with one's forbidden sexual object.

The process of eroticization makes death legitimately desirable on its own. In death, failure and forbidden fruit are both transformed into timeless and acceptable things; consequently, the seeming reversal of categories that exists throughout in the Irish tradition of nationalist violence, where it is sufferers and failures who end up being glorified, is rectified. The sufferer as winner is no longer a contradiction—his work has been completed in death. For the failure who goes to the gallows or to the torture chamber, the victory has been won beyond the constraints of reality. Because ultimate victory is assured, violence becomes a creative act that accomplishes in death what cannot be accomplished in life.

In the eroticization of death that marks the Irish republican tradition, the critical factor is the self-conscious courtship of violence and self-destruction. Parnell's relationship with a married woman is too

---

Republican Tradition and the Sanctification of Political Self-Immolation," in Yonah Alexander and Alan O'Day, eds., *The Irish Terrorism Experience* (Aldershot, 1991), 9–29.

42. There are reasons to suspect that over time the Irish family itself, especially mother-son relationships, provided a family dynamic that has heightened these feelings of inadequacy and encouraged violence in response; see Hasia Diner, *Erin's Daughters in America* (Baltimore: Johns Hopkins University Press, 1983).

obvious an example to be ignored as a manifestation of his courtship of failure. It had to be clear to Parnell, whose political instincts were superb, that the public disclosure of his relationship with Mrs. O'Shea could ruin his career. It is unlikely that a society such as Ireland could have begun to see Parnell as a heroic figure unless he had in some way effected his destruction, or seemed to have done so. In the Irish nationalist cosmology, accidental death and natural death have been insufficient causes for the making of heroes.

The extent to which this tradition of eroticized and spiritualized violence has been passed on is remarkable. The so-called "Manchester Martyrs" of 1867, three men who botched the rescue of two Fenians from prison, were hanged for the killing of a policeman in the attempt, and they became heroic models for the republicans after them. A mock funeral, held in their honor in Dublin's Glasnevin Cemetery, drew upwards of 60,000 people.[43] T. D. Sullivan took Michael Larkin's last speech from the dock and made it into a popular song:

> . . . "God save Ireland," said they all
> "Whether on the scaffold high, or the battlefield
>   we die,
> Oh, what matter when for Erin dear we fall?"[44]

Although Sullivan's lyrics bungled Larkin's actual speech, these verses soon became the rebel song identified with the IRB for the next generation. Ironically, Sullivan had been one of the leading figures in the moral-force wing of Irish nationalists, which had heavily criticized the advocates of violence.[45] Once again the execution of Irishmen committed to the use of violent means overcame ideological differences between groups that normally had widely antagonistic points of view. More important still was the precedent that the

---

43. Malcolm Brown, *Politics of Irish Literature*, 211.
44. Ibid., 212   45. Ibid.

song set for the usually inept Fenians. Malcolm Brown has commented that Sullivan's song "threw a shadow of the death mystique over the whole Fenian movement, subduing its [heretofore] cheerful activism under a lugubrious pall."[46] The elevation of Fenian failures to myth meant that both they and their methods became fixed in the minds of a large segment of the Irish public as ends worthy of pursuit. This process of acceptance occurred at the very time that the republicans themselves accepted failures as legitimate victories within their ideological cosmology.

Brown is correct when he says that, until the "Manchester Martyrs," the IRB had been pragmatic in its use of force and that the Fenians had not generally been susceptible to the "lost cause" mystique that had already grown around people like Tone and Emmet.[47] But the IRB exploited the mystique of the lost cause when it was to their advantage; they not only came to believe in it but also based their recruitment on it. The lost cause gave moral validity to the IRB's tactics and served as an ennobling explanation for their defeats and their tactics.

Not long after the deaths of the "Manchester Martyrs," factions of the IRB split off and became purely terrorist organizations whose goals, except for the use of violence for its own sake, were ill-defined. For example, on 6 May 1882, the most famous assassinations in Irish history took place in Phoenix Park, when several artisans slashed to death both the Chief Secretary and the Undersecretary for Ireland. The organization claiming responsibility for the murders was a new group calling itself the Invincibles.[48] The Invincibles soon disappeared under criminal prosecution, but their existence, along with the tactics they employed, set a precedent. After the Invincibles, Irish nationalism began to resemble violent anarchist movements in

46. Brown claims that Sullivan's family was interested in necrology, (ibid., 213).

47. Ibid., 241–42.

48. T. Corfe, *The Phoenix Park Murders* (London: Hodder and Stoughton, 1968).

Europe and America, which used terrorist violence, "propaganda by deed," as a legitimate expression of political dissension.

This merger of life and death in the Irish revolutionary tradition reached its highest artistic expression in the poetry of the Easter rebels of 1916. Thomas MacDonagh and Joseph Mary Plunkett, both of whom were bona fide poets of some ability, wrote of death in the service of Ireland as the source of life. While Pearse's poetry has probably proven to be more influential and will be discussed in some detail later, both Plunkett and MacDonagh's works merit consideration as expressions of the eroticization of death that captured the Irish republican imagination in the twentieth century.

Plunkett carried the erotic image of death to near-hysterical heights in his poetic works; some are filled with allegories of love, death, and mystical union with God. One of Plunkett's earlier poems, "I See His Blood Upon the Rose," is a prime example.

I SEE HIS BLOOD UPON THE ROSE

I see his blood upon the rose
And in the stars the glory of his eyes,
His body gleams amid eternal snows,
His tears fall from the skies.

I see his face in every flower;
The thunder and the singing of the birds
Are but his voice—and carven by his power
Rocks are his written words.

All pathways by his feet are worn,
His strong heart stirs the ever-beating sea,
His crown of thorns is twined with every thorn,
His cross is every tree.[49]

While Plunkett's poem is a bloody vision of Christ's universal death with universal implications, he identified the source of his

---

49. Desmond Ryan, ed., *The 1916 Poets* (London: Allen Figgis and Co., Ltd., 1963; reprint ed., Westport CN: Greenwood Press, 1979), 192.

inspiration as the Fenians of 1867. The Irish people's rejection of the Fenians, as well as the disastrous Fenian failure in the Rising of 1867, was, to Plunkett, akin to the trials and humiliations of Christ. In Plunkett's mind, the Fenians' sacrifice had to be the source of the revolutionary vision that guided the rebels. The Fenians' failure gave life to him and his fellow revolutionaries.

1867

All our best ye have branded
When the people were choosing them,
When 'twas Death they demanded
Ye laughed! Ye were losing them.
But the blood that ye spilt in the night
Crieth loudly to God,
And their name hath the strength and the might
Of a sword for the sod.

In the days of our doom and our dread
Ye were cruel and callous,
Grim Death with our fighters ye fed
Through the jaws of the gallows;
But a blasting and blight was the fee
For which ye had bartered them,
And we smite with the sword that from ye
We had gained when ye martyred them![50]

To Plunkett, the tradition was life-giving and it was sustained by the deaths of those who died serving it. Thus the failure of the Fenians was the source of the successful passing on of the tradition to later generations, because the death of its martyrs had occurred in service to the holy cause. Patrick Pearse pursued this theme in his speeches and in his writing throughout 1915 and early 1916, but Plunkett's was the voice that raised the cause and not only made it a religious faith but also made Ireland's freedom an object of sexual desire. Unattainable in life, it could be had only in death, through

50. Ibid., 198.

the union of its adherents with the idea of the nation in an allegory
of sexual abandonment. Plunkett identified the force in Irish republicanism as sexual:

THE LITTLE BLACK ROSE SHALL
BE RED AT LAST

Because we share our sorrows and our joys
And all your dear and intimate thoughts are mine
We shall not fear the trumpets and the noise
Of battle, for we know our dreams divine,
And when my heart is pillowed on your heart
And ebb and flowing of their passionate flood
Shall beat in concord love through every part
Of brain and body—when at last the blood
O'erleaps the final barrier to find
Only one source wherein to spend its strength.
And we two lovers, long but one in mind
And soul, are made one only flesh at length;
Praise God if this my blood fulfills the doom
When you, dark rose, shall redden into bloom.[51]

Plunkett's erotic vision of his body's blood passing into the soil of
Ireland equates his blood with life-producing semen that impreg-
nates the flesh of female Ireland.

Desmond Ryan has claimed that Plunkett was deeply affected by
his enthusiastic study of the Christian mystical poets such as Tauler
and St. John of the Cross.[52] If that is so, and Plunkett's imagery
seems to confirm it, then his poetry was another expression of a tradition in Christian mysticism that has used the allegory of sexual
union in describing death and has looked at sexual orgasm as a
metaphor for spiritual revelation. Thompson argues that the historical issue is not whether Plunkett articulated a respectable mystical
tradition but rather his desire to live out a mystical vision in his

51. Ibid., 201.
52. Desmond Ryan quoted in Thompson, *Imagination of an Insurrection*, 134.

life.[53] No doubt Plunkett's health played a great part in this. By 1916 he was dying from consumption; but there is a sense in which Plunkett had, by 1916, already lived a life of adventure, seeking the experience he had read and written about.

Thomas MacDonagh, who in retrospect had the most artistic potential of the Easter Rising poets, was less obsessed with the theme of death than either Plunkett or Pearse. But Thompson believes that MacDonagh's work is important because it expresses the voice of the second-rate melancholic whose artistic inability to express his pedestrian feelings led him to despair, then to revolution.[54] He also believes that all three of the Easter Rising Poets were incapable of sustaining an original artistic vision in their work, and the realization of that inability led them to despair and to choose living out a vision that their poetic voices were incapable of articulating.[55] If so, that sense of failure led MacDonagh to consider death as a way of expressing what he could not express in his poetry. He recreated the image of the holy prophet who speaks a truth not recognized in his own land and who will one day see it triumph over all opposition.

THE POET SAINT

Sphere thee in Confidence
Singing God's Word
Led by His Providence,
Girt with his Sword;

Bartering all for Faith,
Following e'er
That others deem a wraith,
Fleeting and fair.

"Walk thou no ample way
Wisdom do the mark;
Seek thou where Folly's day
Setteth to dark.

53. Thompson, *Imagination of an Insurrection*, 138.
54. Ibid, 138.   55. Ibid., 135–39.

"Darkness in Clarity
     Wisdom doth find,
Folly in Charity
     Doubting the Kind,

"Folly in Piety,
     Folly in Trust,
Heav'n in Satiety,
     Death in Death's dust.

"Though from the dust shalt rise
     Over all Fame,
Angels of Paradise
     Singing thy name."[56]

Ultimately any discussion of the morality or immorality of violence in Irish nationalism is irrelevant to the discussion of the development of those beliefs that uphold the justification of violence on
behalf of Irish independence. For Irish republicans, especially since
1916, Irish nationalism has become more than a political position;
after Patrick Pearse, the republican *believed* in a nationalist theology
that demanded violence and self-immolation.[57] Pearse merely articulated a credo through which the republican could die and kill jus-
tifiably in order to redeem his country and himself.[58]

With the Rising, all of these strands came together in Patrick
Pearse. His conscious equation of Ireland's cause with a holy crusade, along with his stress on the emotional, sexual, and psychic resolution open to those who chose to fight in behalf of that cause,
coalesced the various forces at work in the physical-force movement
of his day. The legacy he left soon became that which carried the
tradition onward for generations after his death. Pearse sanctified
physical-force nationalism, and in doing so his life work became a
part of the tradition of Irish nationalist violence that had been

56. Ryan, *Poets of 1916*, 146.
57. Moran, "Patrick Pearse and Patriotic Soteriology," 26ff.
58. Ibid., 9–10.

bestowed upon him by Clarke. Pearse succeeded far beyond what anyone could have expected, and in the process made violence and death deeply moving spiritual experiences, which had the potential to free not only Ireland but human beings as well. For the IRB and, as we shall see, for Pearse also, death became the medium of personal and national redemption with eschatological implications.

CHAPTER 5

Pearse 1900-1912:
The Shaping of a
National Hero

Journalist and Educator

James Pearse's death in 1900 presented Patrick with both a dilemma and an opportunity. The question of a career loomed before him, complicated by his family's decision to have him run the business.[1] That obligation, however, concealed a hidden blessing, for the estate of James Pearse was considerable and offered security against Patrick's need to find an immediate niche in life. The business was thriving—at James's death it was the largest of its type in the city.[2] The firm's need of Patrick's attention would allow him to forego any commitment to a career and to indulge his pastimes, Gaelic and writing. Unforeseen was the effect of this moratorium on his life; not only did it allow Patrick to follow his interests, it had the additional effect of further stalling his development of an autonomous identity. As a result, Patrick was led to increas-

1. Ruth Dudley Edwards, *Patrick Pearse*, 46.
2. Ibid., 48.

ingly desperate attempts to forge that identity and ultimately to an overwhelming need for action as a way of garnering approval and acceptance.

His father's estate was of a healthy size, but most of the wealth was tied up in the firm.[3] While Patrick had little artistic skill, Willie had shown some talent, and in 1900 he was about to embark on his last year at the Metropolitan School of Art.[4] Because Willie would eventually assume leadership of the firm, the family decided that Patrick should take over the business until Willie finished his studies abroad.[5] At the time there was every expectation that Patrick would mind the store while pursuing his legal education and career, but his changing of the firm's title from "James Pearse" to "Pearse and Sons" might have signified that Patrick was more interested in actual participation than he had originally indicated. He started to identify himself in his new commercial capacity as "Patrick H. Pearse, Sculptor."[6]

Although the family mantle had been placed on his shoulders, Pearse did not inherit his father's business acumen or artistic skills. He had no skill at the stone-carver's craft, and his adoption of the title "Sculptor" for business was most fanciful. One must wonder if the family settlement was agreeable to all parties involved, but it is unlikely, given Willie's subservience to his older brother and the devotion of the family women to Patrick, that any conscious disagreement took place. Actually, Willie was the de facto inheritor of his father's artistic skill, an interesting potential source of conflict between the brothers.[7] The prospective dependence of the family on the business should have caused some concern, as Willie was experiencing academic difficulties, barely passing his preparatory examination and failing two subjects as well[8]—his career as an artist must have been in doubt.

3. Ibid., 46.   4. McCay, *Padraig Pearse*, 18.
5. Ruth Dudley Edwards, *Patrick Pearse*, 46.
6. Ibid.   7. See Appendix.
8. Ruth Dudley Edwards, *Patrick Pearse*, 16.

Not coincidentally, the brothers became even more inseparable at this time. The business was now being looked upon as another joint production of theirs. They took vacations together, studied Gaelic together, and exchanged confidences. There are reports that when they spoke to each other, they often did so in a kind of infantile baby talk, oblivious that this disturbed others, who found that image hard to reconcile with the tediously grave Pearse they usually saw.[9]

In more than one sense, the nature of the continued relationship between Pearse and his family is disturbing. Although living in Dublin at this time was not inexpensive, it was the very time of Pearse's life when he should have established some kind of emotional distance from his family. Instead of asserting his independence, he was being redrawn into his family, away from the possibility of meeting and knowing others—away from freedom as an adult. His enthusiastic acceptance of these developments indicates how unable he was to put distance between himself and his ever-protective relatives. Encouraged to depend on them, he foreclosed any opportunity to depend on others.

Pearse went back to university to further his legal studies, and he continued his involvement in the Gaelic League. In June 1901, he took his finals and passed them both, taking a degree in modern languages and law. Once again, his results were respectable, though hardly outstanding, with a second-class honors.[10]

Immediately upon graduation Pearse started to show how little enthusiasm he had for his prospective career as a barrister; he tried only one case, yet he was proud of his title.[11] Despite his lack of enthusiasm for the law, he had his name recorded on Gaelic League memoranda and publications as "Patrick Pearse, B.A.B.L.," thus revealing the love of titles that followed him throughout his life.[12]

9. Ibid., 46.   10. Porter, *P. H. Pearse*, 40.
11. Ruth Dudley Edwards, *Patrick Pearse*, 47.
12. Ibid., 48.

He continued to teach Irish classes for University College. The family firm was doing well and its continued success mitigated his need to mind it very closely; Pearse therefore chose to pursue the one thing about which he was enthusiastic and confident—Gaelic. He was perhaps typical of the language enthusiasts: keen, zealous, well educated, middle class, and somewhat narrow of vision. Perhaps because of these qualities, but certainly because of his talent and ambition, he had risen quickly to establish himself in Dublin's Gaelic circles with his presence on the League's Publications Committee.

He parlayed this position to his advantage in 1903. After contributing many articles throughout 1902 to *An Claidheamh Soluis* (The Sword of Light), the League's official newspaper, he applied for the job of chief editor of the paper. He got this job in February 1903, and in the process displayed considerable talent in lobbying for support on his behalf.[13] By gaining the editorship of the paper, he had won the use of an important organ for continuing to concentrate on his love of Irish literature. Now he could get paid to do what he had been best at in his youth—fantasizing about the Irish past. His successful landing of the editorship seems a little out of character, until one remembers his esoteric interests and what a small world the Gaelic League really was. When he was very interested in something, Pearse could demonstrate social skills one would never have thought he possessed, and his gifts in Irish were considerable, although he had somewhat prematurely come to regard himself as an authority. His early writings reveal that he thought himself a valuable addition to the field and was confident in his interpretative positions on the various language and literary controversies that swirled through the Cultural Revival at that time.

Before becoming editor of *An Claidheamh Soluis*, Pearse had gone on assignment to the Gaeltacht in Connaught to write a ten-part

13. Ibid., 58-63.

series on the remnants of native traditional Irish life. He wrote about the Irish peasants' way of life with no hint of understanding of the difficult hardships that they had to endure. His view was heavily romanticized, and he grossly idealized the family with whom he stayed, representing them as examples of pure Gaelic life, finding it incomprehensible why these kinds of people were choosing to emigrate from the West of Ireland.[14] Pearse's attitude about emigration was perhaps typical of many in the Gaelic League at the time. Later he was to write that the emigrant "is a traitor to the Irish State."[15]

This lack of insight characterized the way Pearse looked at those around him; although he was unfailingly polite, could be sympathetic and often showed kindness toward others, there is little to indicate that he ever had any sense of real identification with their lives and the problems they faced—he remained isolated and naïve. He was, if anything, vain and self-righteous, a bit of a workaholic, who neither smoked nor drank and strongly disapproved of swearing.[16] His priggishness, combined with his inability to communicate empathy, might account for the blindly self-seeking attitude that many of his early acquaintances remembered as his most distinctive characteristic. Most of them seemed to have regarded him as egotistical, vain, and closed minded.

Part of Pearse's vanity and egotism was obviously attributable to his basic social inadequacy: the self-righteousness and intolerance were masks hiding his sense of inferiority, results of having to operate with all of his emotional deficiencies in a world of adults. In the case of his campaign to get the editor's job at *An Claidheamh Soluis*, he demonstrated an ability to move in adult circles.[17] But his inadequacies really outweighed his abilities, and the rewards of the adult

14. Ibid., 52.   15. *An Claidheamh Soluis*, 18 July 1903.
16. Ruth Dudley Edwards, *Patrick Pearse*, 24.
17. Ibid., 54ff.

world were not so readily forthcoming and fulfilling as those at home had been in childhood. In the seemingly unconditional love of his family, approval had come readily and steadily. Even though he was making a name for himself through his work on the paper, the editorship forced him to confront his lack of maturity.

His immaturity was never more obvious than in the early days as editor. He immediately undertook an expansion of *An Claidheamh Soluis* with no consideration of the possible ramifications of failure. After this expansion, the paper was published at a loss and Pearse was forced to return it to its original size.[18] Edwards is correct in identifying this episode as very important in helping us understand Pearse's psychological makeup.[19] He approached the job at the paper with expectations that could never have been realistically fulfilled, and the subsequent failure of the enterprise left Pearse distraught and puzzled. He thought that whatever he wished could be, and should be, accomplished. He blamed the failure of the paper's expansion on the smallness of others who were not half so committed as he.

As head of *An Claidheamh Soluis*, Pearse was asked to contribute on an impressive variety of topics, especially the endless and often esoteric controversies surrounding the Gaelic League. These topics were ideal for Pearse; having spent a whole childhood thinking about Gaelic Ireland, he considered himself an authority on anything that pertained to the subject. From the very first issue he set out to tell the readership, all of whom were already devoted disciples of the Irish language, where the truth lay and what their own allegiances should be.

In Pearse's mind, the language was everything. From it sprang Irish life, customs, and the peculiarly "Irish" world view, and Pearse accordingly equated the language movement with the national movement.

18. Ibid., 68.
19. Ibid., 67–68.

When Ireland's language is established, her own distinctive culture is assured. . . . All phases of a nation's life will most assuredly adjust themselves on national lines as best suited to the national character once that national character is safeguarded by its strongest bulwark [i.e., the language]. . . .

To preserve and spread the language then is the single idea of the Gaelic League. . . . We have a task before us that requires self-sacrifice and exertion as heroic as any nation ever put forth. . . . Woe to any Irish man who by his lethargy, his pride, his obstinacy, or his selfish prejudice, allows the moments to pass, or impedes this national work until it is too late.[20]

Although Pearse perhaps represented the opinion held by most of his readership, it was not a view held by everyone, and Pearse was challenged immediately by more broad-minded members of the League.[21] In these circumstances, Pearse was exposed as obviously immature in his espousal of narrow-minded and naïve opinions that allowed little room for disagreement. He quietly yet firmly rejected those who did not support him as being less committed than himself. This inflexibility got him into trouble more than once, especially over the issue of political nationalism, which at this time he viewed as desirable but not absolutely essential to the cultural revival. Although he had fallen under the influence of Arthur Griffith's book *The Resurrection of Hungary*, he totally missed the constitutional and political details: he credited Griffith with proving that the revival of the Hungarian language was the primary factor in leading to the eventual Hungarian nation.[22] It became readily apparent that the finer points of politics were not his forte.[23]

In almost every way Pearse's editorship was controversial and at best a mixed success. One letter to Eoin MacNeill (who sat on

20. *An Claidheamh Soluis*, 27 August 1904.

21. Ruth Dudley Edwards, *Patrick Pearse*, 70 - 71.

22. *An Claidheamh Soluis*, 16 June 1904.

23. His family and closest friends knew him to be politically disinterested: see Mary Hayden, "My Recollections of Padraig Pearse," 114.

Coiste Gnothe, the ruling body of the Gaelic League) claimed that
Patrick Pearse was going to destroy the paper by his irresponsible
actions during what was a critical phase of the Gaelic revival.[24]
Pearse's narrowmindedness on certain subjects showed that he was
not the least biased commentator possible in a movement fraught
with internecine strife. Yet, it was a productive period for his personal development as a writer, since he used *Claidheamh* as a
medium for publishing much of his own work.

There is some evidence that this period of controversy bothered
him considerably.[25] He began to see himself as the movement's willing slave, battered and abused by those who did not agree with him
(though he was not beneath attacking others). Hyde wrote later
about these factional disputes and their effect on the Gaelic League,
and he blamed Pearse's work as a typical example of the damage
done to the ideals of the cause.[26] The League was becoming increasingly powerful, and the growing political involvement of its membership brought the cultural revival into the political spotlight. As
the League became politicized, its leadership was forced to take positions on issues not within the usual scope of League interests. Hyde
lamented these developments: "The [Gaelic] League, which was
really a delightful body of men and women so long as it was actuated
by only one desire, that of restoring the Irish language, began to lose
its charm when it became powerful. It was then worth capturing and
people, notoriously Griffith's, set out to do so."[27]

The setbacks at *An Claidheamh Soluis* did not hinder Pearse's
writing, much of which appeared within its pages as well as in other
publications. Two versions of folktales, *Bruidhean Chaorthainn* (The

24. Eoin MacNeill Papers, MacCumhaill to MacNeill, 20 May 1907, National
Library, Dublin.

25. Ruth Dudley Edwards, *Patrick Pearse*, 89.

26. Douglas Hyde Memoirs Manuscript, University College Library, Dublin.

27. Douglas Hyde Memoirs Manuscript, cited by Ruth Dudley Edwards,
Patrick Pearse, 89.

Enchanted Hall of Rowan Tree), and *Bodach an Chotha Lachtna* (The Rustic in the Drab Boat), were published through his connections with the Publication Committee of the Gaelic League. These followed a story for boys that he had pseudonymously written for *Claidheamh* in 1905 and several literary commentaries for the *Gaelic Journal* he had written while still a student. *Bruidhean* reveals Pearse's prudishness: he bowdlerized the original in order to remove a lengthy reference to buttocks.[28]

At this time he sat squarely within the conservative mainstream of the Literary Revival. Since his entire personal being was tied to the language movement, he looked askance at people like Synge and Yeats, who were not as committed to the native sources of literature as he was. While his appreciation of Yeats's work and the Abbey Theater grew with time, he believed that truly national theater was going to be accomplished only by the Gaelic League. He believed that the literature of the so-called "Celtic Twilight School" was inferior to the work of the modern Gaelic writers. "Do Mr. Yeats and his fellows hold a place in the intellectual present of Ireland comparable to that held, say, by an AutAhair Peader [Father Peader O'Leary] or Conan Maol [Patrick O'Shea]? . . . The Twilight People will pass with the Anglo-Irish Twilight."[29]

Pearse could not have been more wrong than in his rejection of the "Twilight People." The artists in the Gaelic wing of the movement could not hold a candle to a Russell, Yeats, or Synge, and their only recourse was to disparage the work of these whose eventual contribution far outweighed their own.[30] Despite the division between the two parties, Thompson believes that the storm over Synge's *Playboy of the Western World* in 1907 discouraged many artists in the cultural movement.[31] At the play's opening perfor-

28. Porter, *P. H. Pearse*, 76.
29. *An Claidheamh Soluis*, 10 February 1906.
30. See Thompson, *Imagination of an Insurrection*, chapters 2 and 3.
31. Ibid., 73-74.

mance the audience rioted over the comically realistic portrayal of Irish character, and forced Yeats to appeal to the police to establish order. To Pearse they represented proof of the final failure of those who believed that Irish art could be represented in English.[32]

Thompson sees in the *Playboy* riots the "note of desperation and intensity" that reflected an ongoing hardening of opinion against the cultural movement and represented the first indication of support for more concrete forms of nationalist agitation that led to political action.[33] As such, the riots appear to mark the popular realization of the failure of the cultural movement to achieve its goals. The rioters were by and large middle class; their dissatisfaction was seen by the more provincial members of the language movement to indicate a rejection of purely "cultural nationalism." While cultural nationalism in Ireland was being led toward politics, its failure to realize an adequate vision of the nation, especially felt by those who criticized such modernists as Synge, led the "poet-patriots" of the future Easter Rising to despair and to take on, in response to their own artistic failures, the self-conscious role of political rebels.[34] The problem with applying this thesis to Pearse is that Pearse was not obviously affected by the failure of Synge's work, which he merely regarded as morally repugnant and worthy of condemnation.

> Irish character does not have to be vindicated against Mr J. M. Synge; and if it did the audience went a strange way about vindicating it. But we do not believe that Mr Synge intended his play either as a picture or caricature of Irish life. The charge we bring against him is greater. Whether deliberately or undeliberately, he is using the stage for the propagation of a monstrous gospel of animalism, of revolt against sane and sweet ideals, of bitter contempt for all that is fine and worthy, not merely in Christian morality,

32. *An Claidheamh Soluis*, February 9, 1907.
33. Thompson, *Imagination of an Insurrection*, 73.
34. Ibid., 74–77.

but in human nature itself. . . . It is not against a nation he blasphemes so much as against the moral order of the universe.[35]

The poor quality of contemporary acting and staging in contemporary Gaelic theater did not deter Pearse, and he pushed to establish an Irish theater under the control of the Gaelic League[36] because of the failures of "Anglo-Irish" drama. Pearse still believed in the power of Irish art, despite Synge.

While the Playboy riots were important in the way that Thompson suggests, the movement of cultural nationalists toward political action did not begin with Synge's play. Clearly, doubt was increasing that cultural nationalism would be sufficient to produce the desired goal of an Irish nation. Pearse was no less affected by these feelings than anyone else, but he did not immediately choose immersion in politics. His way was to explore a more readily rewarding arena, not so open to attack from without and within and more suited to his abilities: he started thinking of founding a school that could teach the noble Irish the lessons he had already learned.

The idea of an "Irish-Ireland" school came to Pearse sometime after he had taken a trip to Belgium with his sister in June 1905 to study bilingual schools.[37] Pearse came back inspired by the teaching of both Flemish and French in the schools of Flanders, and over the next three years he wrote a series of articles about them. Education had become a passion; he had been teaching Irish and Irish history parttime at several schools in Dublin,[38] and his Belgian experience convinced him of the need for a school based on Irish language and culture. In January 1906, Thomas O'Nowlan, a prominent League supporter, approached Archbishop Walsh of Dublin with the idea of establishing such a school, and O'Nowlan named Pearse as a vice-

---

35. *An Claidheamh Soluis*, 2 February, 1907.
36. *An Claidheamh Soluis*, 2 March, 1907.
37. Ruth Dudley Edwards, *Patrick Pearse*, 106.
38. Ibid., 108.

president of the project.[39] This school never came to life, perhaps in part because of a depression Pearse experienced at the end of that year.[40] In the spring of 1908 Pearse wrote to Eoin MacNeill about the idea of an Irish school offering a bilingual education. Though Mac-Neill had doubts, he approved the idea but offered no funds.[41] Eventually Pearse had success getting money from other prominent Gaelic Leaguers, and by June 1908 the school was enough of a reality to allow him to resign his job at *An Claidheamh Soluis*. His prospectus for the school and some additional campaigning in its behalf paid off, and he bought Cullenswood House in Rathmines to serve as the school's main building.

When St. Enda's School opened to seventy pupils in the fall of 1908, its headmaster was no novice in the field of education. Pearse had been teaching Gaelic for years, and during his tenure at *Claidheamh* he had written enough on education to establish himself as perhaps the preeminent theorist on "Irish" education. His goal in founding the school was to educate young Irish minds before they could be Anglicized and to teach them in a compassionate environment the "ways" of Ireland. This was a totally logical extension of the goals of the Gaelic League.

Subconscious motivations for Pearse's choice of education as a career also appear.[42] In every way he was immature for his age: he had no relationships with women other than those in his immediate family; he was still shy and uncomfortable with others; he had as yet

39. Ibid., 111.   40. Ibid., 112.

41. Ibid., 113-14.

42. Thompson argues that the period of 1906-8 was critically important in Pearse's movement toward acceptance of physical force for national ends. Although Thompson's analysis has merit, it is inherently ahistorical; the reasoning stretches the evolution of Pearse's thinking on violence beyond its chronological limits, putting his conscious thought of it well before the point it deserves. Later, when Pearse had begun to recognize that the achievements of Yeats and his colleagues were undeniably important, it is possible to say that a sense of shortcoming began to play a part in Pearse's attitude.

no vision of what he wanted his life to be. The role of educator fulfilled a need to escape the controversies that had besieged him as a
journalist. It allowed him to inspire people who were less likely to
reject him. Pearse loved and idealized children; as a teacher he could
continue to live vicariously in the boy's world of fantasy and dreams
from which realities would be banished.

His enthusiasm for his students raises a troubling issue—Pearse's
attraction to young boys. The only people apart from his family
with whom he seemed ever to be wholly at ease were boys, and there
is no doubt that Pearse found boys attractive in a physical sense. He
wrote much of his prose and poetry to or about them, especially
early in his career, and although his theatrical pieces usually concerned adults, the characters were almost always played by children.
The relationships between his characters are hopelessly idealized
and romantic—as if the author preferred to see adults from a
child's perspective. It is true, however, that Pearse's writing, often
near scandalous in its praise of the beauty of boys, was rarely explicitly sexual.[43]

Boys had captured his imagination as early as 1902, when he had
written "La Fa'n Tuaith," a ten-part serial for *An Claidheamh Soluis*.
He included in his story an incident when Pearse undressed and
shared a bed with a young boy. Edwards is correct in saying that, in
the cultural milieu of which Pearse was a part, homosexuality was
considered grossly aberrant, even among the enlightened.[44] It can
also be said with some assurance that Pearse was not consciously
aware of his attraction to boys, although his repression of references
to the buttocks in his publication of *Bruidhan Chaorthainn* is interesting in this light. He was not a pederast, nor did he leave any
recorded explicitly sexual fantasies regarding boys. There is thus
nothing to indicate that he saw sexual relations with boys as a pre-

43. Ruth Dudley Edwards, *Patrick Pearse*, 52–53.
44. Ibid., 53.

ferred or exclusive way of achieving sexual satisfaction. According to the most recent diagnostic criteria employed in modern psychiatric practice, Patrick Pearse was not a pedophile.[45] What is important is that he obviously was so attracted to boys. They raised in him feelings of pathos and passion that otherwise seemed to be missing from his personality. Boys readily aroused in him the very things he could not feel for others. He viewed them as angelic and pure, but he also saw them as the potential source of sensual fulfillment that he longed to feel.

There is universal recognition amongst his biographers that something was unusual here,[46] especially since it is extremely unlikely that Pearse ever had a sexual relationship with any woman or child. The only possible intimate relationship of any kind with a woman was with Eveleen Nichols, a fellow Gaelic Leaguer who died in 1909 while swimming off the Great Blasket Island, off the coast of Kerry. Edwards has surmised that this supposed relationship is likely to have been the fabrication of one of the Pearse hagiographers.[47]

Women were only ideals to Pearse, who usually portrayed them in his writing as the embodiment of virtue or as a symbol of Ireland. He did write touchingly about mothers but without understanding them as sexual creatures or human beings. One of his only women friends, Mary Hayden, a history instructor at University College, went with Patrick on a tour through the Gaeltacht in January 1903. She was nearly twenty years his senior, old enough to be his mother, and no mention was ever made of any kind of sexual relationship between them, although they briefly became intimate

45. At the present time, the diagnostic criteria for pedophilia involves active and recurrent sexual urges and fantasies involving sexual activity with children; on the basis of the evidence, Pearse was innocent of conscious pedophilia. See the *Diagnostic Criteria from the Diagnostic and Statistical Manual of Mental Disorders*, 3d ed., rev. (Washington: American Psychiatric Association, 1987).

46. See for example, Ruth Dudley Edwards, *Patrick Pearse*, 52-54.

47. Ibid., 126.

friends.[48] She later wrote about his total lack of knowledge of women: "Their lower, or even their lighter side, he very little understood. He looked on the purity, the power of self-sacrifice, which is to be found more commonly in women than in men, as something divine. On this side he could understand them, for these qualities were strong in his own nature. Anything coarse disgusted him; from a doubtful story or subject he shrank as from a blow."[49]

We do know that his interest in and extraordinary knowledge of boys was excessive by most standards, and especially at the time and place in which he lived. How predictable that he should be in excess all that his father had failed to be to him. He was available to and indulged the boys at his school, even felt empathy with their traumas and personal crises, and he proved to be an inspiration to them.[50]

While still a youth, Pearse had written romantic plays that included passionate heterosexual love, but he ceased writing about it when he reached adolescence.[51] Dropping this theme appears to have been almost a conscious decision; at the time in life when sexual identity is confirmed and controlled, Patrick successfully avoided facing his own instinctual drives[52] and retreated into largely patriotic dramas that focused on boys and occasionally had homoerotic themes. It is as if he feared the possible consequences of letting his emotions surface. At the age when the sexual drive anarchically manifests itself, he became overscrupulous in his observation of moral abstinence and purity.[53] Such a reaction suggests a substan-

48. Mary Hayden Diaries, January 1903, National Library of Ireland.

49. Mary Hayden, "My Recollections of Padraig Pearse," 115.

50. Dangerfield, *Damnable Question*, 139.

51. Ruth Dudley Edwards, *Patrick Pearse*, 53.

52. Erikson, *Identity*, 98–99.

53. Erikson goes even further: ". . . the cruel overconscientiousness which is the inner residue in the adult of his past inequality in regard to his parent" (ibid., 99).

tial maladjustment in his personal development. The obsession with boys obviously had its roots in his lack of maturity, a kind of stunted sexuality. It also means, however, that he was able to control his sexual desires by sublimating them into his truly creative and innovative work as an educator.

With Pearse, then, we are talking about a profound form of sublimation. It is not enough to claim that Pearse's innocent productions have to meet a modern standard that is cynical and intolerant.[54] By the standards of his own time, Pearse's emphasis on the liberating life of innocence open to children, and the erotic attraction he felt toward them, albeit in deeply sublimated literary forms, was not novel. "Peter Panism" was at its height during this period. J. M. Barrie's *Peter Pan* was first produced in 1904 and published in book form in 1911.[55] But Pearse's work is at times far more openly homoerotic than other works of the same time. His heroes are almost always young boys, occasionally young girls; he usually portrays adults as enervated failures confronted wih virtuous and heroic youths. Thus his constant dwelling on the subject of boys in his work suggests that, despite the successful repression of his sexual feelings, he could not hide the fact that his desires were with boys.

Political Novice

People acquainted with Patrick Pearse before 1912 knew him to be politically naïve, if not ignorant. Even his students at St. Enda's were aware of his political illiteracy.[56] Friends knew him to be inattentive

54. Ruth Dudley Edwards, *Patrick Pearse*, 53.

55. By time of the publication of Barrie's work, the late Victorian fascination with children as erotic objects was well under way. Lewis Carroll (C. L. Dodgson) published *Alice's Adventures in Wonderland* (1865) and *Through the Looking-Glass* (1871) only after a period of photographing young girls and then the sons of Tennyson.

56. Denis Gwynn, "Patrick Pearse," *Dublin Review* (January-March 1923), 110.

to political issues, but they usually blamed it on his high ideals.[57] His inability to comprehend the essence of politically complex issues led to a common perception that his political thinking was simplistic. Criticism along these lines mounted steadily as he came into the public spotlight, and Pearse often lashed out against his critics. Once, in 1910, he bragged angrily to Desmond Ryan, in response to being attacked once again for his lack of political acumen, "Let them talk! I am the most dangerous revolutionary of the whole lot of them!"[58]

His unfortunate initiation into Irish politics occurred in 1907 when Pearse, in his position as editor of *An Claidheamh Soluis*, had to give his journal's editorial position on the Irish Council Bill, which would have granted Irish control of administrative affairs while legislative power continued to be vested in Parliament. The devolution scheme differed from Home Rule by not providing for an independent Irish Parliament and administration. Mary Hayden wrote that Pearse later attempted to justify the position that he had held at the time in favor of the devolution scheme. He argued that the Liberal's proposal should have been accepted because it would have allowed the Irish control over their own education.[59] Such obtuse reasoning was typical of Pearse and quite incomprehensible to the majority of *Claidheamh*'s readership, most of whom were firm supporters of Home Rule and thus against the bill. His editorial angered separatists as well as Home Rule nationalists; *Sinn Fein*, the official voice of Griffith's party, vehemently attacked Pearse's position, despite Pearse's past sympathy for Griffith's ideas.[60]

Pearse was a quintessential nonpolitical person. He had been brought up in a nonpolitical environment. Although his father had political interests, his mother was utterly without such inclinations,

---

57. Mary Hayden, "My Recollections of Padraig Pearse," 114.
58. Ibid.   59. Ibid.
60. Ibid., 152.

and her interests more than anyone's influenced Patrick. From the female side of his family he received the uncomplicated politics of heroic idealism. The various political intrigues of the Gaelic League and *Claidheamh*, while fascinating to Pearse, confused and disturbed him.[61] He had little understanding of the various political subtleties, a problem that was compounded by his natural acquiescence to a constitutional process he understood little. When fellow nationalists expected him to be consistent, his political insensitivity caused him to stumble. It is understandable that the overly sensitive and unprepared Pearse felt the pressure of this criticism more than many others might have. In reaction to that pressure, he might well have seen a career in education as all the more comforting and appealing. Teaching boys furnished the kind of independence and isolation that allowed his unsystematic mind freely to spin his own brand of nationalism, away from the prospect of critical opinion.

Two factors—increasing financial difficulties and a growing fascination with Robert Emmet—came together to lead Pearse into a leadership role in Irish politics despite his obvious inadequacy.[62] Critical to both of these factors was Pearse's decision to move St. Enda's from Cullenswood House to The Hermitage in 1910. Set against the foothills of the Dublin Mountains, the new facility had one distinct advantage over the old one—it was larger. Pearse's vision had grown to include a girls' school, and the move to The Hermitage allowed him to make Cullenswood House into a new girls' school (St. Ita's), and to expand the size of the student body of St. Enda's. Unfortunately these changes proved to be financially troublesome. The new location for St. Enda's was farther out from the city center and enrollment started to decline almost immediately, thereby exacerbating Pearse's habitual shortage of operating funds.

61. Ibid., 152–53.

62. For the definitive discussion of Pearse's financial situation at this time, see Ruth Dudley Edwards, *Patrick Pearse*, 134–36.

Once again his dream reach had exceeded his grasp, but this time he could not easily return to dreams to answer his difficulties.

To further complicate Pearse's financial picture, the once-profitable firm of "James Pearse" had sunk into debt as "Pearse and Sons;" Willie, like Patrick, proved to be no businessman and only a minor talent as a sculptor.[63] In 1910 "Pearse and Sons" closed its doors after nearly forty years of successful business.[64] By 1916 the family's entire income was connected with the school, and they all moved there to be closer to each other as well as to work for the school. Willie taught there, Patrick was the chief administrative officer as well as a teacher, and their mother and sisters were, in effect, the staff. Everything that the Pearses owned had been sunk into St. Enda's; even their furniture was used by the school.[65] Thus any decline in the school's fortunes meant potential financial ruin to Pearse and his family. He began what became an endless effort of stalling creditors and raising money. That he expanded the school at the same time the business was failing reveals how poor Pearse's judgment could be.

More importantly, Pearse had succumbed to the legend of the Irish patriot, Robert Emmet, who had led an unlikely and doomed rebellion in 1803, only to be hanged and beheaded at age twenty-five. According to legend, Emmet spent many hours with his love, Sarah Curran, on The Hermitage grounds. Pearse was haunted by the romantic image of the two lovers.[66] In the school paper, *An Macaomh*, Pearse wrote about Emmet's importance in the life of the school and in his life also.

> I am not sure whether it is symptomatic of some development within me, or is merely a passing phase, or comes naturally from the associations that cling about these old stones and trees, that

63. Ibid.   64. Ibid.
65. Ibid., 166-67.
66. Desmond Ryan, *Remembering Sion*, 119.

whereas at Cullenswood House I spoke oftenest to our boys of Cúchulainn and his compeers of the Gaelic prime, I have been speaking to them oftenest of Robert Emmet and the heroes of the last stand. Cúchulainn was our greatest inpiration at Cullenswood; Robert Emmet has been our greatest inspiration here. In truth, it was the spirit of Emmet that led me to these hillsides.[67]

Clearly, Emmet's spirit was to fire Pearse's imagination in the subsequent years. Emmet planned a rebellion that was supposed to start in Dublin and spread through the countryside; he went ahead with his rebellion knowing full well, as did Pearse in 1916, that it would fail. And it was Emmet who set the republican standard for speeches in the dock with a moving address linking his eternal reputation and Irish freedom. During the Easter Rising, Pearse spoke of Emmet and praised his men by telling them that their efforts had gone even further.[68]

Before the move to The Hermitage, *An Macaomh* had been entirely devoid of any suggestion of physical-force nationalism. It soon became dominated by Pearse's writings on violence—strange new ruminations on Emmet's national vision and sacrifice, along with new statements of the need for "Irish-Ireland" education in order to "harden" individuals for the inevitable struggle ahead.[69] The fascination with Emmet led to his near-obsessive interest with other Irish patriots who had also been "martyred" in the cause of Irish freedom.[70]

Pearse's developing fascination for Emmet, and his concurrent financial troubles, established a psychological tendency that would follow him to the grave. As his financial troubles increased, Pearse felt helplessness, failure, and frustration; simultaneously, and most importantly, his writing and thinking about the future grew increasingly grandiose and nonrational in response.

67. *An Macaomh* (December 1910).
68. Ruth Dudley Edwards, *Patrick Pearse*, 296.
69. *An Macaomh* (December 1910).
70. Pearse, *Political Writings and Speeches*, 62.

Of equal importance in Pearse's political development was his contact with members of the IRB. Patrick McCartan, a member of the IRB, was very enthusiastic about the work at St. Enda's. A request from Pearse for financial support led McCartan to suggest putting Pearse in touch with a friend of his who, he believed, would also be interested in the school—Tom Clarke.[71] It appears that Clarke's opinion of Pearse at that time was unfavorable.[72] He was concerned with the planning of a revolution, and the acquaintance of a self-centered, vain, and priggish schoolmaster such as Pearse must have seemed to him of dubious value. Furthermore, Clarke was also deeply suspicious of Pearse's past support for the Council Bill and the Irish Parliamentary Party.[73] He put off any meeting with Pearse until he was introduced to him by Sean MacDiarmada in February 1911.[74] This meeting must have gone well, because MacDiarmada convinced Clarke to have Pearse give the oration at the Emmet commemoration only a couple of weeks later.[75]

Little did Pearse or Clarke realize at the time that the Emmet commemoration linked their two destinies inextricably. Either because Clarke was a keen judge of others or because Pearse talked a better show than he usually did, Clarke saw in Pearse the future spokesman for the IRB's cause. After that meeting with Clarke, Pearse attended, or spoke at, practically every nationalist commemorative event or rally of any importance over the next five years. He could have been there only with blessings from someone in the IRB, and Clarke and McCartan are the only logical choices. Despite his

71. Patrick Pearse Papers, McCartan to Pearse, 27 May 1910, National Library, Dublin.

72. Ruth Dudley Edwards, *Patrick Pearse*, 68.

73. Ibid., 154.   74. Le Roux, *Tom Clarke*, 94.

75. See Donagh MacDonagh, "Patrick Pearse," *An Cosantair* (August 1945). MacDonagh has Clarke and Pearse meeting at the Wolfe Tone commemoration. This is unlikely, given both Pearse's and Clarke's presence at the Emmet commemoration.

relationship with Clarke, Pearse was not accepted to be a member of the IRB until November or December 1913, after being sponsored by Clarke over the objections of many of the rest of the organization's leadership.[76] It is not possible at this time to ascertain exactly when Pearse knew about the IRB and the nature of Clarke's role in it, but his association with Clarke grew increasingly intimate, and it seems unlikely that Clarke would have maintained this friendship for long without speaking to him about the IRB.

The father figure that Clarke had become to many young men could not have failed to impress itself upon Pearse. Clarke's advocacy of Pearse, in the face of resistance from IRB men who had not yet forgiven Pearse for his stand in 1907, must have influenced him. Le Roux wrote of Clarke's influence on Pearse: "It was Tom Clarke who was the real patron of Pearse, for it was he who, by facilitating Pearse's progress as a public speaker on Republican platforms, and as a writer in *Irish Freedom*, implanted the Irish-Ireland leader in to articulate the Republican movement. Clarke made it possible for Pearse's evolution to follow its natural, steady and progressive course."[77]

How enthusiastic Pearse was about the IRB per se is difficult to determine. As late as the end of 1912 he was referring to the IRB as full of old men "past all capacity for action" (this, however, was at the same time when his acceptance into the IRB was being resisted by the majority of its leadership).[78] Nonetheless, in Tom Clarke he

76. Le Roux, *Tom Clarke*, 121−22. See the Bulmer Hobson Diaries, National Library of Ireland, Dublin. Hobson claimed to be the one who swore Pearse into the IRB in November 1913. Edwards makes the mistake of equating Hobson's claim with the role of Pearse's mentor within the organization. There is more than enough reason to believe that Hobson was under Clarke's tutelage as much as anyone else within the inner circle. See Ruth Dudley Edwards, *Patrick Pearse*, 121−22.

77. Le Roux, *Tom Clarke*, 121−22.

78. McCay, *Padraic Pearse*, 77.

had found a man fanatically committed to an ideal, who had paid a dear price for that ideal, and who was increasingly dedicated to Pearse. Organizations were not half as comprehensible to Pearse as heroes. He had thought about heroes for a long time, and Clarke's passionate belief in Ireland was much like that passion he had come to admire in Emmet.

Pearse's financial problems were now substantial enough to have consequences, and news of his indebtedness started to spread.[79] Cathal Brugha was surely not the only one in the IRB's inner circle to object to Pearse's membership in the IRB on these grounds.[80] The school's enrollment continued to decline, the girls' school had to be closed, and creditors began to hound him. His personal papers from this period are dominated by his financial matters, but Pearse's habits changed little. Even though he was scrupulous in accounting for school funds, he continued to reach for more than he could afford. For instance, when Clarke urged Pearse to launch his own private paper,[81] *An Barr Baudh*, Pearse did so with absolutely no funds set aside to maintain it.[82]

Pearse wanted a paper of his own because he had new things to say, things that could not be said in a student-run paper or the occasional published poem. *An Barr Baudh* exposed Pearse's new political awareness as he left the ranks of the cultural revivalists to join those committed to action. The paper ran only a few issues and featured some writers of future renown, such as Eamonn Ceannt and Brian O'Higgins, but most of its copy came from Pearse. Its first issue was published the day before St. Patrick's Day, 1912, and considered what was then the major topic in Dublin's political life—the Third Home Rule Bill. Soon afterward, Pearse advocated the use of

79. Ruth Dudley Edwards, *Patrick Pearse*, 155.
80. Ibid.
81. Le Roux, *Tom Clarke*, 120.
82. Ruth Dudley Edwards, *Patrick Pearse*, 158.

violence if Asquith and Redmond failed to secure passage of the bill.[83] How different this was from Pearse's confused views only five years earlier.

Pearse's meeting with Clarke was fortunate for both men. Troubled by the possibility of financial ruin, Pearse had begun to think deeply about his life and his beliefs. As always, his imagination in contact with history—in this case with the inspiration of Robert Emmet—sought solace and fulfillment in fantasy. It is understandable how Emmet became attractive to him, as he felt no doubt a little guilt about the failure of his father's business and the consequences of overexpansion at St. Enda's.

Emmet had achieved greatness and secured an enshrined place in the memory of the nation in spite of—in fact, in part because of— the magnitude of his folly; Pearse had begun to see in Emmet a kindred spirit. Comparing him to John Mitchel and Wolfe Tone, he said in 1914: "Consider how the call was made to a spirit of a different [from that of Mitchel or Wolfe Tone], yet no less noble mould; and how it was answered. In Emmet it called a dreamer and he awoke a man of action; it called to a student and a recluse and he stood forth a leader of men; it called to one who loved the ways of peace and he became a revolutionary."[84] Not coincidentally that revolutionary was also a great failure. Pearse understood this and labeled his rebellion "pathetic."[85] What made Emmet heroic in Pearse's eyes was the fact that he acted despite the inevitability of his failure.[86] Pearse's imagination took him to Emmet, and in Robert Emmet he saw himself. Pearse too was an unlikely revolutionary. He too was a recluse and a dreamer. He began to desire to become a man of action who could lead others—a man who would, even as a failure, change the course of Irish history.

83. *An Barr Buadh*, 27 April, 1912.
84. Pearse, *Political Writings and Speeches*, 73.
85. Ibid., 141–42.   86. Ibid.

CHAPTER 6

The Rising

The Radical Rhetorician

Pearse was enthralled with the attention and notoriety he was receiving from his new political activity. Although *An Barr Buadh* was not a financial success, he considered it a political one because it kept his name in the limelight while allowing him to remain involved at the school. Pearse had become a figure to be dealt with politically, despite the fact that his political acumen continued to be suspect.

At a Home Rule rally at the end of March 1912, Pearse spoke in favor of maintaining ties with Britain and voiced his personal approval of Home Rule. Although he came out in favor of a constitutional solution, Pearse warned the crowd that violence would result if the Liberals failed in their promise to deliver Home Rule for all of Ireland: "But if we are tricked again, there is a band in Ireland, and I am one of them, who will advise the Irish people never again to consult with the Gaul, but to answer them with violence and the edge of the sword. Let the English understand that if we are again betrayed there shall be red war throughout Ireland."[1] That was pretty heady stuff for a crowd of Home Rule enthusiasts in early

1. Pearse, *Political Writings and Speeches*, 60.

1912, especially since Pearse shared the speaker's platform with John Redmond. But Pearse's continued willingness to support Home Rule, in addition to his support for the Irish Council Bill five years earlier, antagonized the very people whose approval he sought. Republicans and separatists alike found Pearse's thinking unfocused, if not hostile to their conceptions of the national cause. Although he was now flirting with the idea of militant resistance, he had not consistently or clearly argued on its behalf.

Pearse continually failed to appreciate even the political positions of those people and organizations he admired most. If he truly wanted to be accepted by republicans, he could not continue to come out in favor of Home Rule. He often expressed bewilderment at the negative reception that nationalists gave his political ideas. His espousal of more violent views in *An Barr Buadh* might have been an attempt to prove his sincerity to the violent radicals in the IRB. Nonetheless, a month after his advocacy of Home Rule, Pearse argued in favor of the legislation because it would allow Irishmen to bear arms, an obtuse argument in the minds of most other republicans.

At the time that Pearse was courting the IRB, many saw him as both excessively vain and possibly emotionally disturbed.[2] He was now somewhat stout of build; by any standard, the unathletic schoolmaster with the romantic ideas was an implausible revolutionary. He usually wore black—no doubt it flattered his figure, but it seems also to have been a device used to convey gravity and purpose.[3] This superficiality on Pearse's part was not lost on his numerous critics, and many dismissed him as a dilettante and a crackpot.

2. Mulcahy MSS, National Library of Ireland, quoted in Ruth Dudley Edwards, *Patrick Pearse*, 161.

3. Erich Fromm's *The Anatomy of Human Destructiveness* (New York: Holt, Rhinehart and Winston, 1973; paperback, 1975) is an exposition of Freud's theory of the "death instinct." See Sigmund Freud, *Beyond the Pleasure Principle*, trans. James Strachey (London: Hogarth Press, 1919) and *Civilization and Its Discontents*, trans. by James Strachey (New York: W. W. Norton, 1962). Freud

An Barr Buadh grew steadily more confrontational in its editorial position. The paper started to heap scorn on the moderate nationalists and to question Redmond's courage. The Gaelic League was soon criticized for its lack of conviction, and the budding labor movement was viewed as being too internationalist and insufficiently nationalist. From his position as editor, Pearse accused the nationalist movement of being weakened by ambivalence and equivocation.

In one sense, *An Barr Buadh* reflects the early development of Pearse's revolutionary ideology. It shows how Pearse moved toward embracing violence, and it demonstrates his desire to be one with the people committed to the use of force. His analysis of the weakness of the nationalist will projected his own lack of inner convic-

---

argues that counter to the erotic instincts of life and self-preservation exists a human desire to be free from the bonds of civilization and its imposition of values, morals, and social restraints. This impulse toward revolution, an inevitable manifestation of civilization, results in destruction and death. Fromm expounded upon Freud's theory by looking at all forms of human destructiveness. Some forms are aimed at others, but all manifestations of destructiveness are self-directed.

Fromm was concerned with noninstinctual forms of aggression and labeled these forms of aggression "malignant." A major form of this kind of aggression is "necrophilia," not merely love of the dead or erotic attraction to the dead, but love of all that is dead, decayed, putrid, sickly; it is the passion to transform that which is alive into something unalive; to destroy for the sake of destruction (369).

Fromm describes what he calls "the necrophilous character" as a personality obsessed with the things of death (366ff). Interestingly enough, Fromm analyzes the constant wearing of dark clothing as a form of necrophilia (377–78). Fromm's work is a convincing explanation of the pervasiveness of aggression and destructiveness in the human condition, but it is suspect because of its cultural limitations. For more on the death instinct, see Karl Menninger, *Man Against Himself* (New York: Harcourt, Brace and World, 1938; paperback, New York: Harcourt, Brace, Jovanovich, 1966); Norman O. Brown, *Life Against Death: The Psychoanalytical Meaning of History* (Middletown, CT: Wesleyan University Press, 1959; paperback, 5th ed., 1977).

tion, as well as his political provincialism. However, his analysis of nationalist politics does not show that he was ready to take up arms on behalf of the cause. His continued support at this time for Home Rule was a conscious rejection of the use of force, unless all else failed. His stand required a certain moral courage, since he deeply desired to become a member of the IRB and his continual temporizing hindered his acceptance into the organization. In fact, his writings in *An Barr Buadh* played a major part in his being denied membership in the IRB for such a long time.[4] Even though Pearse was prepared to talk about violence, he had yet to come to consider it as the only solution.

Pearse's increasingly busy political life deprived the school of much of his attention and nearly led to its failure. By the spring term of 1912, its financial condition was dire, and he was forced to close the girls' school during the summer. He felt that his political activities had to be curbed if the school was to survive, and he resolved to renew efforts in St. Enda's behalf.[5] He was increasingly forced to go out and raise money and was increasingly rebuffed because many people had come to see his lack of business ability as the source of the school's problems.[6] Although he was able to raise enough funds to keep the school going and to keep its creditors off his back, the long-range prospects for St. Enda's remained very gloomy as its enrollment continued to decline. Pearse should have moved the school back into downtown Dublin; keeping St. Enda's in the suburbs was perhaps the single greatest factor in its demise. In spite of his resolve to reduce his political involvement, Pearse did not curb his growing relationship with Tom Clarke and the IRB. In the spring of 1913, Pearse started to contribute articles for the IRB's paper, *Irish Freedom*. This association led to some of Pearse's best writings on

4. Ruth Dudley Edwards, *Patrick Pearse*, 163.
5. Ryan, *Remembering Sion*, 126.
6. Ruth Dudley Edwards, *Patrick Pearse*, 165.

Irish nationalism. The articles reflected both the influence of the IRB on Pearse at the time and his growing disenchantment with the politics of moderation. An even clearer example of Pearse's changing thought and its relationship to the IRB can be found in his speech at the annual republican commemoration at Wolfe Tone's grave in July 1913. Speaking under Clarke's aegis, Pearse raised the rhetoric of violence to stunningly hysterical heights, in the process glorifying the idea of sacrifice for the sake of Ireland. In Tone's sacrifice Pearse found a model for the future.

> This man's soul was a burning flame, a flame so ardent, so generous, so pure, that to come into communion with it is to come unto a new baptism, unto a new generation and cleansing. If we who stand by this graveside could make ourselves at one with the heroic spirit that once inbreathed this clay, could in some way come into loving contact with it, possessing ourselves of something of its ardour, its valour, its purity, its tenderness, its gaiety, how good a thing it would be for us, how good a thing for Ireland; with what joyousness and strength should we set our faces towards the path that lies before us, bringing fresh life to this place of death.[7]

Pearse's espousal of the IRB view helped him to be increasingly accepted in radical circles. As his commitment to violence and sacrifice grew more intense, he met with an ever-increasing enthusiasm from those he admired most. The more he pushed the limits of this vision of violence into language, the more he became acceptable to the still-skeptical members of the IRB's leadership. This acceptance resulted in turn in an escalating rhetoric, which more and more stressed death and violence.

This is not to say that encouragement and acceptance were the sole causes of what became an obsession with death and violence, for Pearse was not considering the political issue in isolation from

7. Pearse, *Political Writings and Speeches*, 55–57.

all other events. The continual financial crisis at the school, as well as its implications for his family, made urgent his need to find release in some course of action; as his financial problems intensified, Pearse's rhetoric grew increasingly apocalyptic. Pearse admitted the connection between his desire for some kind of resolute action and his financial embarrassments, when he told his former student Denis Gwynn that they "made him long for violent actions."[8]

Now that Pearse had a national forum, he envisioned opportunities for success that had not materialized in his artistic and educational careers. He longed for the acceptance and respect that had so often been denied to him, and both the subject and the political climate of the day provided him with the chance to make his mark. In spite of his role as a leading spokesman for Irish nationalism, however, Pearse remained socially awkward. Around most people he was still the shy, quiet, priggish figure he had always been. Though animated with family and his few close friends, he was almost never so forceful or assertive in personal relationships as he could be when on the stage. His political role was limited; it did not force him to be anything more than a propagandist, and it avoided his very real social limitations. We know that when he spoke to crowds, he moved them deeply—a possible result of his own tendency to be transformed by patriotic rhetoric. He was also transformed when he was with his students or when writing—in both cases he was a model of sensitivity and empathy. Those causes that he felt deeply made the clumsy Pearse into the inspired teacher or charismatic political leader, succeeding in ways he never experienced in his personal life. As Pearse came to need every possible success to offset his financial difficulties, he found his own salvation in a vision of selfless sacrifice. The rhetoric of that vision brought him approval and a semblance of success.

While Pearse found success in his political role, his personal life

8. Gwynn, "Patrick Pearse," *Dublin Review* (January-March 1923): 95.

remained unresolved. Now that he was in his thirties, he was also faced with his continuing failure to find someone with whom to share his life. Pearse was no closer at thirty to having a relationship with a woman than he had been before, and we have every reason to believe he died at the age of thirty-seven without ever having had an intimate relationship with anyone. Although there is no evidence to indicate that he or his family ever talked about this issue, his chastity was abnormal for a man of his age and status. For his family, the possibility that he would marry was probably a source of ambivalent feelings, which may explain their silence on the subject.

At the same time, there is reason to suspect that Pearse was beginning to realize his shortcomings as a writer. Although his career as a journalist was active, it was by necessity narrowly propagandistic. His attempts at drama could be called successful only if one could call the productions of his plays at St. Enda's critical artistic successes. He began to realize that neither his work nor the Gaelic art he had advocated for so long would stand the test of time and establish a free Ireland. The Gaelic League he saw now to be a "spent force" outliving its usefulness; Joseph Holloway records Pearse's reluctant recognition that Yeats, Russell, and Synge would receive a fame from posterity greater than that of any of the "Irish-Ireland" writers.[9]

Both Ruth Dudley Edwards and William Irwin Thompson find the source of Pearse's increasing obsession with death in his growing sense of failure. Although there does seem to be an obvious connection, his fear of failure does not fully explain his preoccupation with death. Pearse came to the idea of death not just as a way of salvaging his reputation but as a means to salvation that had the power to give life itself, by tying the individual to a plan of personal and national redemption. In sacrificing himself for Irish freedom, the individual

9. Joseph Holloway Diaries, 24 November 1913, National Library of Ireland, Dublin.

participated in a spiritual war that guaranteed him immortality. Pearse sought more than release from what was beginning to look like an unpromising career. Death would free him from a life that could not fulfill his dreams and would assure his eternal fame. Irish nationalism not only presented him with a resolution of his existential crisis, it offered him an historic role in helping to change Irish history.

Pearse's Vision of Violence and Death

By the end of 1913, Pearse was heavily involved in the formation of the Irish Volunteers, and he had become a member of its ruling Provisional Committee. He was also about to be inducted into the IRB. The rapidly escalating political situation had made some kind of armed conflict seem inevitable, and Pearse's role as an apologist for Irish nationalism had placed him within the mainstream of the movement as well as at the heart of its most radical organization.

There is some reason to suspect that Pearse's reasons for joining the IRB were not altogether selfless. He might have sought IRB membership because it would open doors to new sources of funding. He had decided to go to America to bolster the school's fortunes and to recruit new students. In order to be introduced to John Devoy and Clan na Gael supporters, he badly needed the proper ideological credentials for the ultra-nationalist Irish-American expatriates who supported Irish republicanism.[10] Joining the IRB certainly raised the chances that his American tour would be a success. On the other hand it appears that Pearse genuinely desired to join the IRB. He had been trying to join ever since Tom Clarke first proposed his co-option. Pearse had come to see the Gaelic League as ineffectual, and his speechmaking at republican-sponsored events and his steady

10. William O'Brien and Desmond Ryan, eds., *Devoy's Post Bag, 1871–1928*, 2 vols. (Dublin: C. J. Fallon, Ltd., 1953), 412–13.

writing for *Irish Freedom* indicate that he was both a ready and a logical candidate for membership. Nonetheless he had his detractors, who still remembered his stand on the Council Bill, as well as those like Brugha who found his finances troubling, and his admission to the IRB in December 1913 was not greeted with unanimous enthusiasm within the organization.

He spent most of the first half of 1914 in America, and the trip was to play a very important part in his evolving radicalism. For one thing, the trip was generally a success; yet, even though he raised a substantial amount of money for the school,[11] it was not enough to place St. Enda's on a sound financial footing. More importantly, the American tour placed Pearse in contact with the expatriate Irish community, which had enthusiastically thirsted for and funded an armed revolution for decades. Although he had encountered this kind of conviction before, the continual immersion in the superheated nationalist atmosphere in America was a new and heady experience. The people he met, such as Devoy, were very much like Clarke, and their romantic lust for violent resolution appealed to the impressionable Pearse. Desmond Ryan claims that, when Pearse returned to Ireland from America, he never stopped talking about the "wonderful" Fenians he had met there.[12] Pearse expressed admiration for their conviction, decrying the fact that such men were hardly to be found in Ireland.

Pearse's tour comprised a series of speeches and appearances before various Irish groups up and down the East Coast of the United States. He was introduced to Devoy through a letter from Bulmer Hobson attesting to his character and importance to the nationalist movement. It was decided that in order for him to get a proper hearing, he should be advertised as a "left-wing nationalist";

11. He raised over three thousand dollars. See Patrick Cooke, *Sceal Scoil Eanna* (Dublin, 1986), 28.

12. Quoted in Alan Ward, *Ireland and Anglo-American Relations, 1899–1921*, 24.

this fiction played a part in making his tour a modest success,[13] although it alienated moderate Irish-American nationalists.[14] Pearse was willing to assume the role, as it seemed to pay off in financial dividends; but it also had an uplifting emotional effect on him. Some of his American speeches, delivered to hundreds of rabid Irish nationalists, indicate how radical Pearse was willing to seem. On 2 March 1914, before a crowd of New York Irish, Pearse declared:

> What need I say but that to-day Ireland is turning her face once more to the old path? Nothing seems more definitely to emerge when one looks at the movements that are stirring both above the surface and beneath the surface in men's minds at home than the fact that the new generation is reaffirming the Fenian faith, the faith of Emmet. . . . I cannot speak for the Volunteers; I am not authorized to say when they will use their arms or where or how. I can speak only for myself; and it is strictly a personal perception that I am recording, but a perception that to me is very clear, when I say that before this generation has passed, the Volunteers will draw the sword of Ireland. There is no truth but the old truth and no way but the old way. Home Rule may come or may not come, but under Home Rule or its absence there remains for the Volunteers and for Ireland the substantial business of achieving Irish nationhood. And I do not know how nationhood is achieved except by armed men; I do not know how nationhood is guarded except by armed men.[15]

Pearse usually met with an enthusiastic response, but he once had a minor physical confrontation with members of the rather conservative Ancient Order of Hibernians.[16] This attack did nothing to stop him; in fact, Pearse seems to have drawn strength from it in the same way he did from fights in childhood. He seemed even more provocative when speaking at a commemoration for his hero Robert Emmet less than a week after the incident.

13. Ruth Dudley Edwards, *Patrick Pearse*, 186.
14. Ibid., 188–89.
15. Pearse, *Political Writings and Speeches*, 74–75.
16. Bulmer Hobson Papers, National Library of Ireland, Dublin.

To the grey-haired men whom I see on this platform, to John Devoy and Richard Burke, I bring, then, this message from Ireland: that their seed-sowing of forty years ago has not been without its harvest, that there are young men and boys in Ireland today who remember what they were taught and who, with God's blessing, will one day take or make an opportunity of putting their teaching into practice.[17]

The tour reinvigorated not only Pearse but those whom he touched. Bulmer Hobson was with Pearse in Philadelphia, and both men succumbed to the excitement these meetings generated. Joseph McGarrity recorded his impressions of an evening when he joined Hobson and Pearse in joyous reverie, intoxicated by the excitement they felt confirmed their hopes.

The hours seemed to fly so swiftly, the prospect of Ireland again standing in arms in defense of her ancient rights, the prospect of help from a great power [Clan na Gael was then negotiating for support and arms from Germany], the general awakening that was taking place in Ireland seemed to make us forget everything else for the time being and think only of the fight in prospect.[18]

John Quinn, an Irish-American attorney and a leader in moderate Irish political circles, who had declined Pearse's early requests for an American tour and thus forced Pearse to tour solely among the radical nationalists,[19] wrote about him later with some affection. He recalled looking at Pearse who was caught up in the ecstasy of the tour's success, and hearing him say as he gazed out on snowy Central Park, "I would be glad to die for Ireland . . . anytime."[20]

Pearse's tour of the United States was extremely gratifying and

17. Pearse, *Political Writings and Speeches*, 86.

18. Sean Cronin, ed., *The McGarrity Papers* (Tralee: Anvil Books, 1972), 41.

19. Quinn was getting tired of Irishmen visiting their American brethren to drum up money. See Ruth Dudley Edwards, *Patrick Pearse*, 184–85.

20. Quoted in B. L. Reid, *The Man from New York* (Oxford: Oxford University Press, 1968), 233.

inspiring to him. It confirmed his speaking abilities, and he was cap-
tivated by the determined enthusiasm of the exiled American Irishmen he met. Pearse returned to Ireland carrying tidings from Devoy
to Clarke,[21] inspired and ready for action. The tour had not been a
thorough success[22]—he went to America with the endorsement of
key members of the IRB leadership, but received few of the funds he
had envisioned and recruited only two students for his beleaguered
school. But Pearse returned to Ireland a changed man. Because he
had been billed as a radical, the Americans he met expressed much
more interest in his politics than in his views on Irish education.
Their enthusiastic response gratified Pearse and confirmed in his
mind that he had gifts needing to be explored. Pearse came home
with a renewed sense of purpose and a determination to demonstrate to the scoffers the sincerity of his convictions.[23]

Shortly after he returned from America, the picture in Ireland was
clouded by new and disturbing political developments for the mili-
tants. In June 1914, fearing the loss of his control of the nationalists,
Redmond took over the Provisional Committee of the Irish Volunteers.[24] To the more radical members of the Committee, it appeared
as if Redmond's takeover would blunt the progress made so far; their
fears were soon realized. Redmond's political moderation rapidly
moved the Volunteers more forthrightly behind Home Rule, and the
political machinations of the Redmondites made people such as
Pearse fear that their own voices were being suppressed.[25] When in
September 1914 he pledged Volunteer support for the British war
effort against Germany, the radicals split from the Volunteers and

21. McCay, *Padraic Pearse*, 80.

22. *The Letters of P. H. Pearse*, ed. Seamus O'Buachalla (Atlantic Highlands,
NJ: Humanities Press, 1980), 447.

23. Ruth Dudley Edwards, *Patrick Pearse*, 197.

24. Bulmer Hobson, *A History of the Irish Volunteers*, 2 vols. (Dublin:
O'Laughlin, Murphy, and Boland, 1917), 111–12.

25. Joseph McGarrity Papers, Letter of Pearse to McGarrity, August 1914.

left to form their own "Irish Volunteers" as an alternative to Redmond's now-renamed "Nationalist Volunteers."[26] The Irish Volunteers, under MacNeill, numbered at best some ten to twenty thousand men, while Redmond's followers numbered over one hundred seventy thousand.[27] But neither Redmond nor MacNeill nor the British realized that all of the IRB went into the smaller organization. IRB men now dominated the leadership of the Irish Volunteers, and MacNeill's organization had its ranks filled with republicans. Because of their smaller size, the Irish Volunteers were much easier to coerce than the old Volunteers would have been.

Unbeknownst to anyone except those on the IRB's Supreme Council, the republicans, in August 1915, established a "Military Committee" to plan the use of the Volunteers in an insurrection against the British.[28] That committee was handpicked by Clarke and consisted of men he trusted who were members not only of the IRB but also of the Volunteers Headquarters Staff. The Military Committee was initially Pearse, Joseph Plunkett, and Eamonn Ceannt.[29] The reduced size of the Irish Volunteers made their task far easier than it would have been without the split.

Pearse had moved rapidly through the ranks of the IRB to hold membership on what proved to be the organization's most important committee. He had done so because he was one of the only men on the IRB's Supreme committee who could speak to the entire spectrum of Irish nationalism. This can be clearly seen in Pearse's selection as the keynote speaker at O'Donovan Rossa's funeral on 1 August 1915. The death of the old Fenian warrior provided an opportunity for nationalists of many persuasions to come together in tribute to the republican vision and heritage. The keynote speaker had to be a man who had been within the mainstream of the nationalist

---

26. Hobson, *A History of the Volunteers*, 117.
27. Ibid., 111.   28. Ibid., 71ff.
29. Dangerfield, *Damnable Question*, 141.

movement, had become radicalized, and had the ability requirements and was chosen to be O'Donovan Rossa's chief eulogist.

Pearse had become a major political figure on the strength of his
rhetorical and propagandistic skills. His leadership position in the
Volunteers had come about largely because of the reduced size of
that organization. The critical nature of his position, along with his
long-standing ties to more moderate organizations such as the
Gaelic League, had led to his emergence as the vital person in the
IRB's plan to use the Volunteers in violent action. Pearse had been
groomed by Clarke for his role at the funeral, and his presence was
vitally important to the IRB.

Pearse rose to his occasion as never before. The O'Donovan Rossa
speech, the zenith of his political speaking career, remains one of the
most important speeches in Irish history. Pearse was urged by Clarke
to "make it hot as hell, throw all discretion to the winds,"[30] and
Pearse, with thousands of armed men before him, did as he was told.

> This is a place of peace, sacred to the dead, where men should speak
> with charity and all restraint. . . . Our foes are strong and wise and
> wary; but strong and wise and wary as they are, they cannot undo
> the seeds sown by the young men of a former generation. And the
> seeds sown by the young men of '65 and '67 are coming to their
> miraculous ripening today. Rulers and Defenders of Realms had
> need to be wary if they would guard against such processes. Life
> springs from death; and from the graves of patriot men and women
> spring nations. The Defenders of this Realm have worked well in
> secret and in the open. They think that they have pacified Ireland.
> They think they have pacified half of us and intimidated the other
> half. They think that they have provided against everything; but the
> fools, the fools, the fools!—they have left us our Fenian dead, and
> while Ireland holds these graves, Ireland unfree shall never be at
> peace.[31]

30. Le Roux, *Tom Clarke*, 142.
31. Pearse, *Political Writings and Speeches*, quoted in Ruth Dudley Edwards,
Patrick Pearse, 236–37.

The speech was an immediate national sensation. Even the *Freeman's Journal*, the mouthpiece of the decidedly nonrevolutionary United Irish League, chose to publish the full text.[32] With his speech at O'Donovan Rossa's funeral, Pearse became, in the public's imagination, the official spokesman for the physical-force nationalists. The tremendous impact of the event was not lost on Pearse. Desmond Ryan reports that after the speech was over and the crowd had gone home, Pearse sat alone in his study, aware that "he had spoken the just word . . . to immortalise a man less great than himself."[33]

There is every reason to assume that by now Pearse believed what he said and that he spoke from personal conviction; but it was a conviction he had acquired only recently. Perhaps his new commitment to the republican cause was the source of his unusual power as a speaker—his sincerity did come across powerfully to those who heard him. One listener commented:

> I suppose the people of Dublin never heard quite such speeches as he gave them. He poured out, certainly, the gospel of nationality as they heard it speaking of itself in their own hearts, in that vague first yearning which it's the craft of the orator to turn into self-conscious will and act . . . he would croon to us in that peculiar voice of his about birds and mountains and misty lakes and of the ancient Irish love of colour in costume and of bodily beauty in hero and in hero's Lady-love. A poet, a philosopher, a mystic, one would say, not a leader of the people in the hard tussle of politics, in the desperate onslaught upon a brutally unsensitive organization like the Parliamentary machine. Yet he did lead and the people followed. They hung on his slow, melodious words, dreamed his dream and very largely did his will.[34]

32. Kee, *Bold Fenian Men*, 238–39.
33. Ryan, *Remembering Sion*, 193.
34. Martin Daly [Stephen MacKenna], *Memories of the Dead* (Dublin: n.p., 1917), 176.

The commemorative guide sold after the funeral makes it obvious that Pearse had outdone himself when he spoke over O'Donovan Rossa's grave:

> Cold, lifeless print cannot convey even an idea of the depth and intensity of feeling in which his words were couched. Calm and deliberate, in soft yet thrilling accents, his oration was almost sublime. . . . For some moments after Mr. Pearse had finished there was an intense, an all pervading, silence, then we gave forth round after round of cheers which surely must have gladdened the spirits of Rossa and his colleagues, O'Mahony, Stephens, and O'Leary, who lie so near.[35]

In stressing the erotic and lifegiving nature of the Fenian's sacrifice and in referring to the religious nature of the place, Pearse's speech struck a deep emotional chord within Irish nationalism. Pearse electrified the crowd by identifying the cosmic principles that guided and sustained the republican movement. The O'Donovan Rossa speech not only clearly and movingly stated the Republican creed, it expressed the intense longings of Pearse's heart and won him the approval he desired.

Pearse's Artistic Vision

By 1916, Pearse had matured as an artist and, in spite of his heavy schedule, was writing a great deal. His writing reflected the dramatic changes in his life, and the themes of his later plays, poems, and stories grew increasingly stark and tragic.

Pearse's early writing shows little of this kind of seriousness. Most of his early endeavors were either journalistic pieces on Gaelic Irish life or papers on various Irish-language topics. As he became more confident, he came out with Irish-language versions of traditional

---

35. Commemorative program, quoted in Ruth Dudley Edwards, *Patrick Pearse*, 237.

folktales. By 1905, he was at work on several pieces of fiction. One such was *Poll an Phiobaire* (The Piper's Cave), which received some acclaim; since it was an adventure story for boys, it was put on the curriculum for the Intermediate Examination.[36] The title could also be rendered in English *The Piper's Hole*, a fact not missed by his critics and the cause of consternation to Pearse's publishers. The minutes of the Gaelic League's Publication Committee indicate that they tried and failed to get the author to change the title.[37] Despite this controversy over his first major piece of fiction, Pearse went on to write and publish several children's stories that were issued in a book by the Gaelic League under the title *Iosagan agus Sgealta Eile* (Little Jesus and Other Stories) in 1907. *Iosagan* received even better reviews than *Poll an Phiobaire*,[38] and Pearse's literary career seemed to be on its way, especially given his editorial position at *An Claidheamh Soluis*, which published several of his stories.

There is no doubt that Pearse showed literary abilities, but these must be assessed within the restrictive confines of the Irish-Ireland movement. The language barrier automatically limited his immediate audience, and Pearse, like all the artists of the language movement, never escaped the parochial bounds of native Irish culture and the cultish nature of the movement. Even though the period in question was one of great literary fertility in Dublin, Pearse's art did not impress many outside the movement. For instance, Yeats scarcely mentions Pearse in his autobiography, and then only in passing.[39] Nevertheless, Pearse's early fiction had a kind of romantic, infantile charm, and there was some reason to expect more from him. He did continue to produce pieces of writing, but, apart from

36. Ruth Dudley Edwards, *Patrick Pearse*, 95.

37. Ibid., 94–95. Pearse's sexual obtuseness seems evident in the posthumous acceptance in the 1920s of one of his writings, *La Fa'n Tuaith* by the Department of Education as a recommended reading for children. The piece ends with Pearse sharing a young boy's bed. See Edwards, 53–54.

38. Ibid., 53–54. 39. Yeats, *Autobiography*, 244.

his poetry, they have had little impact or lasting significance except as curious historical artifacts.

As time went on, Pearse wrote more and more pieces for the stage and, together with Willie and Thomas MacDonagh, produced these plays at St. Enda's.[40] They are simplistic but indicative of Pearse's changing temperament over the years. His subject was always Ireland; he always used boys as either messengers of the truth or, as in his play *Iosagan* , the bearers of salvation.

As Pearse became more and more embroiled in political events, these simple themes became complex and pessimistic ones with messages of hopelessness and despair. These dark overtones had been present in some of his earlier writing, but the pessimism now seems portentous. His 1914 production of *An Rí* (The King) is set in an Irish monastic school in the Middle Ages. Students at the school discuss their king's recent series of military setbacks and are told by their priest that his defeats are a result of his sinfulness. When the king approaches the school in retreat from another defeat, the priest tells him he must give his throne to someone more righteous and just than himself. One of the boys in the school is chosen because of his holiness. The boy, named Giolla na Naomh, or "The Servant of the Saints," dies while leading his troops to a great victory.

As early as 1914, then, we have Pearse exploring in dramatic form the subjects that increasingly captured his artistic and political imagination until the Rising. Obviously, Giolla is a "child-hero redeemer" who, like Christ, dies to save his people. Because the boy is pure of heart, his death, like Christ's, is cosmic and atones for the wrongdoing and weaknesses of others. Pearse began to expound these ideas in plays, stories, and poetry, and he also began to explore other means of expression, such as editing a collection of Irish rebel songs in late 1914.

40. Ruth Dudley Edwards, *Patrick Pearse*, 131.

This idea of the child's death in service to Ireland became an obsessive interest for Pearse. It was obviously the theme of a dream his sister says dated from childhood and was with him all his life. Pearse, however, claimed that he had the dream in 1909.

> I dreamt that I saw a pupil of mine, one of our boys at St. Enda's, standing alone upon a platform above a mighty sea of people; and I understood that he was about to die there for some august cause, Ireland's or another.
>
> He looked extraordinary, proud and joyous, lifting his head with a smile almost of amusement; I remember noticing his bare, white throat and the hair on his forehead stirred by the wind, just as I had often noticed them on the hurling-field. I felt an inexplicable exhilaration as I looked down on him, and this exhilaration was heightened rather than diminished.[41]

The vividness of this dream, as well as the ideas it contains, indicate just how important this theme was for Pearse at this time, about 1913. Obviously the boy is also a psychic representation of Pearse himself, the child's exaltation a reward Pearse seems to desire.

By 1915 these ideas were the whole focus of Pearse's most ambitious theater pieces to date. Hand in hand with the ideas of sacrifice and redemption, which he had already explored, was the idea of embracing violence as the necessary means of achieving not only national victory but also individual deliverance. This can best be seen in his play *The Master*, written in late 1915. Pearse's protagonist, Ciaran, is the master of a small school in the forest in pre-Norman Ireland. Ciaran's lack of religious faith is confronted by one of his devout students, a young boy, who calls on the archangel Michael to defend him against attackers. Ciaran's unwillingness to believe in the tenets and powers of the boy's faith, along with his stoic refusal to take up arms to defend himself and the school, leads to his being

41. See *Collected Works of Padraic H. Pearse: St. Enda's and Its Founder*, ed. Desmond Ryan (Dublin, n.d.); Pearse, "My Childhood and Youth," in *The Home-Life of Padraig Pearse*, 32–33.

struck dead by the emotional impact of the boy's faith. Edwards has seen this play as a reflection of Pearse's bewilderment at his own sudden endorsement of physical-force nationalism.[42] She maintains that the child's faith is meant to confirm, despite the horrible consequence, the need to take up arms.[43]

While Pearse was writing *The Master*, he was also writing about war as a source of life. In an essay written in December 1915, Pearse praised the war in Europe because it was so costly, citing the slaughter as proof of the war's value.

> The last sixteen months have been the most glorious in the history of Europe. On whichever side the men who rule the peoples have marshaled them. . . . It is policy that moves the governments; it is patriotism that stirs the peoples. . . . It is good for the world that such things should be done. The old heart of the earth needed to be warmed by the red wine of the battlefields. Such august homage was never being offered to God as this, the homage of millions of lives given gladly for love of country.[44]

By this time, Pearse had been advocating physical force for quite a while, but his essay "Peace and the Gael" presented it in a different light indeed. Not only was blood being used to impregnate the cold earth, Pearse had come to equate the national vision as a religious faith served only by the deaths of those who believed it.

> It is because peace is so precious a boon that war is so sacred a duty. Ireland will not find Christ's sword. What peace she has known in these latter days has been the devil's peace, peace with sin, peace with dishonour. . . We must not flinch when we are passing through the uproar; we must not faint at the sight of blood . . . we (or those of us who survive) shall come unto a greater joy. We and our fathers have known the *Pax Britannica*. To our sons we must bequeath the Peace of the Gael.[45]

42. Ruth Dudley Edwards, *Patrick Pearse*, 142.
43. Ibid., 232–33.   44. *Spark*, December 1915.
45. Pearse, *Political Writings and Speeches*, 218.

This glorification of death and violence had not come to Pearse ex nihilo. He was all too familiar with ancient Irish texts such as the *Tain* which exalted violence, and he had been deeply influenced by the writings of Wolfe Tone and John Mitchel. Denis Gwynn recalled that by 1915 Pearse was almost never without copies of Tone's *Autobiography* and Mitchel's *Jail Journal*, a vitriolic diatribe against Britain.[46] Mitchel's single-minded hatred and his long imprisonment after his participation in the Young Ireland Rising of 1848 bear uncanny resemblance to Clarke's biography—a resemblance that Pearse could not have missed. Mitchel's "holy hatred," as Pearse came to call it, provided the motivation for the violence of the Fenian terrorist campaigns of the 1870s and 1880s, and Tone was Pearse's greatest republican hero.

Pearse wrote about his new conception of physical force nationalism as a spiritual obligation that came complete with its own horsemen of the apocalypse. Most important was Pearse's elevation of Mitchel and Tone to places of honor above his old hero Robert Emmet because of Emmet's unsophisticated development as a nationalist.[47] Emmet was demoted because Pearse's political development had outgrown the romantic insurrectionist. Pearse was becoming more radical by the day and now expressed the depths to which he had come to believe in this radicalism in his poem "Christmas 1915."

> O King that was born
> To set bondsmen free.
> In the *Coming* battle,
> Help the Gael![48]

More and more, Pearse was turning to poetic forms of expression. One can only speculate about the reason for this change. It

46. Gwynn, "Patrick Pearse," 98.
47. Pearse, *Political Writings and Speeches*, 245–46.
48. Ryan, *1916 Poets*, 30.

might reflect a dissatisfaction with the dramatic form, especially since he was unable to produce his plays anywhere but at St. Enda's. But it might be that poetry offered an immediate emotional release that was not to be found in short stories or drama. Whatever the reason, Pearse's only lasting literary contribution has been the poems he wrote during the last few years of his life. In those poems Pearse's militant advocacy of violence reached a crescendo.

In the poetry Pearse wrote in the last three or four years of his life, the ideas of heroism, violence, and dedication became obsessive, wholly unlike their benign and innocent expression in his early writing. At the same time he was developing the ideas of commitment and sacrifice in his political writings, Pearse's poetry came to stress themes of death, the efficacy of blood sacrifice, and the search for redemption.

Some of these themes became the foundation for Pearse's later poetry and had been explored as early as 1912 in his play *An Rí*; at least one commentator has contended that the play consciously raised nationalism to a "religion."[49] This religious aspect of Pearse's conception of nationalism is a major feature of his later poetry, clearly seen in his most famous poem, "Renunciation." Pearse also describes the commitment to the nation as one in which the whole person must accept unequivocally not only violence and death but also sexual denial in order to gain a great personal fulfillment. This denial is exchanged for an eternal existence. Pearse reaffirms the sexual tension at the core of the nationalist commitment to Ireland.

RENUNCIATION

Naked I saw thee,
O beauty of beauty,
And I blinded my eyes
For fear I should fail.

I heard thy music,
O melody of melody,

49. Porter, *P. H. Pearse*, 101.

And I closed my ears
For fear I should falter.

I tasted thy mouth,
O sweetness of sweetness,
And I hardened my heart
For fear of my slaying.

I blinded my eyes,
And I closed my ears,
And I hardened my heart
And I smothered my desire.

I turned my back
On the vision I had shaped,
And to this road before me
I turned my face.

I have turned my face
To this road before me,
To the deed that I see
And the death I shall die.[50]

Thompson has interpreted the first line of this poem as Pearse's recognition of his ultimate failure—the solution being akin to the act of the religious who castrates himself in order to avoid falling into sin.[51] The denial represents a conscious embrace of the merits of death over life. Because of Pearse's Catholicism, the imagery of flesh and sensual experience often has been opposed to that of eternal life, and death represented deliverance. In Thompson's opinion, Pearse was the perfect expression of Irish Catholicism: chaste, pure in motive and deed, no defiler of himself or of the image of women.[52]

Thompson's analysis of "Renunciation" is highly provocative, but it falls on one major point. As an adult, Pearse was probably not as

50. Ryan, *1916 Poets*, 18.
51. Thompson, *Imagination of an Insurrection*, 124.
52. Ibid.

deep or devout a Catholic as legend would have it. He does not seem to have been involved in any of the activities surrounding the major revival rejuvenating much of Irish Catholicism in his lifetime.[53] Thousands of devout Irish Catholics at this time became involved in the support of missionary work or chose to take vows, and yet none of the Pearses appear to have been involved with the church in such a way or to any unusual degree.

In large measure, Pearse's religious reputation rests on the words of his family,[54] Mary Hayden, and the imagery used in his writing. The information obtained from his sisters and mother is a bit suspect, and the imagery he used was a convention of his society and time. Neither is a particularly persuasive argument for his supposedly extraordinary devotion, which was noted with enthusiasm after 1916 in numerous articles in Catholic nationalistic publications such as *Capuchin Annual*. In fact, the only real commentary on Pearse's religiosity we have from an unbiased source is that of the confessor he had as a youth. Father George O'Neill, S.J., is quoted by Patrick Thornley as saying that Pearse's faith, even as a youth, was unremarkable. "He was an [religious] enthusiast of the sombre, humourless kind, with a highly exaggerated sense of the value of old Irish literature, a sincere Catholic."[55] Even his friend Mary Hayden admitted he rarely spoke of his religion.[56] One of his biographers has commented on the problem of determining Pearse's legendary religious devotion and finds the evidence for it to be nonexistent.[57] While we

53. See O'Farrell, *Ireland's English Question*, for an analysis of Irish Catholic revival at this time, 224–30.

54. His sister Margaret is the person most responsible; see Margaret Pearse, "A Few Traits of the Character of Padraig Pearse," in Mary Brigid Pearse, ed., *The Home Life of Padraig Pearse*, 108–9.

55. David Thornley, "Patrick Pearse and the Pearse Family," *Studies* (Autumn-Winter 1971), 340.

56. Mary Hayden, "My Recollections of Padraig Pearse," 116.

57. McCay, *Padraig Pearse*, 46.

can say with certainty that Pearse was a conscientious Catholic, it is difficult to ascribe to him, on the basis of the evidence, anything more.

This question of the nature and fervor of Patrick's faith is an important one. For one thing, it would obviate his Irish Catholic status as a nationalist saint if it were discovered that he had consciously sought death. The question also colors the analysis of his later poetry: Thompson assumed that Pearse was as devout as posterity had pictured him. Pearse's major critics, J. J. Horgan and Francis Shaw, both have attacked Pearse's religious heterodoxy, and more recent scholarship has demonstrated the morphological connections between Pearse's fusion of religion, nationalism, and violence and "nationalist" heterdoxies in the early Christian church and late Middle Ages.[58] What might be said with some degree of certainty is that Pearse was a typical Catholic of no excessive devotion, whose use of the Catholic imagery was due to his cultural upbringing as much as anything else; there is no documented evidence of any visionary experience of great emotional power. Pearse's Catholicism showed little of the characteristic certainties of the devout witness, and there is little mention of his resurrection in his farewell notes to his family.

A more likely explanation than Thompson's suggests that Pearse sought artistic, moral, and spiritual justification for the act he knew he must do in order for his life to have meaning. The choice was between life and eternal life, and an outright suicide would have robbed him of the latter.[59] This is not to say that Pearse was conscious of this choice, but there are other indications, such as his constant wearing of black, that indicate that the idea of death was

58. For more on the doctrinal implications of Pearse's thought and the issue of suicide and martyrdom in Irish nationalism, see Seán Farrell Moran, "Patrick Pearse and Patriotic Soteriology: The Irish Republican Army and the Sanctification of Political Self-Immolation."

59. Ibid., 22ff.

impressing itself upon him. The idea of death was constantly in his mind, a fact revealed in his poetry, his statements to contemporaries, his public appearances, and his other writings. A case in point is his poem "A Rann I Made," written in 1914.

A RANN I MADE

A rann I made within my heart
To the rider, to the high king,
A rann I made to my love,
To the king of kings, ancient death.

Brighter to me than light of day
The dark of thy house, tho' black clay;
Sweeter to me than music of trumpets
The quiet of thy house and its eternal silence.[60]

It is important to note that as Pearse thought more and more of death, his thought was not limited to Catholic terms; increasingly he drew upon the pagan legend of Cúchulainn. In his poem "I am Ireland,"[61] Pearse envisions himself as the land that bore Cúchulainn. Thompson connects Pearse's ideas of Cúchulainn to the translations of the myth by the Anglo-Irish historian Standish O'Grady. O'Grady placed Cúchulainn as a figure in mythic history whose life took place "in the context of a cosmic drama."[62] Adopting an approach that Thompson finds distinctly "Wagnerian,"[63] O'Grady's "reconstruction" of the Irish mythic cycle referred to the era of the *Tain* as "The Heroic Age," because of his less than scholarly ability in Gaelic.[64] In the generation that followed O'Grady, the generation of the Irish literary revival, O'Grady's influence was pervasive among the Irish-Ireland movement of which Pearse was an adherent.[65]

---

60. Ryan, *1916 Poets*, 16.   61. Ibid., 17.

62. Thompson, *Imagination of an Insurrection*, 22–23.

63. Pearse was a devotee of opera and his sister identified that he especially loved Wagner's art—*Gesamtskuntswerk*. See Mary Brigid Pearse, "Our Home Recollections of Padraig," 91.

64. Ibid.   65. Ibid.

Cúchulainn became for Pearse the center of a cosmic drama to save Ireland, representing, by his sacrificial death, a kind of non-Christian Christ for the Irish nation. As a Christ figure, Cúchulainn's example became a central motif in Pearse's later works. For his play *The Singer*, Pearse created a role that put into character what Pearse felt to be the only tool of salvation for Ireland. Written in the months immediately preceding the Rising, *The Singer* was not published in his lifetime. Its rebel hero, MacDara, is forced to leave his homeland in Connaught. He wanders through the countryside as an exile, earning his keep as an itinerant teacher, until loneliness and despair cause him to curse God and deny his fate. This dramatic rejection is MacDara's Gethsemane experience, and he is led not only to new faith but back to his home. All is not well in the land, however, and MacDara is forced, despite the alluring temptations of life, to lead his people, who are too afraid to fight. MacDara does so because he is certain of his eternal survival, even though he is sure to die in battle.

There can be little doubt that the subject matter of Pearse's later writings reflected his own search for meaning and a place in life, and he expressed these problems within the context of his cultural experience. Though Pearse held strange ideas of how the revolution was to be brought about and what it represented, these ideas, however excessive they might appear later, were not alien to those of his time. Bulmer Hobson, who did not follow Pearse's path, believed Pearse's "ideology" was the key to his rapid rise in republican circles, because it reflected the feelings of many of his contemporaries. Looking back, Hobson recognized how troubling Pearse's thinking was: "He had evolved a strange theory that to keep a national spirit alive it would be necessary that there should be a blood sacrifice in every generation. He had visions of himself as the scapegoat for his people."[66]

66. Bulmer Hobson, *Ireland Yesterday and Tomorrow* (Tralee, 1968), 198.

Pearse's writing in his last years reflected his inner emotional struggle. He was still in many ways that young, dreamy, and lonely boy. Those dreams that had sustained him as a child he returned to when he at last appeared to be the master of his own fate.

Above the main door to St. Enda's was a carved panel of the boy warrior Cúchulainn. Inscribed on the panel were Cúchulainn's most famous words from the *Tain*: "I care not though I were to live but one day and one night provided my fame and deeds live after me." Pearse looked upon that saying as a motto for the school, and it can be assumed that the saying had some truth for him as well. He assured himself of fame by coming out on Easter Monday and by speaking the language of those who followed him. One month before the Rising, Pearse gave what was to be his last speech to his students. He gave them the justification for what he was about to do: "As it took the blood of the Son of God to redeem the world, so it would take the blood of Irishmen to redeem Ireland."[67]

In his eulogy for O'Donovan Rossa, Pearse spoke before a crowd disturbed over the possible conscription of Irishmen by Britain to fight at the front in Europe. Conscription had existed as a possibility since the beginning of the war, but the continual loss of men had made it seem ever more probable. John Redmond's pledge of support to the Asquith government at Westminster nearly a year before had had the seeming effect of staving off conscription, but the military disasters in France during the summer of 1915 changed the situation dramatically.

Redmond had pledged himself and his party to recruit Irish volunteers as a demonstration of Irish goodwill. The passage of Home Rule in 1914 raised his reputation at home considerably, and the initial response to his recruitment drives had been good. However, as talk in London turned increasingly toward the need for a military draft, public anxiety in Ireland grew. Some of Redmond's colleagues

67. Quoted in Thompson, *Imagination of an Insurrection*, 98.

in the Nationalist Volunteers began to pressure him to withdraw his pledge.[68] On top of everything else, it was widely perceived in Ireland that Irish volunteers in the field were not receiving their share of glory for their sacrifices at the front. The lack of recognition of the Irish soldiers embittered Redmond[69] and alienated public opinion in Ireland from early 1915 through the early months of 1916.

Irish public resistance to the threat of conscription mounted, and Redmond found it more and more difficult to find recruits. His strongest supporters had enlisted early, and the numbers of potential recruits in Ireland willing to serve the British had diminished substantially.[70] The conscription issue heightened Irish nationalist resentment against Britain, and in late 1915 it presented enough of a threat to the administration's control that the Undersecretary for Ireland wrote that he believed an armed "outbreak" would result from any attempt to institute a military draft.[71] Reports from British intelligence from both Dublin and the countryside indicated that they believed anti-conscription sentiment had grown so rapidly and had become so entrenched that MacNeill's Volunteers, with support from some Redmondites, had planned an anti-conscription uprising as early as October 1915.[72] Eventually Parliament passed a Conscription Act in January 1916 which, although it excluded Ireland, had the effect of exacerbating Irish fears of a draft.

By the end of 1915, Pearse was heavily involved in his work as an officer on the IRB's Military Council and as its official Director of Military Organization at Irish Volunteer's headquarters. He had

68. Kee, *Bold Fenian Men*, 233.

69. Denis Gwynn, *The Life of John Redmond* (New York: Books for Library Press, 1932; reprint ed., 1971), 441–44.

70. Ibid., 441.

71. Ruth Dudley Edwards, "The Decline and Fall of the Irish Nationalists at Westminster," in *The Making of 1916*, 133.

72. Brendan Mac Giolla Chiolle, *Intelligence Notes: 1913–16* (Dublin, 1966), 224.

successfully lobbied for the position with the Volunteers a year earlier, even though a less qualified individual could scarcely have been imagined. IRB men under Clarke's influence now held key leadership positions in the Volunteers, and these posts controlled the military activities of the organization. A Rising led by members of the IRB seemed more than a mere possibility.

Although Pearse had developed into a fire-breathing revolutionary, he had changed little as a man. He had always been gracious to strangers, but he continued to look to his family as his only close friends. He continued to live with his mother and sisters at St. Enda's, and he and Willie were as close as they ever were. The Pearses' life was in most respects typically bourgeois. It seems unlikely that he merited the kind of place in national political life that he had come to hold; and yet in spring 1916 Pearse found himself with the most important combination of political positions of any man in Ireland.

Easter Monday, 1916

Plans for the Rising took on their own momentum. The training of troops went on for many months, and the IRB's Military Council arranged for the smuggling of arms into Ireland from Germany. All of this planning and scheming went undetected by both MacNeill and Dublin Castle. MacNeill believed he had things under control, although he feared that the radicals were up to something.[73] The Government believed that they knew what was going on, but their records indicate that they largely overlooked men like Pearse and Plunkett.

Part of the Castle's smugness was a result of its access to German diplomatic communiques that indicated that Sir Roger Casement

---

73. Leon O'Broin, *Dublin Castle and the 1916 Rising* (Dublin: Helicon Books, 1966; rev. ed., New York: New York University Press, 1971), 26.

would head an attempt to overthrow the government. Casement was in Germany negotiating support for the Volunteers, but he was not privy to the actual planning of the Rising and was hostile to the whole "blood-sacrifice" idea.[74] Even though the British believed incorrectly that something was up as early as 1913, the Castle properly maintained that a Rising could be successful only after a major shipment had taken place, as well as a corresponding German invasion of the island.[75] The Castle had fixed its gaze upon what they called the "Sinn Fein Volunteers" (the Nationalist Volunteers), and it believed they were the force to be reckoned with.[76]

The Castle was several times removed from reality in their analysis of the situation, as the Volunteers themselves were merely unwitting pawns in the IRB's plan by this time. However, it was not even the IRB that the British administration had to fear, for Clarke and his men had not only fooled the leadership of the Irish Volunteers but had also circumvented the Supreme Council of the Irish Republican Brotherhood.

The Military Council had been formed hastily during an IRB Supreme Council meeting gerrymandered in favor of Clarke's followers.[77] The Military Council operated without the supervision of the Supreme Council; it purposely misled the Republican leadership and failed to report its operations.[78] When the Rising occurred, IRB men in the Irish Volunteers recognized Pearse's orders to mobilize as having come from one of their own and they assembled according to his instructions, never realizing that the decision to revolt was not sanctioned by the organization's leadership. For most of the leadership of the IRB—men such as Hobson, who had been cast

74. F. X. Martin, "Eoin MacNeill on the 1916 Rising," *Irish Historical Studies*, 12, 47 (March 1961), 235–36.

75. Ward, *Anglo-American Relations*, 25.

76. Ibid.

77. Ruth Dudley Edwards, *Patrick Pearse*, 241–42.

78. Kee, *Bold Fenian Men*, 236.

out of the Clarke group because of his support for Redmond's takeover of the Volunteers in 1914—the news of the Rising came as a cruel shock. Some men who had been on the outskirts, such as The O'Rahilly, realizing that a Rising was about to begin, joined the rebels on Easter Monday, and died valiantly.[79] The Clarke faction had scored perhaps its greatest strategic victory long before the Rising took place, and those outside their ranks did not recognize it until too late.

Dublin Castle foolishly believed that they completely understood the situation and behaved in an often strangely contradictory manner. Although they had been warned by such reliable sources as Redmond's deputy, John Dillon, that an outbreak was about to occur, they often acted quite blithely about the problem. Sir Matthew Nathan, Chief Undersecretary for Ireland, decided it was safe enough to bring his sister-in-law and her children to Dublin for the Easter holidays.[80] Despite information to the contrary, and in spite of the warnings, military intelligence reported to London that there was no danger of insurrection as late as April 1916.[81] The government succumbed to believing that they knew what was going on, when in fact it knew just enough to obscure the truth.

> They [Dublin Castle] had built up a hierarchy of traitors with Casement at the top position and under him at different levels MacNeill and the rest. The facts were entirely different. Casement was a subordinate, an almost irrelevant figure in the whole business and had come [back from Germany, only to be captured instantly by the British] to stop, not to start a rebellion. . . .[82]

Perhaps MacNeill was more surprised than anyone to read the news, on Thursday, April 20, 1916, that Pearse had ordered a large-

79. Ruth Dudley Edwards, *Patrick Pearse*, 277.

80. Leon O'Broin, "Birrell, Nathan, and the Men of Dublin Castle," in F. X. Martin, ed., *Leaders and Men of the Easter Rising: Dublin, 1916* (Dublin: Harper and Row, 1967), 7.

81. Mac Giolla Chiolle, *Intelligence Notes*, 230.

82. O'Broin, "Birrell and the Men of Dublin Castle," 7.

scale military maneuver for Easter Sunday, April 23. Three days earlier, MacNeill had been presented with a document, supposedly
stolen from Dublin Castle files, which gave instructions for the
arrest of Volunteer leaders and the confiscation of arms. There is
conclusive evidence that the paper was a forgery, written by either
Sean MacDermott or Plunkett;[83] but the threat of this preemptive
strike on the Volunteers forced MacNeill reluctantly to concede the
need to prepare to defend themselves. When MacNeill saw Pearse's
orders in the newspapers, he realized that Pearse had ordered the
mobilization in order to begin an insurrection. When the outraged
MacNeill confronted Pearse that evening at St. Enda's, Pearse admitted that MacNeill's perceptions were indeed correct. MacNeill
issued a countermanding order to stop military activities that was
sent to Volunteer officers. Despite Pearse's assurances that the insurrection had been canceled, it had only been postponed, and Mac-
Neill awoke on Saturday morning to find that a shipment of small
arms, accompanied from Germany by Sir Roger Casement and
essential to the success of the Rising, had been intercepted by the
British in Queenstown harbor—the Rising was still alive.

Like MacNeill, the Government made the mistake of assuming
that the Rising was now dead in the water, but pragmatic objections
and setbacks were not enough to keep Pearse and his comrades
from acting. Even the issue of more orders from MacNeill, printed
in *The Sunday Independent*, countermanding all previous orders to
come out, failed to deter Tom Clarke, who had grudgingly agreed
only to a one-day postponement.[84] Late Sunday evening, Pearse sent
forth an order, which MacNeill could not countermand in time, for
the Volunteers to meet at the ICA's Dublin headquarters, Liberty
Hall, the following morning.

The original plan had been simple, but it suffered from excessive

83. Ruth Dudley Edwards, *Patrick Pearse*, 267.
84. Ibid., 273.

optimism and lack of arms. Without guns, the Rising was destined to fail. More to the point, Casement's failure at Queenstown rendered the plan so untenable that the rebel leadership recognized that its value would be purely symbolic and inspirational. The original plan called for the seizure of strategic buildings and areas of downtown Dublin, with the captors then digging in to await the "rising" of the countryside to support Dublin's example. From the outset, a decisive military victory was never intended. For example, the rebels planned the takeover of St. Stephen's Green, the beautiful public park in the center of Dublin; but the Green was surrounded on four sides by tall buildings—ideally suited for pinning down lightly armed revolutionaries. The sole value of such a move was symbolic, since everyone in Ireland knew of the famous park in the heart of the capital.

The rebel leaders who gathered at Liberty Hall knew they could not win, and most of them seemed resigned to become sacrifices for the nation. James Connolly, who without the knowledge of the IRB's Supreme Council had been secretly co-opted to the Military Council in January 1916, acknowledged to others that he fully expected to die during the fighting.[85] By taking care of his bills on Easter Sunday evening, Pearse also indicated that he did not expect to survive the Rising.[86] Patrick and Willie rode into the city on bicycles Monday morning; several people saw them pedaling along, wearing giant, bulging overcoats. At Connolly's headquarters, they joined the assembling troops, which numbered somewhere around sixteen hundred men. The largest single detachment, about four hundred in number, went with Pearse, Connolly, Plunkett, MacDermott, Ceannt, and Clarke to the General Post Office building in the center of the city.[87] The rest of the troops were deployed to various positions around Dublin.

85. C. Desmond Greaves, *The Life and Times of James Connolly* (New York: International Publishers, 1971), 410.

86. Ruth Dudley Edwards, *Patrick Pearse*, 24.

87. Diarmuid Lynch, *The I.R.B. and the 1916 Rising*, 143–44.

The rebels easily took control of the unprotected positions, with the important exception of Dublin Castle (their only legitimate military target), where they failed to press home an attack even though the administrative center was guarded by only two men. Casual observers throughout the city were shocked to find that the rebels meant business. Most Dubliners had long since become accustomed to bands of armed men on their streets, but the charge of the troops into the helpless GPO must have struck more than a few observers as ludicrous. Ever mindful of the historic nature of events, Pearse asked Tom Clarke to be the first to enter. Members of the Citizen Army under the leadership of musician and silk-weaver Michael Mallin and the eccentric socialist aristocrat Countess Markievicz took over St. Stephen's Green, but not without a fight from disgruntled holiday folk who were basking in the morning sun.[88] Pearse had been chosen by his fellow revolutionaries to be titular head of the new "government" as well as its army. In his roles as "Commandant-General, Commanding in Chief, the Army of the Republic and President of the Provisional Government," Pearse stepped out of the GPO and read to onlookers the "Proclamation of the Republic." The reception was less than gratifying; people laughed and went on with their daily business.

Shortly afterward, sometime in the late afternoon, the rebels fired their first shots. Hapless British cavalrymen unknowingly stumbled into a fusillade of fire from the GPO, and most of the rebels fired without knowing what was going on. The early rebel actions were moderately successful, but the first day or two was the lull before the storm.

The inevitable counterattack was not long in coming. The British

88. Anne Marreco, *The Rebel Countess: The Life and Times of Countess Markievicz* (Philadelphia: Chilton Books, 1967), 202. The first shots of the Rising probably took place between the troops in the park and British officers lunching at the Shelbourne Hotel. See Anne Haverty, *Constance Markievicz: An Independent Life* (London: Allen and Unwin, 1988), 148–49.

moved into position and started lobbing artillery rounds into Pearse's position from the square at Trinity College only a half mile away. The Government troops were helped by many of the indignant local citizenry, who enthusiastically informed on the rebel supporters. Without sufficient firepower or any real military coordination beyond Dublin, the country uprisings never occurred; the rebels' defeat was just a matter of time.

While Pearse had taken the time to wear his rather dapper Volunteer uniform armed with a revolver, he failed to fire a shot during the Rising. He busied himself with writing propaganda and talking about Irish literature with Plunkett, who was bedridden with tuberculosis.[89] Despite knowing full well that Casement's capture had ruined the chances of a mass national rising, Pearse lied and told his men that the leadership was getting information about such activities and that the news was promising. Nonetheless, Pearse had taken the precaution of securing a priest for the purpose of hearing confessions. It does not appear that Pearse led the troops in actual combat; nor did he participate in the building's preparation for battle. The early tactical decisions were made by Connolly, who was probably seen by most of the troops to be the leader of the Rising.[90]

The rebels fought tenaciously and inflicted heavy casualties, but the British shelled the GPO and the surrounding neighborhood around the clock. Faced with the collapse of the burning building around them, Pearse ordered it evacuated. Carrying the severely wounded Connolly on a makeshift stretcher, the rebels got only a couple of blocks away before holing up for the night in an abandoned house. Pearse finally ordered the decimated rebels to surrender when he saw three noncombatants accidentally killed before his eyes.[91] Faced with the Rising's effect on Dublin's citizenry, Pearse

89. Thomas M. Coffey, *Agony at Easter: The 1916 Uprising* (New York: Macmillan and Co., 1969), 102.

90. Leon O'Broin, *Michael Collins* (Dublin: Gill and Macmillan, 1980), 21.

91. Ruth Dudley Edwards, *Patrick Pearse*, 304.

ordered the troops to surrender. At other rebel strongholds in the city, local rebel commanders were stunned to get the surrender order, since they had barely been tested and had largely held their own.

Fighting ceased with the unconditional surrender of rebel forces on Saturday, 29 April, and Pearse was promptly whisked off, first to British military headquarters, then to the Dublin military prison. He and Willie, who had been faithful to his brother despite having had nothing to do with the planning or implementation of the Rising, were both tried before a military tribunal and received the death sentence. Like so many Irish patriots before him, like Emmet and Tone, Patrick had one last speech to make at his trial—he began with his childhood.

When I was a child of ten I went down on my knees by my bedside one night and promised God that I should devote my life to an effort to free my country. I have kept that promise. As a boy and as a man I have worked for Irish freedom, first among earthly things. I have helped to organize, to arm, to train, and to discipline my fellow countrymen to the sole end that, when the time came they might fight for Irish freedom. The time, as it seemed to me, did come and we went into the fight. I am glad we did, we seem to have lost. We have not lost. To refuse to fight would have been to lose; to fight is to win. We have kept faith with the past, and handed a tradition to the future. . . . We . . . love freedom and desire it. To us it is more desirable than anything in the world. If you strike us down now, we shall rise again and renew the fight. You cannot conquer Ireland. You cannot extinguish the Irish passion for freedom. If our deed has not been sufficient to win freedom, then our children will win it by a better deed.[92]

Both Willie and Patrick were sentenced to be shot by a British Army firing squad. Before the fateful hour, Pearse wrote letters to

92. Pearse, *Political Writings and Speeches*, quoted in Ruth Dudley Edwards, *Patrick Pearse*, 318.

his mother and brother. To Willie he wrote a poem that recognized that his younger brother had indeed lived in a subordinate position to his elder brother. It also admitted of the common heritage and maternal origins of the two brothers.

TO MY BROTHER

O faithful!
Moulded in one womb,
We two have stood together all the years
All the glad years and all the sorrowful years,
Own Brothers: through good repute and ill,
In direct peril true to me,
Leaving all things for me, spending yourself
In the hard service that I taught to you,
Of all the men I have known on earth,
You only have been my familiar friend,
Nor needed I another.[93]

In his final letter to his mother, dated 3 May 1916, Patrick told her of papers he had prepared explaining financial affairs and indicated that Willie and the boys from St. Enda's he involved in the Rising would be safe. He then ended it with a love letter to his family.

I have just received Holy Communion. I am happy except for the great grief of parting from you. This is the death I should have asked for if God had given me the choice of all deaths,—to die a soldier's death for Ireland and for freedom.

We have done all right. People will say hard things for us now, but later on they will praise us. Do not grieve for all this, but think of it as a sacrifice which God asked of me and of you.

Good-bye again, dear, dear Mother. May God bless you for your great love for me and for your great faith, and may He remember all that you have so bravely suffered. I hope soon to see Papa, and in a little while we shall all be together again.

Wow-wow [his sister Margaret], Willie, Mary Brigid, and

93. Pearse, *The Letters of P. H. Pearse*, 380–81.

Mother, good-bye. I have not words to tell my love of you, and how my heart yearns to you all. I will call to you in my heart at the last moment.

> Your son,
> Pat.[94]

This letter is a statement of his fidelity to his mother, to the family, to the Church, and to Ireland. It is a letter of love, but it is also an assertion of his independence from the world he had failed to understand and control. It is also a confession of resignation and more than a little accusation. Like his courtroom speech, it is a pleading for respect from all of those Pearse imagined had not believed he could succeed in anything. It is not the letter of a devout Catholic who was concerned about the eternal future of his soul. It is a letter of a man who realized he has won the goal he has sought and is about to be released from the things that held him back. There is no bittersweet expression of a wish that things had gone differently. In fact, in his last two poems to his mother, "A Mother Speaks" and "To My Mother," written from his jail cell, the Christ-like fate he had come to embrace for himself is painfully obvious. In the end his life and death have won an eternal reputation.

TO MY MOTHER

My gift to you hath been the gift of sorrow,
My one return for your rich gifts to me,
Your gift of life, your gift of love and pity,
Your gift of sanity, your gift of faith
(For who hath had such faith as yours
Since the old time, and what were my poor faith
Without your strong belief to found upon?)
For all these precious things my gift to you
Is sorrow. I have seen

94. Ibid., 381–82.

Your dear face line, your face soft to my touch,
Familiar to my hands and to my lips
Since I was little:
I have seen
How you battled with your tears for me,
And with a proud glad look, although your heart
Was breaking. O Mother (for you know me)
You must have known, when I was silent,
That some strange thing within me kept me dumb,
Some strange deep thing, when I should shout my love?
I have sobbed in secret
For that reserve which yet I could not master,
I would have brought royal gifts, and I have brought you
Sorrow and tears: and yet, it may be
That I have brought you something else besides—
The memory of my deed and of my name
A splendid thing which shall not pass away.
When men speak of me, in praise or in dispraise,
You will not heed, but treasure your own memory
Of your first son.[95]

The death and the purpose of that death surely could not have surprised either the mother or the son. A short time before the Rising, Pearse had written a poem, ostensibly to fulfill his mother's wish "to write a little poem which would seem to be said by you about me,"[96] that is, after he had died. This poem is a statement of Pearse's affirmation not of the goodness of life but of his need to die. It serves not to fulfill his mother's wish, but to control her after his death. Instead of speaking "her" words for her, he has forced upon her his own words, making her remember him as he wanted to be remembered.

95. Proinsias Mac Aonshusa, *Quotations from P. H. Pearse,* (Cork: Mercier Press, 1979), 61–62.
96. Ibid., 281.

THE MOTHER

I do not grudge them: Lord, I do not grudge
My two strong sons that I have seen go out
To break their strength and die, they and a few,
In bloody protest for a glorious thing,
They shall be spoken of among their people,
The generations shall remember them,
And call them blessed;
But I will speak their names to my own heart
In the long nights;
The little names that were familiar once
Round my dead hearth.
Lord, thou art hard on mothers:
We suffer in their coming and their going;
And tho' I grudge them not, I weary, weary
Of the long sorrow—And yet I have my joy;
My sons were faithful, and they fought.[97]

The faithful sons died, one after the other, on the third and fourth of May, 1916. Patrick died first, at 3:30 in the morning, shortly after seeing a priest.

97. Ryan, *1916 Poets*, 24.

CHAPTER 7

Patrick Pearse and the European Revolt Against Reason

Though the Dublin Easter Rising of 1916 is commonly regarded as one of the most important events in modern Irish political history, the immediate public reaction against it certainly did not portend its future status. Most immediate opinion, at least that expressed in print, in Ireland as well as from Irish expatriates, seems to have been anger at the high number of civilian casualties and the damage to private property.[1] The reaction by the Bailieborough, County Cavan, branch of the United Irish League was typical of the press's condemnation: "[It is] regretted that the young men who joined in such a movement did not follow the advice of Mr. Redmond."[2] Irishmen as far away as Otago, New Zealand, wrote to Redmond to express their

---

1. The press seems to have been condemnatory at first; there is no sound analysis of general public sentiment in the first days after the Rising. Certainly the lack of first-hand press reports clouds this problem, but it is obvious that the Rising was not a popular success in early May 1916. A skeptical analysis is Joseph Lee, *Ireland 1912-1985: Politics and Society* (Cambridge: England: Cambridge University Press, 1989; paperback, 1989), 29-36.

2. John Redmond, *The Rising* (London: Thomas Nelson, 1916), 44-45.

sorrow, and they offered their continued support for Great Britain and the Allies.[3] Redmond's personal sympathies were split between the Government and the insurrectionists, but the reaction of his party and its supporters was generally outrage, "the characteristic reaction of the middle-class."[4]

While many of the public were angry at the rebels initially,[5] the British execution of most of the leaders of the Rising galvanized public sympathy behind the rebels, making them into martyrs for Ireland[6] and thereby legitimating the physical-force cause. Some leaders of the Parliamentary Party realized that moderate politics stood to lose if the rebels were martyred. John Dillon wrote to Redmond in London and urged him to stop the executions. Dillon agreed with Redmond that the Rising was wrong, but he worried about the effects of martyrdom.

> You should urge shortly on the government the *extreme* unwisdom of any wholesale shooting of prisoners. The wisest course is to execute *no one* for the present. This is *the most urgent matter* for the moment. If there were shootings of prisoners on a large scale the effect on public opinion might be disastrous in the extreme. *So far* public opinion is against the *Sinn Feiners*. But the reaction might very well be created [if the Government executed the rebels]. . . .[7]

At first Redmond, like many others, blamed the Rising on the Germans,[8] and he only reluctantly agreed with Dillon on the ques-

---

3. Ibid., 6.

4. Bulmer Hobson, *A History of the Irish Volunteers*, 198.

5. Casualties were officially listed at 538 for the Army, Royal Irish Constabulary, and Dublin Municipal Police, of whom 132 were killed, with 2,217 civilian casualties, of whom 318 were killed. One hundred sixty were convicted, with fifteen executed. See Mac Giolla Chiolle, *Intelligence Notes*, 238–39.

6. Lee, *Ireland, 1912–1985*, 36–38.

7. Quoted in F. S. L. Lyons, "Dillon, Redmond, and the Home Rulers," in *The Shaping of Modern Ireland*, ed. Conor Cruise O'Brien (Toronto: University of Toronto Press, 1960), 32–33.

8. Redmond, *The Rising*, 9.

tion of reprisals.[9] He never fully recognized, even after the executions, that the Rising changed everything. Dillon was more attuned to the atmosphere in Dublin, and the executions convinced him that the Irish Parliamentary Party at Westminster had to change its tactics.[10] He suggested a turn in the party's tactics toward a kind of "militant constitutionalism" along Parnellian lines, but Redmond never made such a move.[11] Redmond's tragedy was his growing inability to diagnose correctly the Irish political situation. He continued to label all separatist groups as "Sinn Feiners." His reluctance to identify himself with the Rising and its martyrs sealed his, and his party's, demise in 1918 by drawing public support behind the idea of separatism.[12]

Some scholars have questioned the need for the Rising.[13] They argue an opinion popular among parliamentary nationalists at the time that there was no reason to expect that the British would renege on their promise to implement Home Rule at the end of the war in Europe[14] and that the Rising was essentially a meaningless act raised to a mythic level by the stupidity of the British. While this analysis of the Home Rule situation in 1916 is convincing, its analysis of the Rising, why and how it occurred, is shortsighted. The same nonrational motivations that pushed individuals like Pearse to participate in a suicidal insurrection offer a sense of moral conviction to revolutionaries all over the world. These grievances, hopes, and desires, which are the true sources of insurrection and revolution, are not necessarily rational, nor are they addressable by conventional political

9. Ibid.

10. Lyons, "Dillon, Redmond, and the Irish Home Rulers," 32–34.

11. Boyce, *Nationalism*, 288.

12. Brian Inglis, *Roger Casement* (London, 1973; paperback, London, 1974), 311.

13. See Conor Cruise O'Brien, "1891–1916," in *The Shaping of Modern Ireland*, 13–24.

14. Ibid., 21–23.

responses. If these nonrational factors are the cause of insurrectionary violence, it is unlikely that such violence can be fully understood by pragmatic, rationalistic, and perhaps more conventional, historical analysis. Approaches that assume that the primary motivations at work in individuals and political movements are manifestations of reasoned political thinking fail to appreciate those mobilizing forces that often enable ordinary individuals to do extraordinary things.

Ireland's Easter Rising was not, by and large, the result of some rational process. It was rather the manifestation of deep-seated psychological and emotional conflicts, arising from the failures of cultural and constitutional Irish nationalism, which many militant Irish nationalists experienced at the time. Patrick Pearse's unique contribution to Irish political history stems from his personal experience of despair, irresolution, the need to escape his personal situation, failure, and ambivalence—at the same time that many nationalists had to face similar apprehensions about Ireland's future. The road to personal and national deliverance laid out and traveled by Patrick Pearse was in fact the way that the republican movement needed to go for some kind of conclusive deliverance from the modern age and Great Britain, which represented modernity.[15]

This revolt against modernity was hardly restricted to Ireland. At the same time that Pearse and his comrades marshaled the most violent elements of Irish nationalism for an act that was consciously designed to be a symbolic gesture, certain of their deaths, millions of Europeans marched off in defense of equally, if not more, abstract patriotism. World War I occurred after a period of intellec-

15. The issue of modernity in Ireland has been delineated in the critical collision against Patrick O'Farrell's *Ireland's English Question* by Joseph Lee's *The Modernisation of Irish Society, 1848-1918* and more recently in Lee's *Ireland 1912-1985*. It has been most usefully addressed in Tom Garvin, "Priests and Patriots: Irish Separatism and Fear of the Modern, 1890-1914," *Irish Historical Studies*, 25, no. 97 (May 1986): 67-81.

tual revolt against reason as well as escalating terrorism and political violence that bears an uncanny resemblance to political developments in Ireland during the later nineteenth and early twentieth centuries.[16] Yet the tendency of both Irish specialists and European historians to remove Ireland's history from a general European context has served to relegate Pearse and the Rising to the status of an odd, somewhat parochial and idiosyncratic phenomenon. While Ireland's size is small, its political experience was like that of countries on the Continent with oppressed ethnic groups which struggled to achieve independence and/or hegemony. In this sense late nineteenth- and early twentieth-century Ireland is Europe in microcosm. Nationalistic and separatist movements in Poland, Italy, and the Balkans bore close similarities to those in Ireland. Likewise, the development of the Irish Republican Brotherhood's belief that violence was not only a political but also a spiritual and moral force was but another manifestation of the "subjec-tification" of thought that prevailed in Europe in the early twentieth century. No single incident in European political history more clearly demonstrates this phenomenon than the Easter Rising of 1916.

H. Stuart Hughes's *Consciousness and Society*[17] argues that Euro-pean social thought in the early part of this century underwent a major revolt against the rational tenets of positivistic thought. The "revolt" against reason manifested itself across many disciplines,

16. For the reaction of intellectuals and artists to the times and the war, see Paul Fussell, *The Great War and Modern Memory* (New York: Oxford University Press, 1975; paperback, 1977); Robert Wohl, *The Generation of 1914* (Cambridge, MA: Harvard University Press, 1979); Roland Stromberg, *Redemption by War: The Intellectuals and 1914* (Lawrence, KA: The Regent's Press of Kansas, 1982); Modris Eeksteins, *Rites of Spring: The Great War and the Birth of the Modern Age* (New York: Houghton Mifflin, 1989; paperback, 1990); Samuel Hynes, *A War Imagined* (Princeton: Princeton University Press, 1990); Jean Jacques Becker, *1914: Comment les français sont entrés dans la guerre* (Paris, 1977).

17. H. Stuart Hughes, *Consciousness and Society: The Reorientation of Euro-pean Social Thought* (New York: Random House, 1958; paperback, 1961; revised ed., 1971).

from philosophy to the new physics, but was perhaps strongest in social and political theory. Hughes found that this revolt "displaced . . . social thought from the apparent and objectively verifiable to the only partially conscious area of unexplained motivation. In this sense the new doctrines were manifestly subjective. Psychological processes had replaced external reality as the most pressing topic for investigation. It was no longer what actually existed that seemed important: it was what men thought existed."[18] This revolt against positivism's standards of progress and logic found widespread intellectual and cultural expression, and it was not a phenomenon from which Irish intellectuals were immune: Yeats, Synge, Shaw, A.E. Russell, and Joyce were major literary lights of their day. Joyce spent most of his adult life in Europe. Yeats and Shaw were international figures. Before the twentieth century, Irish participation in European political thought was not inconsiderable. Marx and Engels wrote about Ireland.[19] James Connolly was a leading socialist, one of the few working men who rose to leadership in the movement and acquired a noteworthy international intellectual reputation. Little work has been done on Irish politics within this broader European or even Western context, but the presence of an enduring Irish contribution to European letters indicates that the conventional dismissal of Ireland from the general consideration of European intellectual history of this period is mistaken.

In addition to reconsidering Ireland's involvement in the intellectual and cultural life of Europe, there is the need to consider the nearly universal climate of political confrontation and violence that pervaded Western societies during this period. George Dangerfield's *The Strange Death of Liberal England*[20] describes the collapse of

18. Ibid., 66.

19. Karl Marx and Friedrich Engels, *Ireland and the Irish Question* (London: International Publishers, 1978).

20. George Dangerfield, *The Strange Death of Liberal England* (New York: G. P. Putnam's Sons, Ltd., 1935; Perigee Books, 1980).

Britain's Liberal Party as taking place within a climate of almost inevitable violence, in which the politics of moderation and compromise began to founder on the forces of unreason. Dangerfield believed that British politics in the period preceding the Great War was characterized by a deepening political morass of ever more polarized opinions, interests, and issues which succeeded in bringing down the consensus that had dominated political life for decades. Dangerfield demonstrated how force became a tool of both coercion and repression that immobilized a political system based on the idea of rational consensus. As the pattern toward confrontation grew more entrenched, the ideas that were the foundations of these social, political, and intellectual factions assumed the character of articles of faith.

In his *Reflections on Violence* (1907), Georges Sorel maintained that there existed myths that were revolutionary canons of great social movements. These myths "are not descriptions of things but expressions of a determination to act."[21] They represent the desire to destroy the status quo, a search "for a combat which will destroy the existing state of things."[22] Sorel found the greatest example of this in the syndicalist "myth of the general strike," a battle of the collective proletariat to destroy the state and establish a society of the workers. The strength of the myth's hold on its believers is a result of its total avoidance of the contradictory issues and analytical problems that face orthodox socialism.[23] According to Sorel, the myth serves no ideology that needs expression or apology, it exists as an explanation of will, it brooks no academic differences or analytical equivocations that render it meaningless or impossible, and its essential truth is affirmed when it is suppressed or persecuted.[24]

21. Georges Sorel, *Reflections on Violence*, trans. T. E. Hulme and J. Roth (Glencoe: Free Press, 1950), 57.

22. Ibid., 58.

23. Ibid., 140. For an examination of syndicalism in Ireland see Emmet O'Connor, *Syndicalism in Ireland* (Cork: Cork University Press, 1988).

24. Sorel, *Reflections on Violence*, 140–41.

For Sorel the emotional power of the new European political movements of Europe in the early 1900s drew strength from myths that claimed the power to eradicate and change everything. The quibbles of Liberals, Conservatives, Socialists, and Monarchists all would fall before the irresistible power of myth.

> With the general strike all these fine things disappear, the revolution appears as a revolt, pure and simple, and no place is reserved for sociologists, for fashionable people who are in favour of social reforms, and for the Intellectuals who have embraced *the profession of thinking for the proletariat*.[25]

Behind the myth of the general strike operates a basic human desire for apocalyptic catastrophe to which individuals commit themselves at all costs. The myth represents all the hopes and aspirations, emotional and irrational, that political theory, organization and activity never satisfy.[26] The myth of the general strike aims at nothing less than "complete catastrophe"—a cataclysmic overthrow of the past.[27]

Sorel's catastrophe is not aimless. Although its primary manifestation is destruction, the violence of the general strike is ultimately soteriological in nature and aims to save men from a world of oppression and injustice that is based on reason. Thus violence becomes the means by which justice and virtue are at last established in the world of men. Sorel's view was "it is to violence that Socialism owes those high ethical values by means of which it brings salvation to the Modern World."[28] Because violence destroys inequity, it represents the righteous pathway to a new morality that will destroy the modern order, reign triumphant, and redeem the world.

Sorel went on to suggest that the faith and emotional energy committed to the myth were the source of its tenacity. Myth is nei-

25. Ibid., 157.   26. Ibid., 145.
27. Ibid., 153.   28. Ibid., 272.

ther rational nor scientific, it claims no point of debate, it exists as a reality in the mind of the faithful, and it galvanizes them into action because of their hope in the apocalypse to come. Sorel described a religious idea to which men were committed by faith despite, or perhaps because of, never having seen it happen. In this sense faith in the myth is eschatological and apocalyptic, looking toward a future that can be brought about only through the violent destruction of what already exists.[29]

Sorel conceded that there were nonsocialist myths of power as compelling as that of the myth of the general strike.[30] The cases he allowed for were wars of revolution or liberty—both having the same kind of psychological power the myth of the general strike generated.[31] In Pearse's case the myth of a noble Ireland won by violent and resolute action converted him to republicanism. Violent revolution could eradicate the modern morass in Irish society and culture; it could also pave the way for Pearse to reconcile opposites and eradicate equivocations in his own life.

Patrick Pearse's unique contribution to Irish political history was his expression of the "mythic" ideas that served as the moral basis of physical-force nationalism. The source of his success lay in the coincidence of historical events and his own search for things to believe that could make him into a whole person.

By 1900 the politics, culture, and social structure of Pearse's Ireland were all in turmoil. Catastrophic depopulation, especially in rural areas, had reached a peak in Pearse's early adulthood. With emigration came the migration of large numbers of rural Irish into Dublin and Belfast.[32] Social upheaval paralleled an intellectual revolution of major proportions, which began in the 1880s and continued in many ways into the late 1930s. Whatever its considerable con-

29. Ibid., 142.   30. Ibid., 267–70.
31. Ibid., 269–70.
32. Lyons, *Ireland Since the Famine*, 110–11.

tribution was to Irish culture and national identity, the Irish Literary Renaissance represented a major change in ideas and sensibilities. The "rediscovery" of Celtic mythology, folklore, and the Irish language and the Anglo-Irish revival in poetry, drama, and fiction demonstrate that Irish culture was in a period of considerable transition.

While politics appeared to move toward peaceful constitutional resolution in 1914, the process of political failure and compromise clearly pushed many political moderates toward the same kind of confrontational politics that were becoming more evident in Britain. Ireland's political unrest, as Dangerfield demonstrated,[33] manifested the polarization increasingly common in British politics in the early twentieth century. Moderate constitutional politics failed to win a decisive victory in the Irish case and thus ceded to the politics of revolutionary violence—which had survived unsullied by compromise—increasing legitimacy. Irish nationalists evolved into polarized camps, one committed to the politics of reason, consensus, and accommodation, the other committed to an absolute to be won at any cost. This second group was republican and separatist. Despite its history of failures, the myth of violence accepted by Irish republicanism gave physical-force nationalism an apparent integrity constitutionalist politics never possessed. Violence on behalf of Irish freedom came into its own through failure and death, upheld by each generation as an expression of Irish retribution and faithfulness to a holy cause.

Pearse did much more than merely float on a tide that was going his way. He became the leading spokesman for the Irish tradition of armed resistance to Britain. Under the tutelage and inspiration of men of single-minded conviction and experience such as Thomas Clarke, Pearse gave artistic expression to what was for him a new-found political ideology; in the process he became the evangelist for the republican tradition of violence. Pearse was certainly not alone

33. Dangerfield, *Damnable Question*, 57–138 passim.

in glorifying the myth of republican violence, but his unique consciousness of that past, along with his own profound psychological
needs, synergized with republican tradition in a mythopoeia where
violence held personal and national soteriological possibilities.
Because of this synergy of personal experience and revolutionary
tradition, Pearse's impact upon the history of his country was to be
remarkable.

Pearse's thanatic vision was aestheticism that expressed itself
within political action. The rhetoric he brought to bear on the contemporary situation ultimately renewed and continued the tenets of
Irish republican faith. Pearse and his fellow poets of the Rising not
only gave voice to the myth but lived it out in order to appropriate
what was perceived to be its life-giving power.[34]

Pearse's critics have claimed that his vanity and self-aggrandize-
ment were an overcompensation for his inability, and the inability of
the other artists *manques* who followed him into the Rising, to face
reality. In this view, the poets of the Easter Rising self-conceitedly
sought to create politically what they could not achieve in their art,
thus rendering the Rising ludicrous and pitiful. The Rising was
essentially a histrionic re-enactment of myth in which Pearse cast
himself in the lead role.[35]

Certainly Pearse did conceive of himself as a tragic figure and
sought to live out a heroic role in re-enacting a myth. But he did so
believing that the republican myth had power to redeem his life and
his culture. Since he did not expect to survive, Pearse's efforts cannot
be judged to have been simply self-serving.

Patrick Pearse was not the only man in Europe to think this way
at the time. That he expressed a view widespread in Europe is suggested by the lives and views of Rupert Brooke and Charles Péguy,

34. Thompson, *Imagination of an Insurrection*, 124ff.
35. Robert O'Driscoll, "Return to the Hearthstone: Ideals of the Celtic Literary Revival," *Place, Personality, and the Irish Writer*, ed. Andrew Carpenter (New
York: Harper and Row, 1977), 67–68.

among many others. His patriotic poetry has thematic similarities to Rupert Brooke's romantic call to his generation in "The Soldier"—to die for the English national myth as a form of eternal service and cultural redemption. Brooke's "1914 Sonnets" emphasize the same ideas: earth and decay in "The Soldier"; the glory and redemption of violent death and the pouring out of "the Red sweet wine of youth" in "The Dead"; war's ability to free the captive spirit in "Peace."[36] Captivity is the nature of the age, and it is to be overcome by embracing, despite its horror, cleansing violence. The human spirit is to be freed from modernity's clutches by means of war.

> Now, God be thanked Who has matched us with His hour,
> And caught our youth, and wakened us from sleeping,
> With hand made sure, clear eye, and sharpened power,
> To turn as swimmers into cleanness leaping,
> Glad from a world grown old and cold and weary.[37]

For Brooke, a period of personal alienation and morbid introspection ended when he briefly saw action in October 1914.[38] Brooke recounted that the sight of a great city in flames and the threat of death made him feel fulfilled; upon his return to England for more training he was moved to write his war sonnets "1914."[39]

A year before the war Brooke had gone on an extensive trip to North America and the South Pacific, partly to overcome his melancholy with sights of the new culture.[40] This trip was a stimulating one for Brooke, but even before he left England he had come to see some things quite differently from the way he had seen them before.

36. Rupert Brooke, *The Poetical Works of Rupert Brooke*, ed. Geoffrey Keynes (London: Faber and Faber, Ltd., 1946; paperback, 1970; reprint ed., 1981), 19–24.

37. Ibid.

38. Christopher Hassell, *Rupert Brooke* (New York: Harcourt, Brace and World, 1964), 467–69.

39. Ibid.   40. Ibid., 400ff.

Though once a youthful Fabian, at the vanguard of those who accepted modernity, he began to reverse his positions on modernist trends in art. Not the least of these reversals was his decision, contradicting an opinion he had expressed a couple of years earlier, that Henrik Ibsen's "modern" drama was sadly populistic.[41] He now lamented Ibsen's abandonment of classical soliloquy and said that Ibsen was "a great and dirty playwright."[42] As if to emphasize the point, Brooke voiced his admiration of Strindberg for his "honesty" in depicting human relationships, especially because Strindberg would not give in to the feminism that "plagued" Ibsen's work.[43]

Unfortunately Brooke found little in America that encouraged him: American art was being ruined by its commercialization.[44] On the whole he found the spectacular countryside melancholy because "one misses the dead"—because the New World had no history to speak of and consequently "it had no sense of purpose."[45] Finally, before the cataract of Niagara Falls, he had the realization that he was not a modernist. "I am a Victorian after all. . . . I sit and stare at the thing and have the purest nineteenth century thought, about the Destiny of Man, the Irresistibility of Fate, the Doom of Nations, the fact that Death awaits us All, and so forth. Wordsworth Redivivus. Oh, dear! Oh, dear!"[46]

For Brooke the war meant more than an escape from the prosaic and ignoble and the prospect of middle age and dotage. It was an opportunity to side with others who found the modern sensibility so

41. Ibid., 377–78.

42. Ibid., 379. Brooke went so far as to take up the sword against what he saw as the "revolt against Victorian hypocrisy." See Hassell, 378–79.

43. Ibid., 155–56.

44. Rupert Brooke, *Letters From America* (London: Sidgewick and Jackson, 1916), 33–34; 38–39.

45. Hassell, *Rupert Brooke*, 155–56.

46. *The Letters of Rupert Brooke*, ed. by Geoffrey Keynes (London: Faber and Faber, 1968), 491.

enervating. He wrote in a letter to his friend in England, the poet John Drinkwater, in January 1915 that he had come to find the war

> exhilarating and terrible. . . . Still, it's the only life for me, just now. . . . I'd not be able to exist, for torment, if I weren't doing it. Not a bad place to die, Belgium, 1915? I want to kill my first Prussian first. Better than coughing out a civilian soul amid bedclothes and disinfectant and gulping medicines in 1950. The world'll be tame after the war, for those that see it. . . . Certain sleepers have awoken in the heart. Come and die. It'll be great fun. And there's great health in the preparation. . . . If you stay there you'll not be able to start afresh with us when we come back. [Charles] Péguy and [Georges] Duhamel; and I don't know what others. I want to mix a few sacred and Apollonian English ashes with theirs, lest England be shamed.[47]

The war would change him, not because he reveled in the prospect of violence, but because the war's violence would allow Brooke and his generation to find the sense of purpose he had failed to find in poetry as well as in modern culture.[48] Brooke's obituary in *The Times* was written by his close friend Edward Marsh. It began the enshrinement of Brooke as a symbol of his generation. "He expected to die; he was willing to die for the dear England whose majesty and beauty he knew; and he advanced towards the brink in perfect serenity. . . . He was all that one would wish England's noblest sons to be in days when no sacrifice but the most precious is acceptable, and most precious is that which is most freely proffered."[49]

47. Ibid., 654–55.   48. Hassell, *Rupert Brooke*, 472–73.

49. *The Times* (London), 26 April 1915. Robert Wohl comments upon the irony of Brooke's death from an infection (without really seeing combat) and the icon he became after the war. See Wohl's excellent *The Generation of 1914*, 91–92. By coincidence, it is likely that Pearse did not fire a shot during the Rising, and Charles Péguy died in the opening days of the war. This meant that none of these three saw any protracted combat of the kind faced by the disillusioned generation of veterans such as Wilfred Owen, Ernst Junger, Robert Graves, Erich Maria Remarque, or Siegfried Sassoon.

There are even closer parallels between Pearse, a Catholic committed to a gospel of redemptive violence, and the French poet Charles Péguy. Péguy was as obsessed as Pearse and Brooke with the idea that his generation was the last and only hope, that history had presented them with an opportunity and an obligation to save what their nation and culture represented. In 1913 Péguy explained that this generation was to be offered up as a sacrifice "because it had to endure the mediocrity of contemporary history."[50] For Péguy, redemption could be found only in a commitment to faith and belief in the nation of France restored to its glory—this was the source of personal and spiritual integrity without which men lost themselves, and the time for commitment was upon his generation. "We are the last. Almost beyond the last. Immediately after us begins another age, a quite different world, the world of those who no longer believe in anything; those for whom this is a source of pride and glory."[51] The idea of the French nation as the last repository of noble values so attracted Péguy in the last years before the first World War that he condoned violence in service to the nation, and he implied approval of the assassination of socialist Jean Juares because it was a patriotic act.[52] Péguy's notion of the good was evolving into one in which integrity, will, and faithfulness were the determining factors. Hans Schmitt wrote, "The Péguy of 1914 valued constancy over morality. In his eyes even a murderer had become a good man when he killed for the sake of principle."[53] More specifically, Peguy came to see the defense of Catholic France as a divine mission against the modern spirit.

> . . . our Christian sanctities . . . [are] plunged into the modern world, in this *vastatio*, in this abyss of incredulity, of disbelief and

50. Quoted by Wohl, 249.

51. Charles Péguy, *Charles Péguy: Basic Verities, Prose and Poetry*, trans. Ann and Julian Green, 2d ed. (New York: Pantheon Books, 1943), 103.

52. Hans Schmitt, *Charles Péguy: The Decline of an Idealist* (Baton Rouge: Louisiana State University Press, 1967), 174.

53. Ibid.

unfaithfulness . . . isolated like beacons vainly assailed during well-nigh three centuries of raging furious sea. . . . The holy war is everywhere. It is ever being waged. All of us stand in the breach today. We are all stationed on the frontier. The frontier is everywhere.[54]

Péguy posited a national myth to stand against this modern tide. He attempted to raise Joan of Arc as the myth incarnate, not only as the spirit of France but also the refutation of the modern age.[55] For Péguy the battle was between the national myth and the corrupting reason of positivism, and the way was to be won by violence. "Our positivists will learn metaphysics as our pacifists will learn war. Our positivists will learn metaphysics by the firing of rifles."[56]

The national myth required willful self-immolation; without it men were doomed to an impotence that robbed them of their humanity. Péguy found hope in the exercise of the will.

> Nothing is as murderous as weakness and cowardice.
> Nothing is as humane as firmness.[57]

The mythic idea of the nation was served by men who willingly sacrificed themselves on its behalf. Péguy made his sacrifice on behalf of the myth and died early in the war leading a suicidal charge against a German machine-gun position in the First Battle of the Marne.[58] Péguy, like Brooke and Pearse and many others, had come to see that violence in service to a myth had powers of individual and cultural redemption. Serving the myth unto death meant eternal joy and beatification.

54. Péguy, *Basic Verities*, 177.

55. Charles Péguy, *The Mystery of the Charity of Joan of Arc*, Trans. by Julian Green (New York: Pantheon Books, 1950).

56. Ibid., 159.

57. Ibid., 155.

58. For an interesting description of Péguy's death, see Marjorie Villiers, *Charles Péguy: A Study in Integrity* (New York: Harper and Row Publishers, 1965; reprint ed., 1975), 382.

Happy are those who die for a temporal land,
When a just war calls and they obey and go forth,
Happy are they who die for a handful of earth,
Happy are they who die in so noble a band.

Happy are they who die in their country's defense,
Lying outstretched before God with upturned faces.
Happy are they who die in those last high places,
Such funeral rites have a great magnificence.[59]

The outbreak of the First World War led many of less than radical sympathies to view the coming blood-letting as a joyous end to the decadence of a corrupt era. In August 1914 Thomas Mann wrote to his brother Heinrich that whatever the war might bring in terms of personal difficulty it was a great opportunity not to be denied or avoided. "What a visitation! What will Europe look like, inwardly and outwardly, when it is over? . . . Shouldn't we be grateful for the totally unexpected chance to experience such mighty things?"[60]

Mann confessed later that in 1914 he had believed that the war was to be "a purification, a liberation, an enormous hope. . . . The victory of Germany will be a paradox, nay a wonder: a victory of soul over numbers. The German soul is opposed to the pacifist ideal of civilization for is not peace an element of civil corruption?"[61] There is little doubt that Mann at the beginning of the war saw the conflict as a metahistorical struggle in which Germany represented something quite old seeking liberation in the modern age.[62]

Ernest Jones records that the normally pacifistic Sigmund Freud

59. Charles Péguy, *The Myth of the Holy Innocents*, trans. Pansy Pakenham (London: Harvill Press, 1956), 93.

60. Thomas Mann, *Letters of Thomas Mann: 1889–1955*, trans. and ed. Richard and Clara Winston (New York: Alfred A. Knopf, 1971), 69.

61. Quoted in Hans Kohn, *The Mind of Germany* (New York: Macmillan, 1960), 253.

62. Hans Kohn has said that Mann, in a series of now-notorious essays published in 1914, saw the war as yet another example of Germany's ancient struggle against "Rome" and its civilization (ibid., 254).

was no more immune than Mann was to these war enthusiasms in 1914. The declaration of war invigorated Freud.

> [Freud's] response was rather one of youthfulness, apparently a reawakening of the military ardors of his boyhood. He said that for the first time in thirty years he felt himself to be an Austrian. ... He was quite carried away, could not think of any work, and spent his time discussing the events of the day with his brother Alexander. As he put it: "All my libido is given to Austria-Hungary." He was very excitable, irritable, and made slips of the tongue all day long.[63]

Like many European intellectuals in the years before the Great War, Patrick Pearse was concerned about the threat of modernity. Although there is little evidence to show that he was acquainted with these European thinkers directly, the morphological relationship of his ideas to concurrent developments in European thought is striking. His anxiety was more than just coincidence—it was a manifestation of the anxieties of the age, a result of a complex set of influences that affected others in similar ways. Numerous intellectuals had come to fear that spiritual values and categories were eroding before the power of positivism, reason, and science. Theirs was not an original concern, but it was nonetheless an intense and often depressing one, usually expressed in terms of a threat to their nations. Hence for Pearse and many other Irishmen, the sentiments of the "generation of 1914" hearkened back to traditions from the Gaelic past. With Cúchulainn as a starting point, Irishmen could withstand the drift of the modern tide. Pearse believed that the Easter Rising was a blow struck for Irish freedom but also a revolt against the materialistic, rationalistic, and all-too-modern world represented by England. Denis Gwynn claimed that this idea occupied Pearse in the period before the Rising. "[Pearse] used to recur

63. Ernest Jones, *The Life and Work of Sigmund Freud*, ed. and abridged by Lionel Trilling and Stephen Marcus (New York: Basic Books, 1957), 336–37.

continually to the assertion that the people had lost their souls and were becoming vulgarized, commercialized, anxious only to imitate the material prosperity of England."[64] Pearse criticized Synge's *Playboy of the Western World* because the realistic dialogue was "morally repugnant";[65] he thus added his voice to the chorus of those for whom the play's realism was antagonistic to the values of Ireland's heroic past.[66]

Pearse found the source of Irish ills in English influence. As England was responsible for the increasing materialism of the Irish people, it was also responsible for the institutions that acted to subvert Irish values and culture. He committed himself to "Irish-education" schools for children because he believed the English educational system made Irish children into "willing slaves" in more than just the political and economic senses;[67] the true Ireland was losing its soul to Britain's modernity. The educational revolution of which he felt himself to be a part was only a piece of something much bigger.[68] In the end Pearse made Ireland's national cause into a matter of duty against the modern world, which was represented by the empire that held Ireland against her will and corrupted her spirit.[69]

Two points that Pearse stressed helped to establish him as the important figure he is today in Irish political nationalism. Both reveal the political climate of the time and Pearse's personal development; they demonstrate that the resolution and wholeness he sought personally spoke to the needs of many others within the republican movement.

64. Denis Gwynn, "Patrick Pearse," *Dublin Review* (Jan.-March 1923), 93.

65. *An Claidheamh Soluis*, 2 Sept. 1907.

66. Norman Vance, *Irish Literature: A Social History* (Oxford: Oxford University Press, 1990), 166.

67. Pearse, *Political Writings and Speeches*, 16.

68. Patrick Pearse to W. P. Ryan, 18 March 1915, Patrick Pearse Papers, University College, Dublin.

69. Shaw, "The Canon of Irish History," 122-25.

The first point was the paramount need to act in some fashion. He thought, as did many of his contemporaries, that the arming of Orangemen in the North at Larne in 1914 was spiritually the same thing as Fenianism, the difference being only one of goals.[70] Pearse believed that action by Irishmen was more important than anything and that his generation, like generations of Irish patriots before, had a historic obligation it had to discharge.[71] He felt mounting pressure to act, and his anxiety over this found expression in his writing and public statements. He was not above talking about it to friends either, as he replied to Denis Gwynn's statement that a British dreadnought could defeat a rising and ruin Pearse's beloved Dublin: "I would sooner see all Dublin in ruins than that we should go on as we are living at present."[72] Pearse desired an apocalypse to release him and his generation from a present that was shameful.[73] Soon he began to speak of violence as a means of freeing Ireland from its increasing lack of will.[74] Ireland was not free because it had allowed itself to be emasculated, and this emasculation had led to an acceptance of the impotence, the dishonor, of peace.[75] This peace had to be overthrown because it was "the devil's peace, peace with sin, peace with dishonor. . . ."[76]

Self-immolation was the way out, the way to become a hero. Only thus, he believed, could his "generation" (obviously a term for himself) no longer be ashamed of its failure to act.[77] He wished to appropriate the mythic heroic ideal of the old Gaelic Order. But the values exemplified in the Irish epic, the *Táin Bó Cuailnge*, were

---

70. Hobson, *A History of the Volunteers*, 198.

71. Pearse, *Political Writings and Speeches*, 198.

72. Gwynn, "Patrick Pearse," 94.

73. Pearse, *Political Writings and Speeches*, 91–92.

74. P. J. McGill, "Padraic Pearse in Donegal," *Donegal Annual* 3 (1966): 78. For this theme in Pearse's poetry, see his poem "The Renunciation," in *Collected Works of Padraic H. Pearse: Plays, Stories, Poems*, 324–25.

75. Pearse, *Political Writings and Speeches*, 195.

76. Ibid., 218.   77. Ibid., 66.

those of an archaic warrior elite scarcely suited to political action in the twentieth century. While Cúchulainn, the child-hero-redeemer of the *Táin*, wins his battle for glory, he loses the battle on earth. He wins eternal triumph and renown but is killed by his enemies. Vulnerable and mortal, he yet remains invincible.

Pearse's idealization of this myth meant an implicit acceptance not only of the heroic ideal but also of the hero's fate. He came to see that Cúchulainn's death in defense of Ulster provided an example to be emulated by Irishmen in the modern age. Their sacrifice would serve as a work of atonement and redemption like that of Jesus Christ. Pearse's notorious notion of the blood sacrifice on behalf of Ireland came from his merger of the myth of Cúchulainn's self-immolation and the Crucifixion of Jesus. In both cases the shedding of blood won the eternal battle and in fact was, in Pearse's words, "a cleansing and sanctifying thing."[78] Pearse thought he had seen this demonstrated when, on 26 July 1914, four nationalist supporters were killed and thirty-seven wounded by British troops. The "Bachelor's Walk Massacre" had, according to Pearse, served to "re-baptize the movement," and with the bloodshed the Irish Volunteers committed themselves to fight the terrible conflict to come.[79] In the midst of the Rising, Pearse wrote that the sacrifices of the rebels served as "a redemption of Dublin from its innumerable sufferings."[80] By 1916 Pearse believed Cúchulainn's fate offered an example to be emulated that could rescue Ireland from its shameful present and from Great Britain. The Rising was an attempt to embrace the power of the myth in the service of a chiliastic vision. "Patrick Pearse saw in Cúchulainn heroic violence sanctified. . . . Resurrected in the present, Ireland's past glories, pagan and Christian, gave birth to a new

78. Ibid., 99.

79. Patrick Pearse to Joseph McGarrity, 28 July 1914, Patrick Pearse Papers, National Library of Ireland.

80. Pearse, *The Letters of P. H. Pearse*, 372.

messianism which looked forward to that future time when a new
Ireland would rise equal to the old."[81]

Pearse's identification of Irish political and cultural hopes with
the heroic fatalism of the *Táin* and Christian soteriological termi-
nology had ramifications beyond the synthesis of pagan and Christian culture. The self-conscious marriage of these elements in an
apocalyptic political solution indicates just how difficult the search
for an Irish political identity had been. The example of the Gaelic
Order was fraught with peril in the modern world: as the core of a
political commitment it was clearly absurd. The synthesis of
Cúchulainn and Christ[82] required a considerable leap of faith; nevertheless, Pearse fashioned this synthesis into a sacrificial modality
for future republicans to reaffirm in their own sufferings and
deaths.

Embracing the world of the *Táin* meant embracing all of its values and ideals. Pearse maintained that his "Irish" school at St.
Enda's had been established to resurrect the old Gaelic Order's system of education in order to "regenerate Ireland."[83] His school was a
bastion standing in the way of total surrender to English values, the
very values of corrupting civilization itself, the "biggest impediment

81. O'Farrell, *Ireland's English Question*, 239. O'Farrell demonstrates that
these kinds of feelings against modernity as represented by Britain were widespread in pre-Rising Ireland and popularly disseminated in the novels of Canon
Patrick A. Sheehan (230–32). Sheehan was perhaps the most popular of contemporary Irish novelists and his antipathy to Britain was couched in religious
terms, usually contrasting Ireland's spirituality with the enervating materialism
and cynicism of modern English culture and society. A representative work of
Sheehan's in this regard is his novel *Luke Delmege* (New York, 1901).

82. This synthesis can be seen in several places in Pearse's plays and poetry.
The clearest dramatic examples can be found in "The King" and "The Singer."
Pearse's self-identification with Christ can be seen in his poems "The Mother"
and "A Mother Speaks."

83. Pearse, *A Significant Irish Educationalist: The Educational Writings of P. H.
Pearse*, 331.

to these [ancient Irish] ideals."[84] These ideals were to deliver Ireland and renew it through the willingness of disciples to fight and die with them in mind. Ultimately Pearse's own generation would realize the ancient truth and do its duty by dying for Ireland, and in the process redemption would come to his corrupted age. "[W]hen England thinks she has purchased us with a bribe, some good man redeems us with a sacrifice."[85]

In an odd Christmas reflection written from the school in 1910, he said that the student of St. Enda's was being trained to be "an efficient soldier, efficient to fight, when need is, his own, his people's, and the world's battles, spiritual and temporal."[86] To fight battles so would mean suffering and death, but it was only through sacrifice that Cúchulainn's reward could pass down to new generations. In the words Pearse quoted from the *Táin* for the school's motto, the means and the goal were all too clear: self-immolation on behalf of Ireland assured eternal fame. "I care not though I were to live but one day and one night, provided my fame and my deeds live after me."[87] This courting of death and violence borders on the psychopathic.[88] Pearse and those who followed him to certain destruction believed their actions somehow appropriated the transcendent powers of the myth. Pearse failed to see that he was attempting to reinvent the myth mimetically. Since myth is by definition impossible to invent, the motivations for living out a myth are suspiciously irrational if not pathological. Myths cannot be, except perhaps in a psychotic state, *consciously* experienced. By living out the sacrifice at the heart of the myth, Pearse sought what his rational mind could not

84. Ibid., 331.

85. Pearse, *Political Writings and Speeches*, 76.

86. Ibid., 339.

87. Martin Daly [Stephen MacKenna] (Dublin, Pamphlet in the National Library of Dublin), 17.

88. See Erich Fromm, *The Anatomy of Human Destructiveness*, and Karl Menninger, *Man Against Himself.*

furnish. Through ritualizing the hero's death, he hoped to experience the personal transformation that would make his life whole and complete and establish his renown.[89]

Pearse suffered severe psychological limitations that made the prospect of dying on Easter Monday 1916 seem attractive, even compelling. His lack of a secure psychological identity had arrested his emotional development and rendered him unprepared for an autonomous adulthood. The most obvious manifestation of this condition was his sexual backwardness. Pearse's sexual immaturity was severe; in adulthood, the behavioral aberrations of his youth and adolescence gave way to poems praising the beauty of young boys and an almost compulsive interest in their welfare. The heroes of Pearse's writings were almost always children, and his writings were full of negative images of middle and old age. The erotic imagery in his poetry and the mores and values of his culture suggest sexual anxiety and tension. If Pearse's development was arrested, his identification with the emotional world of boys suggests that he wished never to grow up; the onset of maturity would represent yet one more psychological hurdle for which he was spectacularly unprepared. His focus on the transformation and renewal brought about by death has the qualities of another one of his fantastic and infantile dreams. Nonetheless, neither his sexual ambivalence nor his eroticization of death and violence was unusual for his time; moreover, these traits manifested themselves thematically in the works of Pearse's fellow poets of the Rising.

In addition to his considerable sexual immaturity, Pearse had

89. The work of the Jungians is useful within this context. Carl Gustav Jung's *Psychology of the Unconscious*, trans. Beatrice Hinkle (New York: Dodd, Mead and Co., 1916), has a chapter devoted to the heroic ideal and its origins in the unconscious. For an analysis of heroism from a Jungian perspective, see Joseph Campbell, *The Hero with a Thousand Faces* (Princeton: Princeton University Press, 1949). See also Otto Rank, *The Myth of the Birth of the Hero*, ed. Philip Freund (New York: Alfred A. Knopf, 1932; paperback, 1964).

been unprepared psychologically to take up adult responsibilities. His father, who represented what would have been the normal model for establishing the young man's sense of autonomy and ideals, was notably absent from Patrick's life. It does not seem accidental that Patrick, like so many other Irish revolutionaries, should have an English parent, and that he rebelled against his father's English connection while enthusiastically embracing his mother's Irish heritage.

Pearse suffered from the smothering attentions of his female relatives throughout his life, but especially in his childhood. He declined to marry and there is nothing to indicate that either he or his brother ever had romantic or sexual relationships with women. Nonetheless, in his dreams, Pearse was often alone and away from his inescapable family and the realities of this world, and then he was strong and free.

> When people have been talking to me about national policies, I have been listening to the flickerings of the wings of flies on a window-pane that I once knew; in the midst of military plans and organizations I have been watching myself as a child come out of a certain green gate into a sun-lit field; or as a lad breasting great breakers beneath the moon, striving with strong white shoulders, wet and glistening.[90]

Pearse talked constantly about failure, betraying his sexual impotency, emotional inadequacy, intellectual deficiency, and other perceived defects.

The most compelling idea in his life was his oft-stated need to act—not only to express himself, but to act in a decisive way in order to redeem himself. In Pearse's culture the idea of personal redemptive transformation was found in the transformation symbolism of the Eucharist and in the *Táin*, where Cúchulainn was transformed into an unstoppable warrior by his warp spasm. In the

90. P. H. Pearse, "My Childhood," 8.

Christian and Celtic concepts of transformation, base elements are miraculously changed into heavenly and divine ones.[91] In both cases the elements' potentiality was locked within their own natures, only waiting to be liberated for some divine purpose. These ideas were uppermost in Pearse's mind shortly before his death, when he saw himself dying, as Robert Emmet had in 1803, for a divinely ordained purpose—a sacrifice for Ireland like Christ's on the Cross.[92] The transforming power of myth attracted Pearse; he wanted to accept its offer of a wholeness that destroyed all self-doubts and inadequacies. Ultimately that wholeness came from a death that joined the dead to all of the nationalist martyrs of the past and those who suffer for it at present.[93] Pearse spoke of the need of one man who would shed his blood to redeem the nation[94] and hand on the cause, well served by the present generation, to those who were to follow.[95] While death was the inevitable payment for this redemption, the martyr could die with the assurance, as Pearse saw it, that "life springs from death."[96] In 1915 he even went so far as to claim that Ireland could well learn from Europe the transforming power of death. In an anonymously written article in the *Spark* of December 1915, Pearse claimed that Ireland could learn from the war in Europe the transforming power of bloodshed and death.[97]

James Connolly bitterly attacked this tribute to death: "No, we do not think that the old heart of the earth needs to be warmed with

91. See C. G. Jung, "The Transformation Symbolism of the Mass," in *Psyche and Symbol*, ed. Violet S. de Lazlo (Garden City, NY: Doubleday 1958; reprint, Princeton: Princeton University Press, 1958).

92. *Gaelic American*, March 1914.

93. Pearse, *Political Writings and Speeches*, 86.

94. Pearse's self-identification with Christ has played no small part in his status within the republican tradition.

95. Pearse, *Political Writings and Speeches*, 286.

96. Patrick Pearse, *Pearse and Rossa*, ed. Kevin T. McEneany (New York: At-Swim Press, 1982), 10.

97. See p. 152, above.

the wine of millions of lives. We think anyone who does is a blithering idiot."[98] However, only two months after criticizing Pearse for these intemperate remarks, even Connolly adopted Pearse's vision of blood-sacrifice and redemption: "Without the slightest trace of irreverence but in all due humility and awe, we recognize that of us, as of mankind before Calvary, it may truly be said 'without the shedding of Blood there is no Redemption.'"[99]

Patrick Pearse spoke to a time and a society in which many had come to believe as he believed; and many followed him in his desperate action. He had led a life that was emblematic of that lived by many of his contemporaries, and his search for wholeness was mirrored in their search for spiritual wholeness in an age of rationality.

Pearse sought to create through acts of destruction, and his rejection of the modern age that faced Ireland came in a violent refutation of the politics and culture of reason. His personal need for the approval of history, a kind of eternal justification and sanctification, has been granted, and his impact on history has been far greater in death than it ever had been in life. By reconciling life and death in his violent search for wholeness, he paved the way for other Irish revolutionaries to follow. There were others who spoke much as Pearse did, but few communicated with his sense of emotional certainty. As a contemporary who heard him wrote shortly after the Rising: "Men must find some centre of power or action or intellect about which they may group themselves, and I think Pearse became the leader because his temperament was more profoundly emotional than any of the others. He was emotional not in a flighty way, but in a serious way, and one felt that he suffered more than he enjoyed."[100]

The failure of Irish nationalists to find any pragmatic and peaceful solution to their search for cultural and political independence led

98. *Worker's Republic,* 25 December 1915.
99. *Workers's Republic,* 5 February 1916.
100. James Stephens, *The Insurrection in Dublin* (Dublin: n.p. 1916; Gerard's Cross: Colin Smythe, 1978), 91.

many of them to seek solutions that were not bound by the notions of reason. It was Pearse who came to couch the solution in chiliastic terms which promised to free Ireland and to save Ireland from the modern spirit that England represented.

For those who died with Pearse but even more so for those who have followed, the twenty-two men who have starved themselves to death for Ireland since 1916, Pearse's theological definition of their cause is not the propaganda of a revolutionary intellectual elite—a kind of "high culture" that was not easily believable. Pearse's language and ideas went beyond formalistic rhetoric to posit a myth that served as an internalized belief system, which had precedents deep within the western tradition.[101] The extent to which these ideas have a tradition as well as a currency can be seen in republican trials, funerals, and anniversaries, where the "high culture" of the revolutionary has become a part of everyday Irish culture.[102] The myth is not just a belief about the past, substantially true but near enough to the truth to carry conviction. Pearse's myth was a truth, known in the heart and by the spirit, that reason could not (and cannot) deny and constitutional politics could not address, because reason and politics are not heroic—they cannot redeem anyone.

With Pearse to inspire them, republicans win their victory through the self-destructive yet regenerative and ultimately liberating act of self-immolation. In all of this Pearse pointed the way; his lack of maturity and insight did not hinder him from taking on a role that a large portion of his society was all too willing to grant him.

101. Moran, "Patrick Pearse and Patriotic Soteriology," 9ff.

102. The republican movement's rituals bear a striking similarity to those of the Blanquists. See Patrick Hutton, *The Cult of the Revolutionary Tradition: The Blanquists in French Politics, 1864-1893* (Berkeley: University of California Press, 1981). For the standard starting point on an analysis of the discourse between high and low culture, see Mikhail Bakhtin, *Rabelais and His World*, trans. Helene Iswolsky, (Boston: M.I.T. Press, 1968; paperback, Bloomington: Indiana University Press, 1984).

His contribution to that history should not, however, eclipse the fact that he brought to Irish politics concerns not limited to Ireland. Patrick Pearse was not a parochial enigma: like many of his generation, he was deeply concerned that modernity and its culture of reason represented a threat to values and culture. By embracing the subjectivity of myth over the received dictates of reason and pragmatism, Pearse articulated the Irish rejection of modernity at a critical moment in Irish history. That Pearse was Irish should not hide the fact that his vision was shared by many European thinkers of the day.

An undeniably important man in his nation's history, Patrick Pearse was a seemingly ordinary man with an extraordinary life. He won in death what he sought in life, and his success marked a turning point in the history of modern Ireland when the force of reason in politics gave way to myth and unreason. The lasting nature of his vision has vindicated him despite the excesses it has since inspired.

Appendix

The following passage is excerpted from Patrick Pearse's unfinished "autobiography" in *The Home Life of Padraig Pearse. Home Life* was edited by Patrick's younger sister, Mary Brigid Pearse, and the edited version of his work seems to have been little altered from the original documents now kept at the Pearse Museum at St. Enda's school. Its dating is somewhat difficult, for it is not clear whether the entire piece was written all at the same time. This author believes that it had to have been written sometime after mid-1914, because Pearse refers to daydreaming while planning military activities and debating policy.[1] It is unlikely that he participated in such events before 1914, despite his Volunteer membership, because of his trip to America in the early part of 1914. "My Childhood" is brief enough that it was most likely written within a short period, and then work on it ceased, no doubt because of the press of Pearse's political duties.

The issue of the document's reliability is an important one, but can be dismissed on the basis of the honesty and noncalculation that seems to have gone into most of Pearse's writing. His proclivity for honestly exposing his inner thoughts and feelings was great and might be credited to his naïve belief that his inner struggles were profound and tragic. The question of when it was written is important because he was now (in 1914) aware of the possibility of his eminent death because of the nature of his involvement in the IRB.

1. Patrick Pearse, "My Childhood," 16–18.

There is also the issue of the nature of this document. Whether dream or reality, "My Childhood" is Pearse's adult reconstruction of his own past. To Pearse, it told of a past in which he placed his faith as if it were documented reality; his "autobiography" is a faithful presentation of the reality of his childhood as he remembered it. However, this is not an objective historical account of a series of incidents; it is a subjective account of what he understood to be the truth.

NEW ARRIVALS ON THE SCENE

My first great adventure (after those strange migrations which some may look upon as myths) was the coming of Dobbin.

Dobbin was of wood, but apart from the disadvantage he was as gallant a steed as ever knight-errant rode. My father had fashioned him, toiling at him for many nights in his workshop after his apprentices had gone home; building him five hands high; giving him mighty limbs and a proud head and a fiery eye; a broad back and round shapely haunches. He was grey, as all famous steeds have been; and he towered grandly the evening my father set him up on a table for us to see.

"Dobbin is his name," my father said solemnly, not as if he were making a suggestion, but as if he were announcing some fact as old as the Creation.

That night, my mother, who had been ill for a few days, stole down from her room to see Dobbin; and the next morning a little brother came to us mysteriously—a more momentous coming even than that of Dobbin.

And my mother was very ill, and the little brother had to be sent away to Uncle Christy's, where he was fed on the milk of one cow. My mother nearly died; and during all that time Dobbin remained quietly stalled behind the door. Sometimes I climbed up upon him and bestrode him; but oftener I sat with my sister near the fire, and watched the fire-fairy, and studied the ways of Minnie and Gyp.

It was a long time before my mother came down to us again. When she did come, looking very pale, one of the first things she did (after pressing my sister and myself to her heart) was to go over and kiss Dobbin; and in gratitude for that gracious kiss I told her that I would consider the little brother (who returned to us the same day) entitled equally with me to bestride that noble steed, as soon as his little legs should have the necessary length and strength to grip on. For the present they were obviously too fat for any such equestrian exercise. So I alone rode Dobbin, and galloped him to many a battle. Sometimes I harnessed him to a state-coach, and he drew my sister on triumphant entries into cities; often I yoked him to a carrier's cart, and he rattled along country roads at night; there were times when he toiled under loads of hay; I have even known him, suitably draped in black, to pace mournfully with hearse and coffin behind him to Glasnevin. But oftenest I rode him in quest of some Holy Grail, to the relief of some beleaguered Ascalon or Trebizond, or over the slaughtered hearts of some Roncesvalles or Magh Mhuirthemhne.

I have been told it is a marvelous thing that I remember so clearly the days before and after the birth of my brother; for I was only two years and five days old when he was born. It would seem marvelous to me if I did not remember that time and all its little incidents. What greater thing has ever happened to me than the coming of that good comrade? Willie and I have been true brothers—companions! As a boy he was my only playmate; as a man he has been my only intimate friend. We have done and suffered much together, and we have shared together a few deep joys.

While Willie was too small to play with, my sister and I were sufficiently loving companions. Sometimes we quarreled. One of the chief grounds of quarrel was her frequent insisting on my putting Dobbin to what I considered base uses. She was perpetually killing people in the most terrifying and unheard of ways, and calling upon me to bury them. This meant that, instead of driving Dobbin to war, I had to yoke him to hearse and go on a lugubrious progress to Glasnevin. I thought that she should bury her own dead.

In those days she was both bigger and of a more dominating character than I, and she generally had her way. She extracted considerable deference from me as her junior by over a year. She insisted that her wisdom and experience were riper than mine, and, by dint of hearing this again repeated, I came to believe it and to entertain for her a serious respect.

She finally lost my confidence, in the affair of the London Horse's tail.

The London Horse was a present which my father had once brought me from London; he was much smaller than Dobbin, but was more elegant and had real hair. One day my sister instructed me in the properties of hair.

'If hair is cut, it grows. For instance, if I were to cut the London Horse's tail, it would infallibly grow again.'

I was dubious; she was positive. She urged me to dock the tail quite short so as to ensure a luxurious growth. I yielded so far as to reduce the flowing appendage by half its length. Not one fraction of an inch did it ever grow again!

We always tried to persuade ourselves that our toys had life. We quite realised that their life was different from our life, or from Gyp's, or Minnie's. But we felt that they had a kind of mystic *toy* life; and we thought it probable that at night, when the house was still, they disported silently on the carpet; that the dolls rode frantic races on the London Horse; that the cows (I had a fawn and a brindled cow) browsed in secret pastures under the furniture; that my white goat climbed the back of the sofa as if it were a crag.

Once I crept out of bed and downstairs, although sore afraid, to see these esoteric gambols; but all the toys were very quiet. I hoped then that I had come too soon or too late. I could not bring myself to believe that they were merely wooden, without any quickening of joy anywhere within them. But fear of the dark staircase would never allow me to steal down to see them again.

The night at that time was always terrible to me. I thought the house was peopled by strange beings, uncanny and terrifying. My mother and Auntie Margaret knew that visions of some gruesome sort (I never coherently described them) affrighted my sleep, and they used to sit by me if I was restless.

Often and often did Auntie Margaret steal up to me when she was visiting us, and sit silently beside my bed. How good it was to hear her step! And when my mother did not come (thinking I was asleep like the others) how often have I lain tossing from one side to another, trying to call their names, yet fearing to raise my voice lest it might attract the notice of some grisly thing outside the door!

Only when my father and mother came to bed would relief come to me. I used to pray as my mother taught me, but the prayers never drove away the spectres. Only when dawn began to come greyly through the window-blinds did they creep back to their lairs.[2]

The main events at issue in this remarkable passage are the simultaneous coming into existence of two things in Patrick's young life. The first is a wooden hobby-horse; the second is the birth of his brother Willie. The manner in which this story is told obviously suggests that the two events were somehow linked in the infant's mind, and the ensuing action describes his coming to understand what was, in fact, a major psychological upheaval.

Pearse labeled this story an "adventure" in contrast to those "myths" which he had experienced before. The suggestion is that he regarded these incidents as unique, considerably different and of significantly greater importance than those he had known before. There is a sense in which the boy remembered the incident in a way that was also different, a way that gave it meaning, unlike the myths he was so careful to dismiss.

The adventure is that of a boy just barely over two years old. It is the "coming" of a horse named Dobbin. The use of a colloquialism for sexual orgasm is understandable when one considers the various forms of the verb "to come." It can be used to indicate where one has *come from*, in terms of location, existence, origin, background, genealogical lineage, and so forth. To come can be used to indicate a *coming forth* such as the coming forth of a rosebud. It used to be a commonly used expression concerning the age of a horse, as in "she was coming into her sixth year." Thus the verb "to come" has a variety (certainly not exhausted here) of meanings, most of which discuss coming with emanational or existential connotations that support the colloquial term's sexual nature.

2. Ibid., 16–18.

The combination of the horse with the sexual connotation of the word "coming" seems especially significant in this case. Erik Erikson maintains that the age of two is especially important in the formation of autonomous identity. That is to say, autonomy is established in the second or "early infant stage," out of feelings of shame and doubt at this age, when the central psychological crisis is over bodily function.[3] The orientation of a child from two to three years old is necessarily anal, concerned with the issues of control, enjoyment, and elimination. The child's attention is invested in the psychological problem of gaining a sense of self-control while still maintaining self-esteem.[4] Pride and autonomy accompany the feelings of victory over one's bodily function, but the inevitable failures produce shame and doubt, not only about one's abilities, but about the nature of the child's relationship with its parents.[5] Erikson maintains that the question of trust that has been dealt with as an infant is threatened by the parents' role as the guardians of values and standards of social behavior.[6] The parent must tread the narrow line between firm direction on the one hand and allowing freedom on the other.[7] Anality centers on the issues of holding back versus letting go, and learning to do each in an appropriate way. The issue focuses on the very heart of human values and mores, as well as law and order.[8]

In this instance Patrick was struggling not only with the anal problem of controlling his biological urges, but also with a subconscious awareness of his own sexuality. The Horse is the critical figure in this regard, as it represents unbridled passion and the powers of procreation.[9] Dobbin, a hobbyhorse made from living substance, can

---

3. Erikson, "Identity and the Life Cycle," 67–78.

4. Ibid., 71.　　　　　　　　　5. Ibid.

6. Ibid., 71–72.　　　　　　　7. Ibid., 72–73.

8. Ibid., 74–78.

9. See relevant passages of Ernest Jones, *On the Nightmare* (London: Hogarth Press, 1931; reprint ed., 1949) on the symbolic meaning of the horse in dreams.

also be seen as a demonic sexuality waiting to break loose from its superficial incorporeality.[10] Patrick describes the horse in detail, marvels at its beauty and symmetry, but suggests that Dobbin is just a little fearsome as well. Dobbin is full of potentiality, huge, looming, brimming with awesome and mysterious power. Patrick pays special attention to Dobbin's great height and shape, and his description of Dobbin is palpably sensual. Dobbin is grey, a reflection of his heroic nature and gallantry.

As significant as Dobbin is, nothing is more awesome or mysterious than the way he is delivered into the world. He is created, *made,* out of living material by Patrick's father. The work is done a little mysteriously, away from home when the shop was closed. The choice of the word heroic to describe the effort involved in creating Dobbin is peculiar—a recognition of the boy's admiration for the man who made the horse. Dobbin arrives in the arms of his creator. The father gives Patrick the horse and names it, as if he himself were God. The infant boy recognizes this power and likens it to that of the Creator.

At the end of this passage, Patrick talks about his fear of the dark and the strange beings who peopled the house in the dark. His fears over these visions are nearly overwhelming and prayers fail to stop them. Nothing is as effective against these fears as his father going to bed with his mother. The very thought of his father consoles Patrick, which indicates how much the boy needed his father and how much he loved him.

The distance between James Pearse and all of his children was probably not unusual for the time. Nonetheless, the infrequency of Patrick's references to him is striking and leads one to conclude that the separation was great between the father and his son. This is not to imply that there existed an antagonism between them. Patrick

10. Ibid. Jones maintains that the hobby-horse is a reflection of the latent demonic power of the passion of the horse symbol.

invariably spoke well and affectionately of his father, and in most cases related stories about James Pearse with a sense of poignancy. What separated the two was less personal than it was a reflection of mutual inability: both the boy and his father seem shy. The problem was that the boy never received enough affection from James and was being smothered by the attentions of the female side of his family.

What Patrick appears to have wanted in this recollection was the abiding, omnipotent, protective, and quietly benevolent presence of his father. While James probably cared for his son as best he could, Patrick's need far outstripped what went on between them.

After Dobbin arrives, Patrick's mother, "ill" in the child's mind, comes down the stair to see the toy horse. The immediate consequence of this in Patrick's mind appears to be the birth of his brother. Thus Dobbin and Patrick's sexuality are associated in Patrick's mind. Compounding the problem is the way his mother has to "steal" down to see Patrick's new companion—a kind of illicit interest is implied. So Patrick has also associated the coming of Dobbin and his brother. But Dobbin has to be quieted when Willie's birth nearly causes his mother's death, and only occasionally may Patrick ride the horse, which usually must remain quiet behind a door. He and his sister watch the fire and the family pets while waiting for developments. [11]

In this section of "New Arrivals" Patrick has come to an awareness of his sexuality. The discovery is further compounded by his implied responsibility he has for both his brother's birth and his mother's near death. The psychological problem is oriented around his need to control that power and the noncooperative nature of the horse.[12] The horse is barely controllable, but Patrick lets us know that he later "rode him to many a battle." Thus the boy's exercise of his

11. P. H. Pearse, "My Childhood," 17.
12. Erikson, *Childhood and Society*, 85ff.

horse's passion has caused him to be shamed by his failure to be a good steward and control Dobbin.

When his mother at last comes down from her room, she is pale and weak. She is not too ill to bless Dobbin with a kiss. The kiss serves as a benediction and an absolution of wrongdoing. Approved of and sanctified, Dobbin comes out of hiding and is ridden with great vigor. Patrick returns his mother's favor by accepting Willie, even though he is careful to let us know of his privileged and dominant position vis-à-vis his brother.

Several points about the later parts of this passage stand out. One is the nature of this boy's acceptance of his infant brother. Young Willie has been taken away, perhaps to protect him from catching his mother's illness. Patrick, though now accepting of his brother, refuses as yet to share what he alone can do—ride the horse. Thus, though Willie is accepted, his acceptance seems to be somewhat provisional and depends on his riding of Dobbin.

It is important to note that while Patrick received the most honored male name in Irish nationalist culture, Willie received one of the most ignominious. The name William was associated in Irish history with two separate English conquerors. The family's lifelong use of the diminutive form, Willie, served to reinforce the subordinate position of the younger brother, symbolized in the awful historical association of his name. Patrick's description of his relationship with his brother is distinctly patronizing and would continue to be so in adulthood. He glows over him, a result not only of their intimacy, but also of the older brother's being comfortable with his dominant role. Nothing could indicate this more than Patrick's discussion of his own birth in relation to his brother's, a not-so-gentle reminder that he was first.

Second, the passage brings into view Patrick's relationship with his older sister, Margaret. She comes off as a threatening figure, constantly killing off people (dolls?) and forcing Patrick to take them to be buried at Glasnevin Cemetery. She inhibits Patrick, attempting to control both him and Dobbin, and Margaret uses the horse for "base" purposes. He claims she had been a "sufficiently loving companion," a less than hearty endorsement for Pearse, who was effusive in expressing his feelings for his family. In the end Margaret makes Patrick think that the "London" horse's tail is regenerative and fools him into cutting it. The issue between sister and brother is over control of the horse and how it is to be used. In contrast with his relationships with his mother and his brother, both of whom defer to his wishes, Margaret orders Patrick about and in effect gets him symbolically to castrate himself in a denial of his sexual potential.

The trips to the cemetery with Dobbin seem especially important in light of Patrick's adult life. He has to tie his horse to a cart, cover him in black, and make him pull the cart full of bodies to Glasnevin. Dobbin, the early expression of Patrick's sexuality, is relegated to a graveyard detail. It seems to represent an identification of the procreative, life-giving forces within Pearse with a noble mission that resulted in death. Patrick is forced to go on these journeys by his sister; he later does so on his own. His thoughts about his childhood experiences at Glasnevin Cemetery appear highly significant in light of the famous eulogies he later gave there.

This section of "My Childhood" definitively illustrates that Pearse had long associated life with death. His discovery of sexuality seems related in his mind to the near death of his mother. His conflict is between his productive instincts and the potential harm that could result from them. Though his mother's acceptance of the horse and its power is implied, Patrick acquiesces in tying the horse symbolically to life-denying activity.

Selected Bibliography

Published Writings of Patrick Pearse

Collected Works of Padraic H. Pearse. Edited by Desmond Ryan. Dublin: Phoenix Press, Ltd., n.d., but published 1917–22.

The Letters of P. H. Pearse. Edited by Seamas O'Buachalla. Atlantic Highlands, NJ: Humanities Press, 1980.

"My Childhood and Youth." In *The Home-Life of Padraig Pearse*, ed. Mary Brigid Pearse, 7–29. Dublin: Mercier Press, 1934; paperback, 1979.

Pearse and Rossa. Edited by Kevin T. McEneany. New York: At-Swim Press, 1982.

Plays, Stories, Poems. Edited by Desmond Ryan. Dublin: Phoenix Press, Ltd., n.d., but published 1917–22. Reprint ed., 1966.

Political Writings and Speeches. Edited by Desmond Ryan. Dublin: Phoenix Press, Ltd., n.d., but published 1917–22. Reprint ed., 1966.

St. Enda's and Its Founder. Edited by Desmond Ryan. Dublin: Phoenix Press, Ltd., n.d., but published 1917–22.

Scribhinni. Edited by Desmond Ryan. Dublin: Phoenix Press, Ltd., n.d., but published 1917–22.

A Significant Irish Educationalist: The Educational Writings of P. H. Pearse. Edited by Seamas O'Buachalla. Dublin: Mercier Press, 1980.

Songs of the Irish Rebels and Specimens from an Irish Anthology; Some Aspects of Irish Literature; Three Lectures on Gaelic Topics. Edited by Desmond Ryan. Dublin: Phoenix Press, Ltd., n.d., but published 1917–22.

General and Secondary Works

Adas, Michael. *Prophets of Rebellion*. Chapel Hill: University of North Carolina Press, 1979; Cambridge: Cambridge University Press, 1987.

Alexander, Yonah, and Alan O'Day, eds. *Ireland's Terrorist Dilemma*. Dardrecht: Martinus Nijhoff, 1986.

————. *The Irish Terrorism Experience.* Aldershot: Dartmouth Press, 1991.

Alter, Peter. "Symbols of Irish Nationalism." *Studia Hibernica* 14 (1974): 104–23.

————. "Traditions of Violence in Irish Nationalism." In *Social Protest, Violence, and Terror in Nineteenth and Twentieth Century Europe,* ed. Wolfgang J. Mommsen, 137–54. New York: St. Martin's Press, 1982.

Arnstein, Walter. *The Bradlaugh Case: Atheism, Sex, and Politics among the Late Victorians.* Columbia, MO: University of Missouri Press, 1983.

Bakhtin, Mikhail. *Rabelais and His World.* Translated by Helene Iswolsky. Boston: M.I.T. Press, 1968; paperback, Bloomington: University of Indiana Press, 1984.

Banks, J. A. *Prosperity and Parenthood: A Study of Family Planning among the Victorian Middle Classes.* London: Routledge and Kegan Paul, 1954.

————. *Victorian Values: Secularism and the Size of Families.* London: Routledge and Kegan Paul, 1981.

Beck, A. T., H. L. P. Resnick, and D. Letterieri, eds. *The Prediction of Suicide.* Bowie, MD: Charles Press, 1974; paperback, 1986.

Becker, Jean Jacques. *Comment les français sont entrés dans la guerre.* Paris, 1977.

Beckett, J. C. *The Making of Modern Ireland.* New York: Alfred A. Knopf, 1963; reprint ed., 1966.

Behmler, George. *Child Abuse and Moral Reform in England, 1870-1908.* Stanford: Stanford University Press, 1982.

Bell, J. Bowyer. *The Secret Army: The I.R.A. 1916-1979.* Dublin: The Academy Press, 1970; Cambridge, MA, 1983.

Beresford, David. *Ten Men Dead: The Story of the 1981 Irish Hunger Strike.* London: Grafton Books, 1987.

Berman, David, Stephen Lalor, and Brian Torode. "The Theology of the I.R.A." *Studies* 72 (Summer 1983): 137–44.

Bettleheim, Bruno. *The Uses of Enchantment: The Meaning and Importance of Fairy Tales.* New York: Alfred A. Knopf, 1977

Bishop, Patrick, and Eamonn Mallie. *The Provisional IRA.* London: William Heinemann, 1987; paperback, 1988.

Boyce, D. George. *Nationalism in Ireland.* Baltimore: Johns Hopkins University Press, 1982.

Brady, John. *Catholics and Catholicism in the Eighteenth-Century Press.* Maynooth, 1965.

Brooke, Rupert. *Letters from America.* London: Sidgewick and Jackson, 1916.

————. *The Letters of Rupert Brooke.* Edited by Geoffrey Keynes. London: Faber and Faber, 1968.

————. *The Poetical Works of Rupert Brooke.* Edited by Geoffrey Keynes. London: Faber and Faber, 1946; paperback, 1970; reprint ed., 1981.

Brophy, Brigid. *Black Ship to Hell.* New York: Harcourt, Brace and World, 1962.

Brown, Malcolm. *The Politics of Irish Literature.* Seattle: University of Washington Press, 1972.

Buckland, Patrick. *A History of Northern Ireland.* Dublin: Gill and Macmillan, 1981.

Bussy, F. M. *Irish Conspiracies: Recollections of John Mallon.* London: Everett, 1910.

Campbell, Joseph. *The Hero with a Thousand Faces.* Princeton: Princeton University Press, 1949.

Carleton, William. *Traits and Stories of the Irish Peasantry.* 4 vols. New York: Books for Libraries Press, 1971.

Carpenter, Andrew, ed. *Place, Personality and the Irish Writer.* New York: Barnes and Noble Books, 1977.

Carty, Xavier. *In Bloody Protest: The Tragedy of Patrick Pearse.* Dublin: Able Press, 1978.

Casement, Roger. *The Black Diaries of Roger Casement.* Edited by Peter Singleton-Gates and Maurice Girodins. New York, 1958.

Coakley, John. "Patrick Pearse and the 'Noble Lie' of Irish Nationalism." *Studies* 72 (Summer 1983): 119–36.

Coffey, Thomas M. *Agony at Easter: The 1916 Uprising.* New York: Macmillan, 1969.

Collins, Tom. *The Irish Hunger Strike.* Dublin: White Island Book Co., 1986.

Comerford, R. V. "Patriotism as Pastime: The Appeal of Fenianism in the Mid-1860s." *Irish Historical Studies* 22, 87 (1981): 239–50.

Coogan, Tim Pat. *The I.R.A.* Glasgow: Pall Mall Press, 1970; Fontana Press, 1980.

————. *On the Blanket: The H-Block Story.* Dublin: Ward River Press, 1980.

Cooke, Patrick. *Sceal Scoil Eanna.* Dublin, 1986.

Corfe, Thomas. *The Phoenix Park Murders.* London: Hodder and Stoughton, 1968.

Cronin, Sean. *Irish Nationalism: Its Roots and Ideology.* Dublin: The Academy Press, 1980.

————. *Our Own Red Blood: The Story of the 1916 Rising.* Dublin: Irish Freedom Press, 1966; rev. ed. 1976.

————, ed. *The McGarrity Papers*. Tralee: Anvil Books, 1972.

Curran, C. P. "Griffith, MacNeill and Pearse." *Studies* (Spring 1966): 21–28.

Curtis, L. P. "Moral and Physical Force: The Language of Violence in Irish Nationalism." *Journal of British Studies* 27, 2 (April 1988): 150–89.

Daly, Martin [Stephen MacKenna pseud.]. *Memories of the Dead*. Dublin, 1917.

Daly, Mary. *Dublin, The Deposed Capital: A Social and Economic History 1860–1914*. Cork: Cork University Press, 1985.

Dangerfield, George. *The Damnable Question: A Study in Anglo-Irish Relations*. Boston: Little, Brown, 1976.

————. *The Strange Death of Liberal England*. New York: G. P. Putnam's Sons, 1935; Perigee Books, 1980.

de Búrca, Marcus. *The G.A.A.: A History of the Gaelic Athletic Association*. Dublin: Cumann Luthchleas Gael, 1980.

Devoy, John. *Recollections of an Irish Rebel*. New York: Chas. Young Co., 1929.

Diner, Hasia. *Erin's Daughters in America*. Baltimore: Johns Hopkins University Press, 1983.

Donnelly, James S. "The Whiteboy Movement, 1761–65." *Irish Historical Studies* 21, 81 (March 1978): 20–54.

Dunleavy, Janet Egleson, and Gareth W. Dunleavy. *Douglas Hyde: A Maker of Modern Ireland*. Berkeley: University of California Press, 1991.

Ecksteins, Modris. *Rite of Spring*. Boston: Houghton Mifflin, 1989; paperback, 1989.

Edwards, Owen Dudley, and Fergus Pyle, eds. *1916: The Easter Rising*. London: Victor Gollancz, 1968.

Edwards, Owen Dudley, and Bernard Ransom, eds. *James Connolly: Selected Political Writings*. New York: Grove Press, 1974.

Edwards, Ruth Dudley. "The Decline and Fall of the Irish Nationalists at Westminster." In *The Making of 1916: Studies in the History of the Rising*, ed. Kevin B. Nowlan, 127–56. Dublin: The Stationary Office, 1969.

————. *Patrick Pearse: The Triumph of Failure*. London: Victor Gollancz, 1977; paperback, Faber and Faber, 1979; rev. ed., 1990.

Erikson, Erik. *Childhood and Society*. 2d ed. New York: W. W. Norton, 1963.

————. *Identity and the Life Cycle*. New York: International Press, 1959; paperback, W. W. Norton, 1979.

————. *Life History and the Historical Moment*. New York, W. W. Norton, 1975.

————. *Young Man Luther: A Study in Psychoanalysis and History.* New York: W. W. Norton, 1958; paperback, 1962.

Evans, Glen, and Norman L. Farberow. *The Encyclopedia of Suicide.* New York: Facts on File Publications, 1988.

Fallis, Richard. *The Irish Renaissance.* Syracuse: Syracuse University Press, 1977.

Fallon, Charlotte. "Civil War Hunger Strikes: Women and Men." *Eire-Ireland* 22, no. 3 (Fall 1987): 75–91.

Farberow, N. L., ed. *The Cry for Help.* New York: McGraw Hill, 1961; paperback, 1965.

Feehan, John M. *Bobby Sands and the Tragedy of Northern Ireland.* Dublin, 1986.

Fitzgerald, Desmond. "The Geography of Irish Nationalism, 1920–1921." *Past and Present* 78 (1978): 113–44.

Fitzgerald, Garrett. "The Significance of 1916." *Studies* (Spring 1966): 29–37.

Fitzpatrick, David. *Politics and Irish Life, 1913–1921: Provincial Experience of War and Revolution.* Dublin: Gill and Macmillan, 1977.

Foster, John Wilson. *Fictions of the Irish Literary Revival: A Changeling Act.* Syracuse: Syracuse University Press, 1987.

Foster, R. F. *Modern Ireland, 1600–1972.* London: Oxford University Press, 1988.

Freud, Sigmund. *Beyond the Pleasure Principle.* Translated by James Strachey. London: Hogarth Press, 1919.

————. *Civilization and Its Discontents.* Translated by James Strachey. New York: W. W. Norton, 1962.

————. "Group Psychology and the Analysis of the Ego." In *The Standard Edition of the Complete Psychological Works of Sigmund Freud,* ed. James Strachey, 18: 69–143 London: Hogarth Press, 1953–1974.

Fromm, Erich. *The Anatomy of Human Destructiveness.* New York: Holt, Rhinehart and Winston, 1973; paperback, Fawcett Crest Books, 1975.

————. *Escape from Freedom.* New York: Holt, Rhinehart and Winston, 1941; paperback, Avon Books, 1969.

Fussell, Paul. *The Great War and Modern Memory.* New York: Oxford University Press, 1975; paperback, 1977.

Garvin, Tom. *The Evolution of Irish Nationalist Politics,* Dublin: Gill and Macmillan, 1981.

————. *Nationalist Revolutionaries in Ireland 1858-1928,* Oxford: Oxford University Press, 1987.

————. "The Politics of Language and Literature in Pre-Independence Ireland." *Irish Political Studies* 2 (1987): 49–63.

————. "Priests and Patriots: Irish Separatism and Fear of the Modern, 1890–1914." *Irish Historical Studies* 25, 97 (May 1986): 67–81.

Gilley, S. "Pearse's Sacrifice: Christ and Cúchulainn Crucified and Risen in the Easter Rising, 1916." In *Ireland's Terrorist Dilemma*, ed. Yonah Alexander and Alan O'Day, 29–48. Dardrecht: Martinus Nijhoff, 1986.

Goldring, Maurice. *Faith of Our Fathers: The Formation of Irish Nationalist Ideology 1890–1930*. Dublin: Repsol Press, 1982.

Greaves, C. Desmond. *The Life and Times of James Connolly*. New York: International Publishers, 1971.

Gwynn, Denis. "Patrick Pearse." *Dublin Review* (January-March 1923): 92–105.

Hachey, Thomas E., and Lawrence J. McCaffrey, eds. *Perspectives on Irish Nationalism*. Lexington, 1989.

Hassell, Christopher. *Rupert Brooke*. New York: Harcourt, Brace and World, 1964.

Haverty, Anne. *Constance Markievicz: An Independent Life*. London: Pandora Books, 1988.

Hayden, Mary. "My Recollections of Padraig Pearse." In *The Home Life of Padraig Pearse*, ed. Mary Brigid Pearse, 113–16. Dublin: Mercier Press, 1934; paperback, 1979.

Hayes, James. *Patrick H. Pearse: Storyteller*. Dublin: Talbot Press, 1919.

Hegarty, P. S. *A History of Ireland Under the Act of Union*. London: Metheun, 1952; reprint ed., New York: Kraus Reprint, 1969.

Heaney, Seamus. *Selected Poems, 1965–1975*. London: Faber and Faber, 1980; paperback, 1981.

Hobsbawm, Eric. *Labouring Men*. London, 1971; paperback, 1973.

————. *Primitive Rebels*. New York: Frederick A. Praeger, 1959.

Hobson, Bulmer. *History of the Irish Volunteers*. 2 vols. Dublin: O'Laughlin, Murphy, and Boland, Ltd., 1917.

————. *Ireland Yesterday and Tomorrow*. Tralee: Anvil Books, 1968.

————. *A Short History of the Irish Volunteers*. Dublin: The Candle Press, 1918.

Holland, Jack. *Too Long a Sacrifice: Life and Death in Northern Ireland Since 1969*. New York: Dodd, Mead and Co., 1981; paperback, 1981.

Hughes, H. Stuart. *Consciousness and Society: The Reorientation of European Social Thought*. New York: Random House, 1958; paperback, 1961; rev. ed., 1971.

Horgan, J. J. *From Parnell to Pearse*. Dublin, 1948.

Howarth, Herbert. *The Irish Writers 1880–1890*. London, 1955.

Hutchinson, John. *The Dynamics of Cultural Nationalism: The Gaelic*

Revival and the Creation of the Irish National State. Boston: Allen and Unwin, 1987.

Hutton, Patrick H. *The Cult of the Revolutionary Tradition: The Blanquists in French Politics, 1864–1893*. Berkeley: University of California Press, 1981.

Hynes, Samuel. *A War Imagined*. Princeton: Princeton University Press, 1990.

Inglis, Brian. *Roger Casement*. London: Hodder and Stoughton, 1973; paperback, London: Coronet Books, 1974.

Jalland, Patricia. *The Liberals and Ireland*. Brighton, 1980.

Johnston, Edith Mary. *Ireland in the Eighteenth Century*. Dublin: Gill and Macmillan, 1974.

Jones, Ernest. *The Life and Work of Sigmund Freud*. Edited and abridged by Lionel Trilling and Stephen Marcus. New York: Basic Books, 1957.

———. *On the Nightmare*. London: Hogarth Press, 1931, reprint ed., 1949.

———. *Psycho-Myth, Psycho-History: Essays in Applied Psychoanalysis*. 2 vols. New York: Stonehill Publishing, 1974.

Jones, Francis P. *History of the Sinn Fein Movement and the Irish Rebellion of 1916*. 3d ed. New York: P. J. Kennedy and Sons, 1920.

Joy, Maurice, ed. *The Irish Rebellion of 1916 and Its Martyrs: Erin's Tragic Easter*. New York: Devin-Adair, 1916.

Jung, Carl G. *Psychology of the Unconscious*. Translated by Beatrice Hinkle. New York: Dodd, Mead and Co., 1916.

———. "The Transformation Symbolism of the Mass." In *Psyche and Symbol*, ed. Violet S. de Lazlo, 22–52. New York: Random House, 1958.

———. *The Undiscovered Self*. New York: Little, Brown, 1957.

Kain, R. "A Diary of Easter Week: One Dubliner's Experience." *Irish University Review* 10, 2 (Autumn 1980): 200–211.

Kearney, Richard. "Faith and Fatherland." *Ireland: Dependence and Independence*. RTE/UCD Lectures. *The Crane Bag* (1984).

———. "The I.R.A.'s Strategy of Failure." *The Crane Bag* 4, 2 (1980): 62–70.

Kedourie, E. *Nationalism*. 3d ed., London, 1966.

Kee, Robert. *The Bold Fenian Men*. First published in a single volume under the title *The Green Flag*. London: Weidenfield and Nicholson, 1972; Quartet Books, 1976.

———. *That Most Distressful Country*. London: Weidenfield and Nicholson, 1972; Quartet Books, 1976.

Kelly, James. "We Were Framed." *Hibernia* (31 July 1980).

Kennelly, Brendan, ed. *The Penguin Book of Irish Verse.* Baltimore: Penguin Books, 1970.

Keogh, Dermot. *Twentieth Century Ireland: Unequal Achievement.* Dublin: Gill and Macmillan, 1988.

Kilcullen, James. "Appreciation: Headmaster of St. Enda's." *Eire-Ireland* (Summer 1967): 72–78.

Kohn, Hans. *The Idea of Nationalism.* New York: Macmillan, 1961.

———. *The Mind of Germany.* New York: Alfred A. Knopf, Inc., 1960.

Laffan, Michael. "Violence and Terror in Twentieth-Century Ireland: I.R.B. and I.R.A." In *Social Protest, Violence, and Terror in Nineteenth and Twentieth Century Europe,* ed. Wolfgang Mommsen and Gerhard Hirshfield, 155–74. New York: St. Martin's Press, 1982.

Laing, R. D. *The Divided Self: An Existential Study of Sanity and Madness.* New York: Tavistock Publications, 1959; paperback, 1965; reprint ed., 1977.

Lazlo, Violet S. de, ed. *Psyche and Symbol.* Garden City, NY: Doubleday, 1958.

Lecky, W. E. H. *The History of European Morals from Augustine to Charlemagne.* 2 vols. New York, 1872.

———. *A History of Ireland in the Eighteenth Century.* Chicago: University of Chicago Press, 1972.

Lee, Joseph. "In Search of Patrick Pearse." In *Revising the Rising,* ed. Máirín Ní Dhonnchadha and Theo Dorgan, 122–38. Derry: Field Day, 1991.

———. *Ireland 1912-1985: Politics and Society.* Cambridge: Cambridge University Press, 1989; paperback, 1989.

———. *The Modernisation of Irish Society: 1848-1918.* Dublin: Gill and Macmillan, 1976.

Lemass, Seán F. "I Remember 1916." *Studies* (Spring 1966): 7–9.

Le Roux, Louis N. *Patrick H. Pearse.* Translated by Desmond Ryan. Dublin: Talbot Press, 1932.

———. *Tom Clarke and the Irish Freedom Movement.* Cork: Talbot Press, 1936.

Loftus, Richard J. *Nationalism in Anglo-Irish Poetry.* Madison: University of Wisconsin Press, 1964.

Longley, Edna. "The Rising, the Somme and Irish Memory." In *Revising the Rising,* ed. Máirín Ní Dhonnchadha and Theo Dorgan, 29–49. Derry: Field Day, 1991.

Lynch, Diarmuid. *The I.R.B. and the 1916 Rising.* Edited by Florence O'Donoghue. Cork: Mercier Press, 1957.

Lyons, F. S. L. *Charles Stewart Parnell.* New York: Oxford University Press, 1977.

————. *Culture and Anarchy in Ireland, 1890-1939*. Oxford: Clarendon Press, 1979; paperback, 1982.

————. *Ireland Since the Famine*. London: Oxford University Press, 1971; paperback, 1973.

————. *The Irish Parliamentary Party, 1890-1910*. London: Oxford University Press, 1951.

————. *John Dillon*. Chicago: University of Chicago Press, 1968.

Mac An Tsoir. "Padraig MacPiaras-I." *Comhair* 21, no. 5 (Beltaine, 1962): 26-27.

Mac Aonshusa, Proinsias. *Quotations from P. H. Pearse*. Cork: Mercier Press, 1979.

McCaffrey, Lawrence J. *The Irish Question, 1800-1922*. Lexington: University of Kentucky Press, 1968.

McCardle, Dorothy. "James Connolly and Patrick Pearse." In *The Shaping of Modern Ireland*, ed. Conor Cruise O'Brien. Toronto: University of Toronto Press, 1960.

McCartney, Donal. "Hyde, D. P. Moran and Irish Ireland." In *Leaders and Men of the Easter Rising: Dublin, 1916*, ed. F. X. Martin, 36-51. Dublin: Harper and Row, 1967.

————. "The Sinn Fein Movement." *The Making of 1916: Studies in the History of the Rising*, ed. Kevin B. Nowlan, 31-51. Dublin: Stationary Office, 1969.

McCay, Hedley. *Padraic Pearse: A New Biography*. Cork: Mercier Press, 1966.

MacDonagh, Augustine. "To Make a Right Rose Tree: Reflections on the Poetry of 1916." *Studies* 55, 217 (Spring 1966): 38-50.

MacDonagh, D. "Patrick Pearse." *An Cosantair* (August 1945): 46-62.

————. "Plunkett and MacDonagh." In *Leaders and Men of the Easter Rising: Dublin, 1916*, ed. F. X. Martin, 165-76. London: Harper and Row, 1967.

MacDonagh, Oliver. *Ireland: The Union and Its Aftermath*. Englewood Cliffs, NJ: Prentice Hall, 1968; rev. ed., London: Allen and Unwin, 1979; paperback, 1979.

————. *States of Mind: A Study of Anglo-Irish Conflict 1780-1980*. London: Allen and Unwin, 1983.

McGill, P. J. "Padraic Pearse in Donegal." *Donegal Annual* 3 (1966): 67-82.

Mac Giolla Choille, Breandan, ed. *Intelligence Notes, 1913-16*. Dublin, 1966.

Mack, John E. *Prince of Our Disorder: The Life of T. E. Lawrence*. Boston: Little, Brown, 1976; paperback, 1976.

McGloughlin, Emily Pearse. "An Elder Sister's Recollections of Padraig

Pearse." In *The Home Life of Padraig Pearse*, ed. Mary Brigid Pearse, 43 – 45. Dublin: Mercier Press, 1934; paperback, 1979.

McHugh, Roger, ed. *Dublin 1916*. Dublin: Arlington Books, 1966.

Mann, Thomas. *The Letters of Thomas Mann: 1889-1955*. Translated and edited by Richard and Clara Winston. New York: Alfred A. Knopf, 1971.

Mansergh, Nicholas. *The Irish Question, 1840-1921*. 3d ed. Toronto: University of Toronto Press, 1966; paperback, 1975.

Marcus, Stephen. *The Other Victorians: A Study of Sexuality and Pornography in Mid-Nineteenth Century England*. New York: W. W. Norton, 1964.

Marreco, Anne. *The Rebel Countess: The Life and Times of Countess Markievicz*. London: Wiedenfield and Nicholson, 1967; paperback, 1967.

Martin, Augustine. "To Make a Right Rose Tree." *Studies* (Spring 1966): 38 – 50.

Martin, F. X. "1916 — Revolution or Evolution." In *Leaders and Men of the Easter Rising: Dublin, 1916*, ed. F. X. Martin, 239 – 52. London: Harper and Row, 1967.

———. "1916 — Myth, Fact, and Mystery." *Studia Hibernica* 7 (1967): 7 – 126.

———. "The 1916 Rising — Coup d'etat or Bloody Protest?" *Studia Hibernica* 8 (1968): 106 – 37.

———. ed. *The Irish Volunteers, 1913-1915*. Dublin: James Duffy and Co., Ltd., 1963.

———. ed. *Leaders and Men of the Easter Rising: Dublin, 1916*. Dublin: Harper and Row, 1967.

Marx, Karl, and Friedrich Engels. *Ireland and the Irish Question*. London, International Publishers, 1978.

Meacham, Standish. *A Life Apart: The English Working Class 1890-1914*. Cambridge, England: Cambridge University Press, 1977.

Menninger, Karl. *Man Against Himself*. New York: Harcourt, Brace and World, 1938; paperback, 1966.

Menninger, W. C., and Leon Chidester. "The Role of Financial Loss in the Precipitation of Mental Illness." *Journal of the American Medical Association* (6 May, 1933).

Mommsen, Wolfgang, and Gerhard Hirshfield, eds. *Social Protest, Violence, and Terror in Nineteenth and Twentieth Century Europe*. New York: St. Martin's Press, 1982.

Montague, H. Patrick. *The Saints and Martyrs of Ireland*. Gerard's Cross: Colin Smythe, 1981.

Moran, Seán Farrell. "Patrick Pearse and the European Revolt Against

Reason." *Journal of the History of Ideas* 50, 4 (October-December 1989): 625–43.

———. "Patrick Pearse, The Easter Rising, and Irish History." *Graduate Review* (Summer 1989): 2–19.

———. "Patrick Pearse and Patriotic Soteriology: The Irish Republican Tradition and the Sanctification of Political Self-Immolation." In *The Irish Terrorism Experience*, ed. Yonah Alexander and Alan O'Day, 9–29. Aldershot: Dartmouth Press, 1991.

Morgan, Austen. *James Connolly: A Political Biography*. Manchester: Manchester University Press, 1988.

Munck, Ronnie. "Rethinking Irish Nationalism: The Republican Dimension." *Canadian Review of Studies in Nationalism* 14, 1 (1986), 31–48.

Murphy, Brian P. *Patrick Pearse and the Lost Republican Ideal*. Dublin: James Duffy, 1991.

Murphy, John A. *Ireland in the Twentieth Century*. Dublin: Gill and Macmillan, 1975.

Neeson, Eoin. *The Book of Irish Saints*. Cork: Mercier Press, 1967.

Newsinger, John. "'I Bring Not Peace But a Sword': The Religious Motif in the Irish War of Independence." *Journal of Modern History* 13, 3 (July 1978): 609–28.

Ní Dhonnchadha, Máirín, and Theo Durgan, eds. *Revising the Rising*. Derry: Field Day, 1991.

Norstedt, Johann A. *Thomas MacDonagh*. Charlottesville: University of Virginia Press, 1980.

Nowlan, Kevin B. *The Politics of Repeal, 1841–50*. London, 1965.

———. "Tom Clarke, MacDermott, and the I.R.B." In *Leaders and Men of the Easter Rising: Dublin, 1916*, ed. F. X. Martin, 104–22. Dublin: Harper and Row, 1967.

———, ed. *The Making of 1916: Studies in the History of the Rising*. Dublin: The Stationary Office, 1969.

———, and O'Connell, Maurice, eds. *Daniel O'Connell, Portrait of a Radical*. New York: Fordham University Press, 1985.

O'Balance, Edgar. *Terror in Ireland*. Novato: Presidio Press, 1981.

O'Braonair, Cathoir. "Poets of the Insurrection II—Patrick Pearse." *Studies* 5 (September 1916): 339–52.

O'Brien, Conor Cruise. "1891–1916." In *The Shaping of Modern Ireland*, ed. Conor Cruise O'Brien, 13–24. Toronto: University of Toronto Press, 1960.

———. *States of Ireland*. London: Hutchinson, 1972; paperback, 1973.

———, ed. *The Shaping of Modern Ireland*. Toronto: University of Toronto Press, 1960.

O'Brien, Joseph. *Dear, Dirty Dublin: 1899-1916* Berkeley: University of California Press, 1982.

O'Brien, William, and Desmond Ryan, eds. *Devoy's Post Bag, 1871-1928.* 2 vols. Dublin: C. J. Fallon, 1953.

O'Broin, Leon. *Dublin Castle and the 1916 Rising.* Dublin: Helicon Books, 1966; rev. ed., New York: New York University Press, 1971.

———. "The Invincibles." In *Secret Societies in Ireland*, ed. T. Desmond Williams, 113-26. Dublin: Gill and Macmillan, 1973.

———. *Michael Collins.* Dublin: Gill and Macmillan, 1980.

———. *The Revolutionary Underground: The Story of the Irish Republican Brotherhood, 1858-1924.* Totowa, NJ: Rowman and Littlefield, 1976.

O'Casey, Seán. *The Story of the Irish Citizen Army.* London, 1919; reprint edition, 1980.

O'Connor, Emmet. *Syndicalism in Ireland, 1917-1923.* Cork: Cork University Press, 1988.

O'Day, Alan, ed. *Reactions to Irish Nationalism.* London: Hambledown Press, 1987.

O'Driscoll, Robert. "Return to the Hearthstone: Ideals of the Celtic Literary Revival." In *Place, Personality, and the Irish Writer*, ed. Andrew Carpenter, 46-68. New York: Harper and Row, 1977.

O'Farrell, Patrick. *England and Ireland Since 1800.* Oxford: Oxford University Press, 1975; paperback, 1979.

———. *Ireland's English Question.* New York: Schocken Books, 1971; paperback, 1975.

———. "Millenialism, Messianism and Utopianism in Irish History." *Anglo-Irish Studies*, vol. 2 (1976).

O'Hegarty, P. S. "P. H. Pearse." *Irish Commonwealth* (March 1919): 93-99.

O'Malley, Padraig. *Biting at the Grave: The Irish Hunger Strikes and the Politics of Despair.* Boston: Beacon Press, 1990.

O'Muirithe, Diarmuid. "O'Connell in Irish Folk Tradition." In *Daniel O'Connell, Portrait of a Radical*, ed. Kevin Nowlan and Maurice O'Connell, 53-69. New York: Fordham University Press, 1985.

O'Neill, Eamonn. "Patrick Pearse, Some Other Memories." *Capuchin Annual* (1935): 29-41.

———. "Some Notes on the School and Post-School Life of Padraig Pearse." In *The Home Life of Padraig Pearse*, ed. Mary Brigid Pearse, 103-6. Dublin: Mercier Press, 1934; paperback, 1979.

O'Nolan, F. "Prophet and Martyr." In *The Home Life of Patrick Pearse*, ed. Mary Brigid Pearse, 121-24. Dublin: Mercier Press, 1934; paperback, 1979.

O'Tuama, Seán, and Thomas Kinsella, eds. *An Duanaire 1600-1900: Poems of the Dispossessed.* Translated by Thomas Kinsella. Philadelphia: University of Pennsylvania Press, 1981.

Pearse, Margaret. "A Few Characteristics of Padraig Pearse." In *The Home Life of Padraig Pearse,* ed. Mary Brigid Pearse, 108-9. Dublin: Mercier Press, 1934; paperback, 1979.

————. "Patrick and Willie Pearse." *Capuchin Annual* (1943): 86-93.

Pearse, Mary Brigid, ed. *The Home Life of Padraig Pearse.* Cork: Mercier Press, 1934; paperback, 1979.

————. "Our Home Recollections of Padraig." In *The Home Life of Padraig Pearse,* ed. Mary Brigid Pearse, 30-102. Dublin: Mercier Press, 1934; paperback, 1979.

Péguy, Charles. *Charles Péguy: Basic Verities, Prose and Poetry.* Translated by Ann and Julian Green. 2d ed. New York: Pantheon Books, 1943.

————. *The Myth of the Holy Innocents and Other Poems.* Translated by Pansy Pakenham. London: Harvill Press, 1956.

————. *The Mystery of the Charity of Joan of Arc.* Translated by Julian Green. New York: Pantheon Books, 1950.

Piaget, Jean. *The Child's Concept of the World.* New York: Harcourt, Brace, 1929.

Pollard, H. B. C. *The Secret Societies of Ireland: Their Rise and Progress.* London: Phillip Allan, 1922.

Porter, Raymond J. *P. H. Pearse.* New York: Twayne Publishers, 1973.

Rank, Otto. *The Myth of the Birth of the Hero.* Edited by Philip Freund. New York: Alfred A. Knopf, 1932; paperback, 1964.

Raymond, Raymond James. "Irish Nationalism in the Early Twentieth Century: A Reappraisal." *Canadian Review of Studies in Nationalism* 14, 1 (1987): 19-30.

Reddin, Kenneth. "A Man Called Pearse." *Studies* 34 (June 1943): 241-51.

Redmond, John. *The Rising.* London: Thomas Nelson, 1916.

Reid, B. L. *The Man from New York.* Oxford: Oxford University Press, 1968.

Rohrich, Wilfred. "Georges Sorel and the Myth of Violence: From Syndicalism to Fascism." In *Social Protest, Violence, and Terror in Nineteenth and Twentieth Century Europe.*, ed. Wolfgang Mommsen and Gerhard Hirshfield, 246-56. New York: St. Martin's Press, 1982.

Rose, Paul. *The Manchester Martyrs: The Story of a Fenian Tragedy.* London: Lawrence and Wishart, 1970.

Rumpf, Erhard, and A. C. Hepburn. *Nationalismus und Sozialismus in Irland: historich-soziologischer versuch über die Irische Revolution seit 1918*. Hain: Masenheim am Glan, 1959; revised translation, *Nationalism and Socialism in Twentieth Century Ireland*. Liverpool, 1977.

Ryan, Desmond. *The Man Called Pearse*. Dublin: Maunsel, 1919.

———. *Remembering Sion*. London: Arthur Baker, Ltd., 1934.

———. *The Rising: The Complete Story of Easter Week*. 4th ed. Dublin: Golden Eagle Books, Ltd., 1969.

———. "St. Enda's—Fifty Years After." *University Review* (1958): 108.

———. "Stephens, Devoy, Tom Clarke." In *The Shaping of Modern Ireland*, ed. Conor Cruise O'Brien, 34–41. Toronto: University of Toronto Press, 1960.

———, ed. *The 1916 Poets*. London, 1963; reprint ed., Westport, CN: Greenwood Press, 1979.

Sands, Bobby. *One Day in My Life*. Dublin: Mercier Press, 1983.

Schneidman, Edwin S., and Norman L. Faberow, "Suicide and Death." In *The Meaning of Death*, ed. Herman Feifel, 284–99. New York: McGraw-Hill, 1959; paperback, 1965.

Schneidman, Edwin S., Norman L. Faberow, and Robert Litman. *The Psychology of Suicide*. New York: Science House, 1974.

Schmitt, Hans A. *Charles Péguy: The Decline of an Idealist*. Baton Rouge: Louisiana University Press, 1967.

Shannon, Catherine. *Arthur J. Balfour and Ireland: 1874-1922*. Washington: The Catholic University of America Press, 1988.

Shaw, Francis, S.J. "The Canon of Irish History—A Challenge." *Studies* 61, 242 (Summer 1972): 115–53.

Short, K. *The Dynamite War*. Atlantic Highlands, NJ: The Humanities Press, 1979.

Somerville-Large, Peter. *Dublin*. London: Hamish Hamilton, 1979.

Sorel, Georges. *Reflections on Violence*. Translated by T. E. Hulme and J. Roth. Glencoe: Free Press, 1950.

Stephens, James. *The Insurrection In Dublin*. First published in Dublin in 1916; reprint ed., Gerard's Cross: Colin Smythe, 1978.

Stewart, A. T. Q. *The Ulster Crisis: Resistance to Home Rule, 1912-1914*. London: Faber and Faber, Ltd., 1967; paperback, 1969.

Stromberg, Roland N. *Redemption by War: The Intellectuals and 1914*. Lawrence, Kansas: The Regent's Press of Kansas, 1982.

Thompson, William Irwin. *The Imagination of an Insurrection: Dublin, 1916*. London: Lindisfarne Press, 1967.

Thornley, David. "Patrick Pearse." *Studies* (Spring 1966): 10–20.

———. "Patrick Pearse and the Pearse Family." *Studies* (Autumn-Winter 1971): 332–46.

Townsend, Charles. "The I.R.A. and the Development of Guerrilla War, 1916–1921." *English Historical Review* 94 (April 1979): 318–45.

———. *Political Violence in Ireland: Government and Resistance Since 1848.* Oxford: Clarendon Press, 1983.

Travers, Pauric. *Settlements and Divisions: Ireland 1870–1922.* Dublin: Helicon Limited, 1988.

Tynan, Patrick. *The Irish Invincibles and Their Times.* First published 1894; reprint ed., Millwood, NY: Kraus Reprint, 1983.

Vance, Norman. *Irish Literature: A Social History.* Oxford: Basil Blackwell, Ltd., 1990.

Villiers, Marjorie. *Charles Péguy: A Study in Integrity.* New York: Harper and Row, 1965; reprint ed., 1975.

Walkowitz, Judith. *Prostitution and Victorian Society.* Cambridge, MA: Harvard University Press, 1982.

Wall, Maureen. "The Background to the Rising, From 1914 Until the Issue of the Countermanding Order on Easter Saturday 1916." In *The Making of 1916,* ed. Kevin Nowlan, 157–201. Dublin: The Stationary Office, 1969.

Walsh, Seán Patrick. *Free and Gaelic: Pearse's Idea of a National Culture.* Dublin: Coiste Chomoradh an Phiarsaigh, 1979.

Ward, Alan J. *Ireland and Anglo-American Relations, 1899–1921.* Toronto: University of Toronto Press, 1969.

Watson, G. J. *Irish Identity and the Literary Revival: Synge, Yeats, Joyce and O'Casey.* London, 1979.

Whyte, John H. "1916—Revolution and Religion." In *Leaders and Men of the Easter Rising: Dublin, 1916,* ed. F. X. Martin, 215–26. Dublin: Harper and Row, 1967.

Williams, T. Desmond, ed. *Secret Societies in Ireland.* Dublin: Gill and Macmillan, 1973.

Wohl, Robert. *The Generation of 1914.* Cambridge: Harvard University Press, 1979.

Wright, Arnold. *Disturbed Dublin: The Story of the Great Strike of 1913–1914.* London: Longmans, Green, 1914.

Yeats, William Butler. *The Autobiography of William Butler Yeats.* New York: Macmillan, 1965; paperback, New York, 1974.

Unpublished Materials

Stephen Barrett MSS, National Library, Dublin.

Eamonn De Barra, University College, Dublin.

Martin Daly [Stephen MacKenna] Pamphlet, National Library, Dublin.

Roger Casement Papers, National Library, Dublin.
Eamonn Ceannt Papers, National Library, Dublin.
Gaelic League Letter Book, National Library, Dublin.
Gaelic League Minute Books: Minute Books of Coiste Gnotha,
    National Library, Dublin; Minute Books of the Publication
    Committee, National Library, Dublin.
Mary Hayden Diaries, National Library, Dublin.
Bulmer Hobson Papers, National Library, Dublin.
Joseph Holloway Diaries, National Library, Dublin.
Joseph Holloway Papers, National Library, Dublin.
Joseph McGarrity Papers, National Library, Dublin.
Eoin MacNeill Papers, National Library, Dublin.
Richard Mulcahy Papers, University College, Dublin.
James Pearse Papers, National Library, Dublin.
Mrs. Margaret Pearse Papers, National Library, Dublin.
Patrick Pearse Diary Draft, St. Enda's School, Dublin.
Patrick Pearse Papers, National Library, Dublin.
Pearse Family Papers, University College, Dublin.

Index

"After Death," 90
An Rí, 150, 154

Blanquist "cult of the revolution-
ary tradition," 201
Bodach an Chota Lachtna, 117
Brophy, Brigid, 98–100
*Bruidhean Chaorthainn: Sgeal
Fiannaidheachta,* 116–17, 121
Brooke, Rupert: anti-modernist
ideas, 186; fear of old age, 187; and
"1914 Sonnets," 184-87; obituary
of, 187; visits United States, 186

Carson, Edward, 64, 75–77
Casement, Roger: and arms shipment, 162–63, 165; distrust of
Pearse, 80
Cathleen Ní Houlihan, 90
Celtic Revival: anti-modernist
ideas, 53–55, 57–59; defined,
52–53; history of, 52–61, 68;
impact on Pearse's generation,
60; limited appeal of, 57–60, 68;
racialist ideas, 58–59; and
Roman Catholicism, 69
"Christmas 1915," 153
Clarke, Thomas: background of,
71; dedication to Irish republicanism, 71; helps resurrect IRB,
71–72, 74; grooms Pearse to be
IRB spokesman, 129–31; initial
distrust of Pearse, 129; and IVF,
80; mentors new generation, 71,

74–75. *See also* Pearse, Patrick,
influences
"The Clogher Massacre," 90
Connolly, James: and "blood-sacrifice," 200; and Easter Rising, 6n,
168; and IRB, 82; joins IRB Military Council, 166; as leader of the
ICA, 80–81; links nationalism
and class struggle, 81; and Patrick
Pearse, 199–200; historical reputation, 200; syndicalism of, 6n
Cúchulainn: as child-hero
redeemer, 92; myth of, 92; and
transformation symbolism,
198–199
"cultural nationalism," 53n
Cumann na nGaedheal, 65. *See also*
Pearse, Patrick, influences

"Dark Rosaleen," 88–89
Defenders, the, 92–93
developmental analytical theory,
17–19
De Vere, Aubrey, 89
Devoy, John, 140–41, 143–44
Dillon, John; 63, 164, 175–76
Dublin Castle, 162–64

Easter Rising: irrationalism in,
176–77; plan, 165; as political
act, 6–7; public reaction to,
174–75; as suicidal action, 12–13;
as symbolic act, 1
ego psychology, 16–17

Patrick Pearse and the Politics of Redemption was composed in
Adobe Minion by Marathon Typography Service, Inc. of Durham, North Carolina.
It was printed on 60 pound Booktext Natural and bound by BookCrafters, Inc.
of Chelsea, Michigan. The design of the book and cover is by
Kachergis Book Design of Pittsboro, North Carolina.